Kids' Vancouver

by Victoria Bushnell

RAINCOAST BOOKS

Vancouver

First published in 2000 by

Raincoast Books
8680 Cambie Street
Vancouver, B.C.
V6P 6M9
(604) 323-7100

Visit our website: www.raincoast.com

1 2 3 4 5 6 7 8 9 10

CANADIAN CATALOGUING IN PUBLICATION DATA

Bushnell, Victoria
Kids' Vancouver

ISBN 1-55192-290-8

1. Family Recreation — British Columbia — Vancouver — Guidebooks.
2. Vancouver (B.C.) — Guidebooks. I. Title

FC3847.18.B86 1999   917.511'33044   C99-910971-5
F1089.5.V22B88 1999

Cover illustration by Greta Guzek
Interior artwork and text design by Bruce Collins

Printed in Canada

THE CANADA COUNCIL | LE CONSEIL DES ARTS
FOR THE ARTS | DU CANADA
SINCE 1957 | DEPUIS 1957

Raincoast Books gratefully acknowledges the support of the Government of Canada, through the Book Publishing Industry Development Program, the Canada Council for the Arts and the Department of Canadian Heritage. We also acknowledge the assistance of the Province of British Columbia, through the British Columbia Arts Council.

Contents

Introduction

I remember the first time I came to Vancouver. As my plane flew in we seemed to hover above the city for several minutes, a period that allowed me to take in the landscape. I immediately fell in love with what I saw. Years later I am still stunned by this city that sits in the middle of a rainforest, watched over by the Coast Mountains to the north, their peaks covered with snow much of the year. To the west the immediate waters of the Pacific Ocean are dominated by Vancouver Island, flecked by the tiny and numerous Gulf Islands, landforms in misty tones of blue and grey. Waterways surround Vancouver, with Burrard Inlet neatly separating the city from the North Shore, the Fraser River dividing it from Richmond and Surrey. It *is* a rainforest, and consequently has so much precipitation that at times it's quite maddening. When the skies clear, however, there is a clarity to the air that is almost luminescent, and all rain is forgiven.

On top of that there is actually a *city* here, a rapidly growing place with a vibrant downtown area, shops, restaurants and clubs, and people who love literature and the arts. Thousands of people from other countries have made this area their home, so there's a great opportunity to experience a diversity of cultures and to meet people from a diversity of backgrounds. For the most part people here are very easygoing and progressive, which is typical of the West Coast lifestyle, and most of them have a deep sense of respect for others. I can only believe the natural landscape somehow inspires us, reminding us of something greater within ourselves.

It's no wonder this is such a wonderful place for families. Vancouver society is very inclusive of children, with lots of parks and community centres, arts classes and family events. At the same time it can be difficult to discover all the city has to offer, particularly if you're a parent already overworked by diapers and feeding times, homework and dinner. That's why I wrote *Kids' Vancouver*.

Kids' Vancouver is both a guide to activities *and* a reference book for parents and other caregivers. Here you'll find activities for kids, restaurants that cater to kids, and kid-related services and shopping. Vancouver's best parks, nature spots, museums, galleries, and theatre and music venues are also described. You'll find out who offers swimming lessons, where to take a train ride, where you can go indoor rock climbing, where to hire a clown for a birthday party and who cuts children's hair. The chapter on shopping for kids covers everything from kid-size Doc Martens to secondhand maternity clothes, from home-schooling supplies to naturopathic shops. Kid-friendly restaurants that reflect a diversity of cuisines, in various geographical locations and with a range of prices are reviewed. The chapter on babies (and their parents) covers prenatal courses and postpartum counselling, diaper services and shops that sell nursery items. In this book you'll also find a list of family places, community centres, 24-hour drugstores, and shelters and support organizations.

This book is for visiting families as well. Knowing where to go and what to do can turn a tedious trip into a fun adventure. Visitors will find an overview of the area's neighbourhoods, information on how to get around, where to stay and where main attractions are. There is also a separate chapter on taking a trip to Victoria with kids.

The intention of this book is to reflect the diversity of the city, to help you stimulate your children and to help them think and experience new things. Writing about "children's activities," as such, can be difficult because there is a certain tendency to exclude adult-oriented activities, many of which do hold significant interest for kids. Ultimately this book is a guide to having fun. Use your own discretion when considering some of the activities described here. Kids need to be encouraged, and sometimes gently prodded, but beyond that the experience will be no good for anyone if they're miserable. Despite my love of art, I won't torture my children by making them walk through a gallery if they really don't want to be there. Also, allow for a margin of failure. Many times I've taken my kids to a restaurant I thought they'd like, only to have them hate the food or behave in some horrific manner. Sometimes we've gone off on an adventure only to have it be a day of whining and complaining; another day might have been different. That's just the way it goes sometimes.

Most of the Lower Mainland is covered in this book. This is a guide not only to Vancouver, but to the North Shore (North Vancouver and West Vancouver), Burnaby, New Westminster, the Tri-Cities (Coquitlam, Port Coquitlam and Port Moody), Richmond and Surrey. Entries are categorized by area for the most part; sections with a smaller number of entries present the entries in alphabetical order with the corresponding city highlighted in boldface type.

Deciding what to include and exclude was an arduous task, but the general criteria applied was how much fun the activity is for kids and how open the establishment is to families. When faced with choices too numerous to include, as with some of the shops and hotels, I tended to go with what is most popular and interesting, relying heavily on feedback from other parents, as well as, of course, extensive field research on my part. (My kids have been taken to so many stores, restaurants and establishments, it's a wonder any of us survived.)

I've tried to indicate age-appropriateness where applicable, as well as ease of access by public transit. Cross-references to other chapters are provided whenever I thought they'd be helpful; otherwise consult the index if you're looking for a particular entry or category. Main cross streets are indicated, but I strongly suggest buying a good map to help you locate places. When price ranges are given, they do not include taxes. Incidentally, all phone numbers begin with the area code 604, except those on Vancouver Island (and some of the smaller islands and areas just north of Vancouver); the area code for these areas is 250.

Although I've made every effort to make this book as up-to-date as possible, prices do change, places close down and new owners take over. Call ahead before visiting any of the places mentioned, and please write to me care of the publisher to let me know your comments and suggestions, both good and bad.

Visitor Information

The majority of families visit Vancouver in the summer. The city is at its most beautiful then, with less rain and longer days; the sun doesn't set until around

10:00 p.m. Regardless of the time of year, however, bring raincoats for you and your kids, as well as good sturdy shoes for walking and a pair of light rain boots. In the summer the weather is usually warm enough for shorts and T-shirts, but be sure to have long pants and sweatshirts in your suitcase. In the winter the temperature rarely gets to the freezing point, but bring a warm jacket and gloves and a hat. Rain pants, or "muddy buddies," are essentials for kids; lots of parks can be muddy, and pulling these on over your child's clothes saves a lot of washing. (For recorded weather forecasts for the Lower Mainland, call 664-9032.) Collapsible umbrellas can be handy, but they're hard to hold onto if you're already clutching a toddler's hand; hats or raincoats with hoods are a better idea. Like the United States, Canada operates on 110-volt, 60-cycle electric power, so if you're coming from the U.S. you can bring your blow-dryer or bottle warmer.

Visas are not required of Americans, nor of travellers from nearly all Western countries. Americans are not required to show passports to cross the U.S. border into Canada, but going through the immigration line at the airport will probably take less time if you and your kids have them. Otherwise, photo identification is generally acceptable. As with travelling to any other countries, if you are a single parent coming into Canada with your kids, you may be asked to show proof of legal custody or a letter of consent from your partner (preferably notarized). Going through customs is usually very straightforward, provided your passports are up-to-date and you have any necessary documentation. (For U.S. and Canada customs information, call 1-800-668-4748.)

English is spoken throughout most of the Lower Mainland. Although French is Canada's other official language, you'll probably hear Chinese spoken more often. Overall this is a safe city, but the Main and Hastings area is rather seedy, characterized by a lot of drug activity and not great to walk through. Exercise the same caution you would anywhere: keep your car locked with no valuables inside, have your money in a safe place close to your body and keep watch of your children at all times.

> *Rain pants, or "muddy buddies," are essential for kids in Vancouver*

Generally Vancouver provides good value in terms of shopping and excursions, but hotel prices can be high as a result of the whopping 17 percent tax that is added on. (See "Where to Stay with Kids," page 131.) Canadian currency is similar to American, but one U.S. dollar is currently worth about $1.50 Canadian, which makes Vancouver (and Canada) a particularly good deal for Americans. As well as the standard quarters, dimes, nickels and pennies, Canadian currency includes gold-coloured one-dollar coins called loons or loonies (named after the bird that appears on one side of the coin) and newer two-dollar coins, called toonies, which have an aluminum bronze core and nickel outer ring. Bills come in five-, 10-, 20- and higher-dollar increments, but if you're getting money at a bank, try to stay with 20-dollar bills; they're easier to change than 50- or 100-dollar bills. Most restaurants and shops accept U.S. dollars, but their exchange rate won't be as good as a bank's (and change is given in Canadian currency, of course). Money can be exchanged easily at any bank; try the **Bank of Montreal** downtown (665-7265), at 401 West

Georgia Street (at Homer). **Thomas Cook Travel** (687-6111) has several offices in Vancouver, including one at 701 Granville Street, in Pacific Centre. The **American Express Travel Agency** (669-2813) is at 666 Burrard Street (the money exchange entrance is behind the building at the corner of Hornby and Dunsmuir Streets). The airport also has a money exchange area just past the baggage claim area. Most shops and other establishments use Interac. For cash, there are plenty of automated teller machines (ATM); some foreign cards work on them.

A seven percent Provincial Sales Tax (PST) must be paid on all purchases (excepting some food items at grocery stores). In addition, a seven percent Goods and Services Tax (GST) is charged on nearly every product, service and transaction in Canada. Visitors can get a GST rebate on hotels (for stays of less than 30 days) and goods that are being brought out of the country. Taxes paid on services and transportation are not refundable. A cash rebate is available by filling out an application and providing original receipts; application forms are available at all duty-free stores or from **Revenue Canada**'s tax services office (666-7577), 1166 West Pender Street (at Burrard).

Those needing emergency medical care can go to **Vancouver General Hospital** (875-4995), 855 West 12th Avenue (at Oak). Other hospitals and emergency services are listed in "Emergency, Medical and Other Resources" (see page 229). There are walk-in medical clinics all over Vancouver. Unlike many in the United States, clinics here are clean, safe, very reasonably priced and staffed by excellent nurses and doctors. They're good resources if you're visiting and one of your kids suddenly gets sick with an ear infection or other ailment. To find out the clinic closest to you, call the City of Vancouver Health Services at 736-2033. If you're staying at a hotel, the concierge will undoubtedly know of several; they're also listed in BC Tel's Yellow Pages. Check your insurance policy before you come to Canada to see if you and your kids are covered should medical treatment be necessary; travel insurance is always a good idea. There is no need for any specific health precautions or immunizations before coming here.

Canada Post's main postal outlet (662-5722) is at 349 West Georgia Street (at Homer). Those who collect stamps might want to stop in here; they have a good selection of souvenir and collectible Canadian stamps.

For information on, and rules and regulations for driving in the city as well as other transportation information, see "Getting Around," page 1. The following are some useful phone numbers for visitors.

Tourism Vancouver
210 – 200 Burrard St
Tel: 683-2000 or 683-2772
Tourism Vancouver provides assistance with bookings for accommodation, tours, transport and activities. They also have a free visitors' guide; phone the number above to have it sent to you.

Tourism British Columbia
Tel: 663-6000
Call for information on province-wide travel and accommodations.

North Shore Tourism
131 E. 2nd St
Tel: 987-4488

Tourism Richmond
11980 Deas Throughway (at Hwy 99)
Tel: 271-8280

Websites

Many of the places mentioned in this book have websites. Although websites for
some public places and for some larger venues or organizations have been given,
I have not included commercial websites, since they are often simply advertisements for the company being described and do not provide much valuable
information. However, some websites are good entry points to Vancouver as well
as being useful links to some main attractions and services; those are noted here.

www.vcn.bc.ca
This is the website for the **Vancouver Community Network**, founded in 1993
in order to bring a working CommunityNet, a community-based computer
information system, to the people of the Greater Vancouver area. It has helpful
links to a lot of community services.

www.city.vancouver.bc.ca
This is the **City of Vancouver**'s website, with listings of city services, parks,
community groups, support services, daycares and more.

www.discovervancouver.com
This is a good site for tourist attractions, accommodations, transportation,
attractions, restaurants and more, plus links to kids' activities.

www.travel.vancouver.bc.ca
Tourism Vancouver's website lists attractions, kids' stuff, as well as sightseeing,
camping and other information for visitors.

www.travel.bc.ca
This site covers travel and tourism information for the whole province of B.C.,
including camping, lodging and other activities.

www.localdir.com
This is a great site, with listings of local websites and e-mail addresses for both
Vancouver and Victoria.

Publications

Both *B.C. Parent* and *Westcoast Families* are free monthly publications that have
many articles on parenting, on where to go, on summer camps and so on. These
publications are available by subscription, but most people pick them up at any
shop that sells kids' supplies. Their websites contain past articles, which have lots
of information on what to do in the city. The *Georgia Straight*, another free publication, comes out weekly, on Thursdays, and is a great source of information on
what's going on in the city, with movie reviews, articles on the local environment

and more, as well as a small section on events for kids. The *Georgia Straight* is readily available throughout the city at newsstands, stores, restaurants and other venues. Also on the free-newspaper stands is the **Vancouver Courier**. Although not as popular as the *Georgia Straight*, it's delivered free every other day to most households and is packed full of advertisements and inserts; it occasionally has information about stuff for kids.

The city's two daily newspapers are the **Vancouver Sun** and **The Province**. The *Vancouver Sun* is a decent paper focusing on the city's news; its Thursday section lists weekend activities. *The Province* is shorter, smaller and less in-depth, with a minimal amount of information relating to children. The magazine **Vancouver** comes out once a month and costs a few dollars at the newsstand. (Many households get it delivered to their door free.) The magazine focuses on trends and fashions, with little information on outings with children, but it's still a good source of information for what's going on in the city. Their website links to the Visitors Bureau and has information on bars, shopping and other municipalities besides Vancouver. Every year *Vancouver* puts out *City Guide* ($5.95), an excellent resource for visitors and residents, with information on restaurants, neighbourhoods and shopping, plus maps and tips.

B.C. Parent
P.O. Box 72086, 4479 W. 10th Ave
Vancouver, B.C. V6R 4P2
Tel: 221-0366
Website: *www.bcparent.com*

Georgia Straight
2nd Floor, 1770 Burrard St
Vancouver, B.C. V6J 3G7
Tel: 730-7000
Website: *www.straight.com*

The Province
200 Granville St
Vancouver, B.C. V6C 3N3
Tel: 605-2222

Vancouver Courier
1574 W. 6th Ave
Vancouver, B.C. V6J 1R2
Tel: 738-1411

Vancouver *Magazine*
300 – 555 West 12th Ave
Vancouver, B.C. V5Z 4L4
Tel: 877-7732
Website: *www.vanmag.com*

Vancouver Sun
200 Granville St
Vancouver, B.C. V6C 3N3
Tel: 605-2111
Website: *www.vancouversun.com*

Westcoast Families
8 – 1551 Johnston St
Vancouver, B.C. V6H 3R9
Tel: 689-1331
Website: *www.family.com*

Chapter 1

Getting
Around

Public transit in the Greater Vancouver area is safe, inexpensive and commonly used. You usually don't have to wait an inordinate amount of time for a bus, the SkyTrain or the SeaBus. The main deterrent is the weather: Vancouver's rainy skies make it easy to rely on your automobile or even stay at home! Provided you and your kids are dressed for the weather in good boots and rain gear, you'll find it's quite simple to get around Vancouver on public transit. Save your car for trips to those out-of-the-way places that are off the main bus or SkyTrain lines and avoid driving into downtown – it's full of one-way streets and traffic, and parking is expensive and can be difficult to find.

Keep in mind that bicycles are an accepted form of transportation in Vancouver, even for families. There are bike routes posted all over the city, although some that are on the city streets can be a bit hectic for children (riding on the sidewalk is illegal). For information on bike routes, rentals, laws and more, see page 48.

Finally, taking a trip can be just as fun as the final destination. Smaller kids love riding on buses, the SkyTrain and the SeaBus, while all seem to enjoy watching or flying on planes, riding the ferry or taking a train ride. For more ideas on transportation adventures, see "Get Up and Go!" page 102.

Public Transit

Greater Vancouver's transit consists of the bus, the SkyTrain and the SeaBus, operated by TransLink, all of which interconnect and operate seven days a week, including holidays. The transit network services all the areas covered in this book: Vancouver, the North Shore, Burnaby, New Westminster, the Tri-Cities, Richmond and Surrey, as well as areas farther afield.

The **SeaBus** is a passenger-only ferry that operates between Lonsdale Quay in North Vancouver and the SeaBus terminal in downtown Vancouver. The SeaBus operates daily every 15 to 30 minutes and the crossing takes 12 minutes. The **SkyTrain** is an automated, light-rail train that travels above ground, except in the downtown area, where it goes underground. Trains run about every five minutes and make 20 stops between Vancouver, Burnaby, New Westminster and Surrey.

TransLink buses serve the Greater Vancouver area. (West Vancouver has a separate transit system, called the **West Vancouver Blue Bus**.) Transit schedules are available at hotels, libraries, tourist centres and various retail outlets, and on their website, at *www.translink.bc.ca*. Some schedules can be picked up right on the bus from the driver. You probably won't be up with kids really late at night, but do keep in mind that the SkyTrain and SeaBus stop running at around one in the morning, resuming between 5:00 and 6:00 a.m. The buses also have a hiatus in the wee hours – you won't see many after 2:30 a.m.

Fares are the same for the bus (including the Blue Bus), the SkyTrain and the SeaBus. Fares are determined according to the time of day and what zone you're travelling in: Zone One (Vancouver), Zone Two (Richmond, Burnaby and North Vancouver) and Zone Three (the Tri-Cities and Surrey). The fare you pay depends on the number of zone boundaries crossed. Fares for the various zones are as follows: for Zone One, a single adult fare is $1.50, a concession fare is $1; for Zone Two, a single adult fare is $2.25, concession fares are $1.50; for Zone Three, a single adult fare is $3, concessions fares are $2. Concession fares apply to children between five and 13, to secondary school students aged 14 to 19 who are in grades eight to 12 and have a valid GoCard, and to HandyPass holders and seniors 65 and over (with proof of age). Children under five ride free.

Transfers, which you should request when you board the bus, are valid for 90 minutes of travel in any direction whether you're using the bus, SeaBus, SkyTrain or Blue Bus. If you want to board the SkyTrain or SeaBus and are not using a transfer, you must either buy a ticket (or validate a ticket already purchased) at the terminal. Keep hold of your ticket or transfer in case a transit attendant asks for it.

The above fares are based on regular day travel until 6:30 p.m. every day. After 6:30 p.m. on weekdays and all day on weekends and holidays, the fare is reduced – adults pay $1.50 no matter what zone they're travelling in; concession fares are $1.

A DayPass (adults $6, concession $6) is good for one day's travel and may be purchased in advance at FareDealer outlets. Packs of 10 tickets, called

FareSavers, can be purchased for $13.75 (Zone One), $20.50 (Zone Two) and $28 (Zone Three). Monthly passes, called FareCards, can also be purchased, for $54 (Zone One), $78 (Zone Two) and $103 (Zone Three). Tickets and monthly FareCard passes are sold at all 7-Eleven stores, Safeways and Scotiabanks. (Scotiabanks sell monthly passes only.) Look for the FareDealer symbol at Money Marts, and at Mac's and other convenience stores. FareSaver tickets and DayPasses are available throughout the month. FareCards are only sold on the last five business days and first five business days of each month.

GoCard applications are available through high school offices. Residents of the GVRD who have a permanent disability may apply for a HandyPass; call 540-3400. Not covered by the pass is HandyDART, a custom transit system for people with disabilities. Lift-equipped vans provide door-to-door transportation for passengers in wheelchairs and others with disabilities that restrict mobility. Call one of the HandyDART numbers below for fare information.

Average waiting time for the buses is 10 minutes, but this varies depending on the time of day. Bus stops are clearly marked; route numbers are often listed. Enter by the door at the front of the bus and leave by the rear door; pull the cord if you want to get off at the next stop. Exact change is required; again, make sure you request a transfer when you board. Young children can't ride in a stroller on the bus, so be sure to fold it up ahead of time. People with small children often sit in the front seats reserved for the elderly and disabled, but if you're standing and looking suitably uncomfortable, someone may

Young children can't ride in a stroller on the bus; fold it up ahead of time.

offer you their seat anyway. If possible, avoid travelling at rush hour, when there is standing room only. It's really dangerous with kids and people are too grumpy to give up their seats. As with the SeaBus and SkyTrain, keep your transfer as proof of payment; occasionally someone asks for it, especially if you are travelling between zones. Call the numbers listed below if you need assistance; the operators are very friendly and will give you the best route to take to get from one place to another. The Coast Mountain BusLink website lists all their bus routes and other schedule information.

TransLink, 521-0400, *www.translink.bc.ca*
HandyDART, 430-2692 or 430-2892 in Vancouver, 980-3691 in North Vancouver, 524-3655 in Burnaby, New Westminster and Tri-Cities, 279-7090 in Richmond, 591-8234 or 591-3346 in Surrey
West Vancouver Blue Bus, 985-7777

Taxis

Taxis can be found at the airport and in front of hotels, as well as at a few taxi stands located downtown. It's possible to flag down taxis that cruise through downtown, but when they're in any other part of town, people tend to phone a taxi to come and pick them up. There are normally seat belts in taxis (but no car seats) and drivers are usually very friendly and honest, though sometimes they drive a bit fast and dart in and out of traffic in a somewhat precarious manner.

Bel-Air Taxi 433-6666
Services Burnaby and the Vancouver airport.
Black Top and Checker Cabs...731-1111
Bonny's Taxi 435-6655
Services Burnaby, New Westminster and the Vancouver airport.
Coquitlam Taxi 937-3434
Services Coquitlam and the Vancouver airport.
Maclure's Cabs 731-9211
North Shore Taxi..987-7171
Richmond Cabs 272-1111
Vancouver Taxi..871-1111
Wheelchair-accessible taxis.
Yellow Cab 681-3311

Car Travel

U.S. highways connect directly with the Canadian highway system at numerous points; the most common in the Vancouver area being Highway 99 north of Blaine. During weekends and in summer months border crossings can get very busy; many people choose to take the truck crossing east of the 99 instead. Visitors with U.S. passports are allowed to bring their cars in for up to six months. Insurance companies usually provide coverage in Canada, but check ahead to be sure. In any case, it's a great, inexpensive way to get to Vancouver; many people do drive up from California and other points south. For a taped message of an updated B.C. highway report, call 299-9000. If you are coming from out of the country, the British Columbia Automobile Association (BCAA) has a 24-hour breakdown service (293-2222) for its members as well as those who belong to other automobile associations, such as the American Automobile Association (AAA).

There are no freeways in Vancouver so all driving is done through the city, which can be pleasant in nice weather but wretched in rain and rush hour. Driving anywhere during rush hour (between 7:00 a.m. and 9:00 a.m. and between 4:30 p.m. and 6:00 p.m.) is a headache, especially on the main bridges (except Burrard and Cambie) and on Highway 1 going east and Highway 99 going south. Free parking in Vancouver is rare; keep lots of loonies and quarters in your car to feed the inevitable parking metres.

Some rules of the road: speed limits are posted in metric (30 km is 18 mph, 50 km is 30 mph, 60 km is 36 mph and 90 km is 54 mph). Seat belts are mandatory, as are motorcycle helmets and car seats for children under 18 kg (40 lbs). Car seats must not only be buckled in, but attached with a heavy strap to a metal clip secured to the car's frame behind the seat. A valid driver's license from any country is good in Vancouver for three months; auto insurance is mandatory. You can make a right turn on a red light after you stop and yield; you can make a left turn on a red light if you are turning left off a one-way street onto another one-way street. A flashing red light is a stop sign; a flashing green or yellow light gives you the right of way, but you must slow down at the yellow. Pedestrians have the right of way. Be sure to keep a watch out for bicyclists – give them enough space and don't cut them off. There are strict drunk-driving laws, with roadblocks in place from time to time.

For those renting a car, there are car rental offices both at the airport and at several offices around Vancouver. Car rental prices run about $50 a day and up; most places rent car seats.

Avis Rent a Car	606-2872
Budget Rent a Car	668-7000
Discount Car and Truck Rentals	682-2413
Dollar Rent a Car	1-800-465-0045
Enterprise Rent-a-Car	1-800-736-8222
Hertz Rent a Car	606-4711
Lo-Cost Rent-a-Car	689-9664
National/Tilden	1-800-227-7368
Rent-a-Wreck	688-0001
Thrifty Car Rental	606-1666

The Airport

Vancouver's main airport is the Vancouver International Airport (276-6101), located 10 km (6 mi) south of Vancouver on Sea Island, just west of Richmond, about a 20-minute drive from downtown Vancouver. In the terminal, just past the baggage claim, is a money exchange booth and an information desk, where you can book a hotel or get other travel help. At the airport there are also car rental counters and taxis waiting out front.

A taxi to downtown Vancouver usually runs around $27. Frankly, unless you're renting a car, I think it's the easiest way to get into the city, especially after you've been on a plane for hours and just want to get to your destination. You can also take a public or private bus to or from the airport. The public bus (see "Public Transit," page 2) is the best deal – only $1.50 per adult – and usually takes about an hour, but it is a hassle if you've got kids and luggage (and who reading this book won't?). The **Vancouver Airporter** (946-8866) leaves the airport every half hour and stops at most downtown hotels. It's only $10 one-way (kids five to 13 are $8), but if you've got at least three people in your party, a taxi is still a better deal. There are also two limousine services to consider. **Air Limo** (273-1331) is $29; limousines are waiting outside the airport 24 hours a day. **Star Limousine Service** (685-5600) has nicer cars and amenities and trained, well-dressed chauffeurs (at $65 a ride, they should be!); these cars need to be booked a day in advance. If you're travelling *to* the airport from downtown Vancouver, call one of the bus or limousine services to arrange for a pickup. Taxis are usually waiting outside all major hotels or you can call one of the numbers listed (see "Taxis," page 3).

To get to the airport from downtown Vancouver, take the Granville Bridge and follow Granville Street south to the Arthur Laing Bridge, which leads directly to the airport. If you're picking someone up from the airport, short-term parking, though a bit pricey, is really convenient, especially if you have kids in tow. If you're the one travelling with kids, don't drive to the airport. Long-term parking is expensive and a hassle; take a cab or bus or get a friend to drive you. Inside the domestic terminal there is a great indoor play area with a climb-on tugboat, castle and see-saw, a good place to hang out if you are meeting a friend in transit or seeing someone off. Nearby is a large nursery with a number of cribs, chairs for nursing and a changing table, and even a washroom with a kid-size toilet. Bill Reid's large sculpture, *Spirit of Haida Gwaii*, is a good meeting point and an interesting sight. And young kids always appreciate a ride in a luggage trolley.

The airport has undergone tremendous expansion. To help cover costs, passengers to the United States are charged a $10 airport improvement fee; international passengers are charged $15. Those flying within Canada are charged $5.

Over 40 airlines are serviced by the airport, including the following.

Air Canada (Air BC) 688-5515
Air China 685-0921
Air France..1-800-667-2747
Air India..879-0271
American Airlines 1-800-443-7300
British Airways 1-800-247-9297
Canadian Airlines..279-6611
Cathay Pacific 606-8888
Continental Airlines 1-800-231-0856
Delta Airlines...1-800-221-1212
Hawaiian Airlines 1-800-367-5320
Horizon Air 1-800-547-9308
Japan Airlines...1-800-525-3663
Korean Air 1-800-438-5000
Lufthansa German Airlines 1-800-563-5954
Malaysia Airlines...1-800-552-9264
Mandarin Airlines 682-6777
Northwest Airlines/KLM 1-800-447-4747
Qantas Airways..1-800-227-4500
Singapore Airlines 689-1223
United Airlines 1-800-241-6522

BC Ferries

BC Ferries operates out of two terminals in Vancouver. The ferries that leave from the Horseshoe Bay terminal (about a 20-minute drive northwest from downtown Vancouver) go to Bowen Island, to Langdale on the Sunshine Coast and to Departure Bay in Nanaimo. The ferries from the Tsawwassen terminal (about a 30-minute drive south from downtown Vancouver) go to Victoria and the Gulf Islands, as well as to Duke Point in Nanaimo. The islands are popular summer spots for Vancouverites. If you go to one of them, you'll see why: they're idyllic retreats full of forests and beaches. (See "A Side Trip to Victoria" for a possible weekend trip, page 173.)

In the summer it's not uncommon to have a "two-ferry wait," during which you'll have to wait for two ferries (or more!) to fill up and depart before it's your turn to go. This can mean hours in line at a crowded outdoor terminal (hot in summer; worse if it's raining). Reservations for some ferries are accepted; the cost for reserving is a steep $15 per one-way trip, but *it's worth it.* By the way, if you do find yourself waiting for a ferry at Horseshoe Bay, you can leave your car in the lineup and walk the short distance to the town, where there are a number of kid-friendly restaurants (see page 120) and a tiny waterfront park with playground equipment. On board the larger ferries are cafeterias, play equipment, video games, gift shops and newsstands. I'd still recommend bringing cards, colouring books or other tabletop activities. The cafeteria food is predictably mediocre; bring a lunch or snacks if you want to eat something decent and don't want to spend a fortune on a hamburger. Sadly, **Duthie Books** (see page 161) no longer stocks the gift shop with local literature; they were underbid by another outfit that tends to favour pulp fiction.

For information about **Aquabus** and **False Creek Ferries**, the two mini-ferries that service False Creek, see page 102.

BC Ferries
Tel: 1-888-223-3779 (information and reservations), 1-888-724-5223 (automated reservations)
Website: *wwwbcferries.bc.ca*

Out-of-Town Bus Travel
The following outfits offer travel between Vancouver and destinations as close as Victoria as well as all across North America. Except as noted below, all buses depart from Pacific Central station, 1150 Station Street at Terminal (683-8133).

Greyhound Lines of Vancouver
Tel: 482-8747 or 1-800-231-2222
Bus service across North America.

Pacific Coach Lines
Tel: 662-8074 or 662-7575
Prices: $23 one-way adult fare
Daily scheduled service between Vancouver and Victoria.

Perimeter Transportation
Tel: 266-5386
Prices: $43 one-way adult fare
Service between Vancouver Airport and Whistler.

Quick Shuttle Bus Service
Tel: 940-4428
Service between Seattle and Vancouver. Vancouver arrival is at the Sandman Hotel, 180 W. Georgia Street (at Beatty).

Train Travel

As by bus, you can make short jaunts to locations such as Whistler and longer trips across the country by train. It's not within the scope of this book to get into long-distance travel, but here are some outfits to keep in mind if you want to give it a try. BC Rail and the West Coast Express (see "Get Up and Go!" page 106) go to places outside Vancouver.

Amtrak

Tel: 1-800-USA-RAIL (872-7245)

From Vancouver to Seattle; departs from Pacific Central station; one-way adult fare is $21.

Rocky Mountaineer Railtours

Tel: 606-7200 or 1-800-665-RAIL (7245)

Two-day trips between Vancouver and Jasper, Banff or Calgary. Prices vary widely depending on trip and time of year, but a one-way trip to Jasper, which takes two days and one night, is $665, including hotel, breakfast and lunch.

VIA Rail

Tel: 1-800-561-8630

Goes across Canada as far east as Ontario; trains depart from Pacific Central station. Prices vary.

chapter 2

Neighbourhoods

From the bustling density of Chinatown to the rainforest community of Deep Cove to the farmlands of Richmond, there are multitudes of neighbourhoods in and around Vancouver. The city and its environs are a fabulous mix of the rural and the urban, the quaint and the cosmopolitan, and have a wealth of places for families to explore. Have a slumber party with the whales at the Vancouver Aquarium! Take a trip to Mars at the Pacific Space Centre! Explore Commercial Drive or brave the Capilano Suspension Bridge, the end of which is in the middle of an old-growth forest with fir trees even Dad can't put his arms around! This chapter is an overview of the major neighbourhoods in Vancouver, each of which has attractions that will engage your children's senses and teach them about science, history and the environment. Out-of-towners who get a taste of all these neighbourhoods will leave with a good idea of the variety of Vancouver life.

The City of Vancouver is roughly, although not officially, separated into two areas: East Vancouver and the West Side, both of which are described below. Across Burrard Inlet lies the North Shore (as it's commonly known), which is divided into the Municipality of West Vancouver, the City of North Vancouver and the District of North Vancouver. And there are neighbourhoods within neighbourhoods. Parts of Vancouver's West Side, for example, are commonly known as Kitsilano, Kerrisdale, False Creek, and so on. To make matters more complicated, the West Side is not West Vancouver, or even the West End! This can all seem confusing to visitors (and to some locals as well). It's worth buying a good map and taking a few minutes to study the layout of the area. There is far more to the Lower Mainland than downtown Vancouver, so take time to explore what each neighbourhood has to offer. Each of the areas listed below are very kid-friendly and most importantly, they're loads of fun.

Downtown

Roughly bordered by the Burrard Inlet to the north, False Creek to the south, Main Street to the east and English Bay to the west, Downtown is the area's central business district. **Downtown** is also home base for out-of-town families as most of the city's hotels (particularly of the five-star variety), are located here. It does make a good central starting point, especially if you're a first-time visitor; there are a lot of places within walking distance and it's easy to get to Stanley Park, the North Shore and many beaches and destinations. (By the way, if you're staying downtown and want to explore any of the attractions described here, don't drive to them. Parking is difficult and expensive and the numerous one-way streets are confusing to all but the most seasoned Vancouverites. Walk or take a bus if need be. See page 2 for transit information.)

Robson Street is downtown's "main drag" and it's full of shops and restaurants, particularly to the west of Burrard Street. Visitors love it here, though kids, understandably, are not thrilled with being dragged from store to store. Younger ones may be appeased, however, by watching fudge being made at **Rocky Mountain Chocolate Factory** (1017 Robson). Older kids will undoubtedly appreciate **Virgin Megastore** at the corner of Burrard and Robson (generally considered downtown's core intersection) and **Planet Hollywood** next door to it, as well as **MAC Cosmetics** a half-block east. Just kitty-corner to that you'll find the **Vancouver Art Gallery** (see page 64), which has excellent children's interactive events the third Sunday of every month, and **Robson Square**, which has a nice outdoor ice skating rink in the winter. The architectural monolith just short of the dome of **B.C. Place** (see page 12) is the downtown branch of the **Vancouver Public Library** (see page 22), which has a huge children's book floor, with computers, a toddler play area, children's books in languages other than English and lots of events for kids.

If you want to take your kids to a movie, there are a number of theatres on Granville Street, just a few blocks east of Burrard. The area is funkier and has lots of street youth but it's just as safe as the rest of Vancouver. There's also a huge underground mall, **Pacific Centre**, which runs north–south along Granville between Robson and Pender Streets and connects with the **Four Seasons Hotel** (see page 133). Here you'll find **The Bay** which stocks reasonably-priced children's clothes and toys.

Another popular downtown spot, within walking distance of the core, is **The Lookout! Harbour Centre Tower** located next to the downtown campus of **Simon Fraser University** (SFU). The price for the elevator up is $8, which seems like a bit of scam (it's more if you bringing kids older than six) but once you get on – whooosh! The glass-enclosed skylift thrusts upwards, giving you the distinct impression of being Charlie Bucket or Willy Wonka in *Charlie and the Great Glass Elevator*. Instead of bursting through the roof of a chocolate factory, however, the elevator lets you out onto a circular viewing tower 168 metres (553 feet) above the ground. Small signs indicate landscape features such as **Stanley Park** (see page 32), **Burnaby Mountain** (see page 37) and the **Port of Vancouver** (see page 18), but little kids are more interested in where the train tracks go or what's on top of the buildings (a tennis court, in one case). It's fun to watch a helicopter land on the heliport or to observe the **SeaBus** go in and out of North Vancouver. Depending on your child, you may spend five or 50 minutes here. There's a small snack bar if you're peckish, and **Top of Vancouver Revolving Restaurant** (669-2220), a floor above, has average food (no kids' menu) with an above-average view. (If you eat here the elevator ride is free.) This attraction is mainly popular with tourists (many long-time locals I've met have never been), but it's a great place from which to see the layout of the city on a clear day.

On the waterfront, just north of Harbour Centre, is **Canada Place**. The five-sailed complex was built as a pavilion for Expo 86 and houses the cruise ship terminal, the **Pan Pacific Hotel**, the **World Trade Centre**, the **Vancouver Trade and Convention Centre**, as well as shops and restaurants and the **CN IMAX Theatre**, with its five-storey-high screen and wraparound IMAX digital sound. The IMAX films, many of which are in 3-D, celebrate themes such as Canadian wildlife, natural wonders, popular destinations and amazing adventures. Films last approximately 35 to 45 minutes. Walking around the exterior of Canada Place is quite pleasant; there are great views of the North Shore and of the surrounding area. Canada Place's website address is *www.canadaplace.ca*.

Just to the east is **Waterfront Station**, where you can take the **SkyTrain** (see page 2) and get tickets for the **West Coast Express** commuter train (see page 106). Waterfront Station is also the Vancouver terminal for the **SeaBus**, which goes to North Vancouver (see page 103).

Gastown is Vancouver's birthplace (named for "Gassy" Jack Deighton, one of Vancouver's first prominent businessmen), and is located west of downtown along Powell, Water, Alexander, Carrall and Cordova Streets, also within walking distance of the downtown core. Basically it's a maze of cobblestone courtyards, Victorian architecture and shops, shops, shops. I'm always put off by the masses of tourist paraphernalia, but it's a good spot if you're in the market for a Cowichan sweater or other aboriginal artwork. Some kids get a kick out of the **Gastown Steam Clock** (at Cambie and Water), which blows out steam and pipes a tune every 15 minutes.

There are several sports and conference facilities to the southeast of downtown, a 10-minute walk from the downtown core. The most noticeable of these is **B.C. Place**, distinguished by a huge white dome-shaped roof that is held up by air and steel wires. Rock concerts and trade shows are hosted here, and this is where the Canadian Football League's **B.C. Lions** play (see page 74). It's also home to the **B.C. Sports Hall of Fame and Museum** (see page 62), a great interactive venue for kids who are sports fanatics. Next door is **General Motors Place**, home to the National Hockey League's **Vancouver Canucks** and the National Basketball Association's **Vancouver Grizzlies** (see page 75). Just behind B.C. Place is the **Plaza of Nations**, once the main gathering place for Expo 86 and now a locale for various restaurants, clubs and casinos. The Plaza of Nations also hosts the annual **Alcan Dragon Boat Festival** (see page 245) as well as **Molson Indy Vancouver** (see page 250). Good for families is the plaza's **Score-Virtual Sportsworld**, which, like B.C. Place, has an amazing interactive sports facility (see page 99).

Don't go to Yaletown's pricey shops with toddlers who like to touch everything.

Farther south along Pacific Boulevard is the high-rise community of **Yaletown**, a small residential and shopping district. There are some fabulous but expensive shops here (go alone; these are not good spots for toddlers who like to touch everything). Do take your kids to the **Roundhouse Community Centre** (see page 215), however, where they can climb on the old train or play in the park. Aside from the shops and the Roundhouse, there's not much to do in the immediate area, although major residential construction continues to occur and the area will undoubtedly get even livelier.

Back at the downtown core, on the other side of Burrard Street, extending all the way to Stanley Park, is the **West End**. This is within walking distance of downtown, but it's just far enough away that with kids you might prefer to hop on a bus (see page 2 for transit information). Don't drive into the West End – there are a very few metered parking spots on the busier streets, the rest of streets are permit-only parking and many of the streets have blockades to prevent "through" traffic. Head for gorgeous **English Bay** (see page 42) at Denman and Davie, a fun and lively (and very crowded) beach, with lots of restaurants and shops close by. The **Sylvia Hotel** (see page 136), located at English Bay, is a charming, ivy-covered hotel very popular with visiting families; some rooms have kitchens. An excellent bike and foot path runs along the beach north to **Stanley Park** and continues through it. South, the path runs to the Burrard Bridge (and beyond). Just short of the bridge is **Sunset Beach** (see page 42), and just beyond it is the **Vancouver Aquatic Centre** (see page 86), with three great indoor pools, one of which is quite shallow – just for kids and their parents. Outside the Aquatic Centre (it's the ugly triangular building) is a **False Creek Ferry** dock (see page 102), which drops off passengers at various points around False Creek. Another mini-ferry, the **Aquabus** (see page 102), has its dock just under the Burrard Bridge.

A five-minute walk from downtown along English Bay takes you to **Stanley Park** (257-8400)(see page 32). This world-renowned park, one of the largest urban parks in the world, is essentially a huge forest with lots of other treats thrown in, including **Second Beach Pool**, the **Lost Lagoon Nature House**, the **Children's Farmyard and Miniature Railway**, and the exceptional **Vancouver Aquarium**. The **Seawall** runs around the perimeter of the park, but I wouldn't try the whole stretch with kids unless they're teenagers or you've got time to do it leisurely on bicycles. Drive your car, or better yet, take the **Stanley Park Shuttle Bus** (see page 104), a free shuttle that stops at numerous points around the park.

The **Vancouver Aquarium**, located in Stanley Park, is top-notch, well worth the hefty admission prices. (See the end of this section for more information.) There are over 56,000 underwater creatures to encounter, and kids run from one tank to another, pointing out the giant starfishes and sea anemones, the grumpy-looking octopus and the colourful rainbows of tropical fish. Check out the sharks, piranhas, electric eels, snakes and tarantulas. There are changing exhibits, many of which encourage kid participation. Try on a frog costume or look through a kid-size "swamp bubble" that gives you a frog's-eye view of a freshwater pond alive with wetland critters. Gaze through the porthole of a submarine while discovering the wonder of the ocean's floor in the Twilight Zone deep sea exhibit. Outside are tanks of seals and sea otters as well as the two resident whales. Whale shows are held throughout the day, and if you go to the lower observation room, you can watch the cetaceans shoot past the glass partition. There is also an Amazon rainforest environment where you can hunt for the sloth.

Some people avoid the aquarium because of the crowds and high prices, but one mom I know played it smart and bought a family pass. She takes her kids to the aquarium right after school whenever the mood strikes them; the two-hour period before it closes is a relatively quiet one. She recommends avoiding weekends "unless you want to queue up to see the octopus." The $69.95 family pass fee is worthwhile when you consider its educational value. The aquarium has overnight adventures and birthday parties as well as occasional hour-long "ed-ventures" for preschoolers. There is also a small restaurant near the whale pool. Unfortunately, the only way to exit the aquarium is through the gift shop, but if you're willing to part with a few more dollars, you can pick up inexpensive but well-made kids' items, such as educational colouring books and rubber whales for the bathtub.

The Lookout! Harbour Centre Tower
555 West Hastings St, at Waterfront Skytrain station and SeaBus terminal
Tel: 689-0421
Hours: Daily 8:30 a.m. to 10:30 p.m. in summer; daily 9:00 a.m. to 9 p.m. in winter
Prices: Adults $8; seniors $7; kids 6 and up $5; kids under 6 free; family $22 (2 adults and up to 3 kids under 17). Tickets valid all day.

CN IMAX Theatre
999 Canada Place, at Waterfront SkyTrain station and SeaBus terminal
Tel: 682-4629

Hours: Call ahead for show times
Prices: Adults $12.50; kids $6

Vancouver Aquarium Marine Science Centre
Off Georgia St, east of Denman St, in Stanley Park
Tel: 659-3474
Website: *www.vanaqua.com* or *www.vancouver-aquarium.org*
Hours: Daily 9:30 a.m. to 7:00 p.m. from June to Sept.; daily 10 a.m. to 5:30 p.m. from Oct. to May
Prices: Adults $12; seniors, students and kids 13 to 17 $10.50; kids 4 to 12 $8; kids under 4 free; family (five related people) $40 in summer. Adults $10; seniors, students and kids 13 to 17 $8.75; kids 4 to 12 $6.75; kids under 4 free; family rate $35 in winter

Chinatown

What began as a small Chinese settlement in the late 1800s has since become North America's second-largest **Chinatown** (San Francisco being the first). Located along Main Street and along the three blocks of Pender Street between Gore and Carrall, Chinatown is the place to shop for Chinese goods (though a strong Chinese presence makes Richmond a contender; see page 24). Visiting Chinatown is a great way to expose your kids to a vital part of Vancouver culture. Even small children are stimulated by the diverse shops, which sell everything from persimmons to duck eggs to lotus seeds coated with sugar. Ask your kids to figure out how many of the vegetables they can identify. Take them to a Chinese bakery and treat them to egg tarts, steamed pork buns or almond cookies. The world's thinnest building is at the corner of Carrall and Pender. (My son's comment: "You have to be really small to work there.") Your kids will probably jump for joy if you take them to **N&S Trading** (122 East Pender), which sells inexpensive items like wooden pop guns, wind-up toys, back-scratchers and diaries that lock. **Oriental Dragon Holdings** (112 East Pender) sells "everything" – Hello Kitty stuff and more.

There are a multitude of Chinese restaurants in this area (see page 122), nearly all of which are inexpensive, appropriate for families and have portions large enough to share easily. Close by is the **Dr. Sun Yat-Sen Classical Chinese Garden** (see page 47), a tranquil spot you may favour more than your children do. The **Chinese Cultural Centre**, at 50 East Pender (see page 214), is a good place to go if you want to find out about classes in Mandarin, Cantonese or the martial arts. The centre is also very involved in the community's festivals and performances, one of which is the **Chinese New Year Parade** (see page 242) each year. This is a really fun and interesting event (and *loud* – lots of firecrackers and drums), but be prepared to perch your child on your shoulders in order for him or her to see the dragon costumes and performers. It's often hard to navigate a stroller through Chinatown's midst, even on an ordinary day, so avoid sunny Saturday afternoons if you can't leave the buggy behind. Street parking can be hard to find; if it's crowded find the nearest pay lot and save yourself a headache. Otherwise, many buses service this area (see page 2). It's fun to go here in the summer, when it doesn't get dark until ten and the shops stay open late.

Older kids will like the **Vancouver Police Centennial Museum**, located at Main and Cordova (see page 65). Younger kids, particularly those into transportation, will appreciate the plethora of trains, boats, seaplanes and helicopters at **Portside Park** (see page 31). Gastown, Chinatown and places like Portside Park are good to explore with kids, but bear in mind that the immediate area around Main and Hastings can be grim – it's much more rundown and has a lot of petty crime and drug trafficking.

West Side

The West Side refers to the area of Vancouver west of Main Street. It's bordered by Burrard Inlet, the Strait of Georgia and the Vancouver International Airport. There are three bridges that go here from downtown: Burrard Bridge, Granville Bridge and the Cambie Street Bridge. The Granville Bridge is the best route if you want to get to the airport (see page 5).

At Cambie Street and 33rd Avenue you'll find **Queen Elizabeth Park** (see page 32). The park's gorgeous, manicured flower garden is a site very popular with wedding photographers. (Weekends are the best days to spot these parties.) Its accompanying **Bloedel Floral Conservatory** is a great spot on a rainy day.

Burrrard Street Bridge brings you directly into the heart of Kitsilano from downtown. "Kits," as it's commonly known, was a vibrant community in the sixties and remnants of that culture still linger. It has since become popular with middle-class families (those who can afford the housing) because of its strong community base and its proximity to the beaches. **Kits Beach** (see page 42) is a lively summer spot and has an enormous outdoor pool popular with families. There aren't really any hotels here, only the odd bed-and-breakfast, but the area is only five minutes from downtown by car, and not much farther by bus. (See page 2 for transit information.)

There's lots to do in Kits. A big family favorite is the **Pacific Space Centre** in Vanier Park (see page 33). Here your kids might take a pulse-pounding trip to Mars or travel back in time to be a sauropod – only two of the different types of adventures you might expect to find on **Virtual Voyages**, B.C.'s only full-motion simulator and one of the Pacific Space Centre's key attractions. Because the rides are so realistic and sometimes a bit frightening, this is generally not a good ride for kids under six. (One stalwart four-year-old boy I know adores it, however. After four visits, his father is not so keen.) There's plenty more to do here, all the activities having to do with outer space. One computer game shows how baseball might be played on other planets, according to the gravity present. Another game shows you what to pack when travelling to another planet. Pacific Space Centre is home to a planetarium and the **Star Theatre**. Multimedia presentations are held here and at **GroundStation Canada**.

One computer game shows how baseball might be played on other planets.

The **Gordon MacMillan Southam Observatory**, housed in a separate building nearby, has a half-metre telescope. It's open to the public on weekends from 7:00 to 11:00 p.m. if the weather is clear, if volunteers are available and if the equipment is working. On a cloudless night your kids will feel like they can touch the stars. (Call the Observatory at 738-2855, after 7:00 p.m. on Friday or Saturday nights, to see if it's open). The Space Centre is right next door to the **Vancouver Museum** (see page 65) and the **Vancouver Maritime Museum** (see page 64), both of which are also located in Vanier Park, a great place for a picnic and for watching kite-flying enthusiasts. Vanier Park is also home to the **Vancouver International Children's Festival** (see page 245), held here each May.

If you keep travelling along Cornwall Avenue, which parallels the water, from the park (again, take the bus or drive – the West Side is too big to explore on foot with kids), you'll hit some excellent beaches, namely **Jericho** and **Spanish Banks** (see pages 31 and 43). Farther west of these is the **University of British Columbia** (UBC) which has a number of excellent museums, the most impressive being the UBC **Museum of Anthropology** (see page 63), as well as the UBC **Botanical Gardens** (see page 48) and the **Nitobe Memorial Gardens** (see page 47). Much of this area is home to **Pacific Spirit Regional Park**, also known as the **University Endowment Lands** (see page 31), which is laced with beautiful walking trails, some short enough for small children to enjoy. The UBC **Observatory** (822-6186) atop the geophysics and astronomy building is open for free public viewing on clear Saturday nights. The observatory opens an hour past sunset and remains open for three hours; it's a great place to see star clusters and the rings of Saturn. Park at the West parkade or the Health Sciences parkade.

For the most part West Side shopping is done along 4th Avenue, Broadway, Granville Street and 41st Avenue. These areas also have good restaurants (see "Where to Eat with Kids").

South of Pacific Spirit Park is the **Musqueam Reserve**, home to some of the area's First Nations peoples, as well as the wealthy areas of Kerrisdale and Shaughnessy. South of the West Side are numerous golf courses and the **Fraser River Park** (see page 30). Don't miss the kid-friendly gardens (not an oxymoron) of **VanDusen Botanical Garden** at Oak St and 33rd Avenue. (Its restaurant, **The Shaughnessy**, is a bit stuffy for children.)

If you've headed out of downtown across Granville Bridge, you've passed directly over **Granville Island**. This destination is not an island at all – originally it was formed by two sandbars that were filled in back in 1915 and turned into an industrial area. Part of it has since been transformed into an impressive public market, but there's much more here. Granville Island is one of Vancouver's highlights. Make a point of going here at least once if you're a visitor and numerous times if you're a resident.

Just past the entrance is the **Kids Only Market**, an indoor market full of the most kid-friendly shops, selling everything from books and art supplies to kites and wooden toys. There's even a store devoted to Thomas the Tank Engine (**All Aboard**) and another that only sells water-oriented paraphernalia, from rain boots to rubber ducks (**Everything Wet**). **The Hairloft** makes haircuts fun for kids and you'll be pleased with the results. Very popular with kids is the **Adventure Zone** and **Circuit Circus**, a four-level indoor playground and amusement centre (see page 98). Outside is a fabulous summer water park, **Granville Island Water Park** (see page 43), a small lake with residents that quack and croak, and **False Creek Community Centre** (see page 214). There's also a tiny shop there, the **Crystal Ark**, which has a "pool" of rocks that kids can play in; they can also pick out their own bags of stones to buy and take home. Beyond that is **Arts Umbrella** (see page 198), which offers some of the city's best children's courses in dance, theatre and visual arts. If physical activity is more your family's style, you can rent a kayak or a small motorboat, arrange scuba adventures or take boating classes (see page 52).

You won't find a string of five-star restaurants here, but with kids in tow you'll probably be quite happy with **Bridges** or **The Keg**, both of which have kids' menus (see pages 112 and 115). Those with more of a culinary bent will be enchanted by the **Public Market**, which is full of fresh fish, yummy baked goods, two Italian delicatessens, an exquisite cheese shop and numerous fresh produce stands plus much, much more. My kids inevitably want to visit the fudge maker (**Olde World Fudge Co. Ltd.**), the donut shop (**Lee's Donuts**) and the tiny but charming candy stall (**Candy Kitchen**), but can often be distracted by goggly-eyed fresh salmon on beds of ice, towering pyramids of strawberries or the guy making fresh linguini at **Zara's Pasta**. Another great spot is the **Granville Island Sport Fishing Museum** (see page 62), with its display of model boats and trains – this is a good spot to take kids.

Maritime activity is big on Granville Island but so is handiwork, and you'll find local craftspeople at work in their studios. Watch someone blow glass, weave a rug, print a book, make a kayak or piece together a guitar. People here are friendly and don't seem to mind noses pressed up against the glass; after all, watching craftspeople in action is the best part of being here. Local crafts are sold around the island at a variety of shops. During the summer, jugglers, musicians and clowns entertain for free (performances are their livelihood, however, and they do appreciate donations). Numerous festivals are hosted here throughout the year, including the **Blue Grass Festival**, the **du Maurier International Jazz Festival**, the **Vancouver International Comedy Festival**, and the **Vancouver International Writers (& Readers) Festival** (see "Calendar," page 241). Three theatres – **Performance Works**, the **Waterfront Theatre** and the **Arts Club Theatre** are located here (see "Live Entertainment," page 53). Parking is available at the many covered garages for a small fee (bring extra change), but on a Saturday afternoon it might take you 15 minutes to even get near one of the lots. Save yourself the trouble and take one of the mini-ferries from downtown, a treat for kids in itself (see page 102). If you're already on the West Side, access the island by walking along the bicycle and walking path that goes through the area.

Pacific Space Centre
Vanier Park, 1100 Chestnut St (at Cypress)
Tel: 738-STAR (7827)

Hours: Mon. to Sun. 10:00 a.m. to 5p.m.
Prices: Adults 19 to 60 $12; kids 11 to 18 $9.50; kids 5 to 10 $8; kids under 5 free; family (5 people with a maximum of 2 adults) $38.

Granville Island

Off 2nd Ave or 4th Ave (2 blocks east of Burrard)
Tel: Info Centre 666-5784; Kids Only Market 689-8447
Hours: Public Market open Tues. to Sun. 9 a.m. to 6 p.m.; Kids Only Market open daily 10:00 a.m. to 6:00 p.m.

East Side

East Side (often referred to as East Van), is the part of Vancouver which lies east of Main Street, bordered on the north by Burrard Inlet, on the south by the Fraser River and on the east by Burnaby. If you look on a map you'll see that the "dividing line" (two "zero hundred" blocks between Quebec and Manitoba Streets), is just west of Main. If you're going to explore this area you can drive or take the bus. The bus services this area well (see page 2).

At the foot of Quebec Street, on the east side of False Creek, is **Science World**. It's hard to miss Vancouver's trademark silver geodesic dome. You won't want to, either. A legacy building from Expo 86, Science World is a great place for kids to learn about science hands-on. And I do mean hands-on. Kids can physically participate in loads of permanent exhibits – search for gold, blow square bubbles or dance on a giant synthesizer. Watch their hair stand on end when they touch the Vandergraaf Generator. Admission includes numerous rotating exhibits, demonstrations and a 3-D Laser Theatre. The **Alcan OMNIMAX Theatre** has a wraparound digital sound system and one of the world's largest dome screens (best for older kids). You might find yourself in the midst of a "real" astronaut mission or a neck-snapping car race. Science-based shows change every six months or so. Browse the gift shop for one-of-a-kind items to encourage the scientist in your child. If you live in Vancouver, consider getting a membership, which enables you to bypass the long lines; children never seem to get bored from repeat visits.

Science World is a great place for kids to learn about science hands-on.

There's a **White Spot** café on the main level and lots of pay parking close by. Incidentally, the mini-ferries service this attraction from downtown (see page 102).

The **Port of Vancouver**, located at 1300 Stewart Street (666-3226), is one of two places you take your kids when they ask why there are so many ships in the harbour. (The other place is the **Vancouver Maritime Museum** (see page 64). Daily logs at the museum indicate the boats' countries of origin and what cargo they're carrying). This is a huge port; 60 million tons of cargo are exchanged here annually and 30 ships pass through daily. The viewing centre (free!) looks out over the shipping yard where kids can watch the enormous green and orange lifts moving containers from place to place. Maps and displays inside the centre show what cargo comes in and out of the port. Kids like finding out some of the products western Canada exports (forest products, coal, sulphur, potash, grains, chemicals and petroleum products). Unfortunately, the viewing centre doesn't enable kids to see the containers actually being loaded onto the ships; you can get a better view of dock activity from **Portside Park** (see page 31) or **New Brighton Park** (see page 90). The centre has educational programs for school-age children and the very friendly and informative staff loaded down my kids with stickers, colouring sheets and port-related word search puzzles (and no, I didn't tell them I was doing a kids' guidebook to Vancouver!).

Probably the most interesting and well-known area in East Vancouver is **Commercial Drive**, also known as "The Drive." Originally an Italian neighbourhood (**Abruzzo Cappuccino Bar**, 1321 Commercial Drive, 254-2641, has what I think is the best coffee in town – strong and delicious – and the place is simple and unpretentious, with customers sitting around watching Italian sports on television), Commercial Drive is now popular with artists. There are a lot of families here, and **Britannia Community Centre** (see page 214) has the **Britannia Skating Arena** (an indoor rink; see page 79) and the **Britannia Swimming Pool** (also indoor; see page 87). There are also good shops and cafes along the Drive, at the foot of which is the **Vancouver East Cultural Centre** (see page 58). Affectionately known as "The Cultch," the centre puts on unusual and very worthwhile kids' theatre throughout the year.

Southeast of Commercial Drive, at around Renfrew St. and Hastings St. is **Hastings Park** (see page 30), home to the **Pacific National Exhibition** (PNE) every summer. Every year looks to be the last for this huge exhibition (it's now projected to stick around yet another few years) which will eventually be relocated in order to turn the park back into, well, a park. But what a project! Projected to take another fifteen years in the making, the eventual result will be a 65-hectare (162-acre) landscape refuge (for more information see "The Out of Doors," page 27). Small portions of the greenspace are now open. In the meantime the PNE continues to be a Vancouver summer institution and the 2nd largest exhibition in Canada, with concerts, livestock displays, pig races, the Pacific Classic Horse Show, exhibits, arts & crafts, inventions and more. Arrive at opening time before the crowds get heavy; a mid-week visit is best as the kids won't get impatient with long lines and adults may be more tolerant of this overflow of noise and hubbub.

A main part of the PNE is **Playland**, Vancouver's equivalent of Disneyland. It may be lacking Mickey Mouse, but no kid is ever disappointed by the 35 attractions and rides. Older kids will love riding one of the best rollercoasters in North America, as well as the Corkscrew, visiting the Nintendo Power Zone, and various other rides. Smaller kids will love Kids Place, which has a lot of rides for people their size. Playland opens earlier in the year than PNE (see hours below).

If your kids are toddlers and not begging to go on rides, you could avoid Playland and visit the rest of the PNE instead; it's much cheaper. A smart parent I know took her young kids to the PNE where they saw the pig races, animals, and other live shows, and they brought their own lunch. Total cost for that family: $12 for two adults. Kids were free. A visit to Playland, including buying lunch (but the donut stand is yummy) will run you at least $50. A pricey venture, but your kids will probably be eternally grateful if you treat them once a summer.

Pacific National Exhibition
East Hastings St. (at Renfrew St.)
Tel: 255-5161
Hours: middle of August to beginning of September daily 10:30 a.m. to 10:30 p.m.
Prices: Adults $6; kids free

Playland
East Hastings St. (at Renfrew St.)
Tel: 255-5161
Hours: Mar 28th to June 20th weekends and holidays 11:00 a.m. to 7:00 p.m.;
June 21st to Aug. 22nd daily 11:00 a.m. to 9:00 p.m.
Prices: All Day Ride for kids 4' and over: $17.95. Kids under 3 are free. Adult accompanying a child 12 & under: $8. All-Day Ride tickets can be purchased in advance at Shoppers Drug Mart for $14.95.

Other jewels in East Van are **Trout Lake**, near 12th Avenue and Nanaimo Street, in **John Hendry Park** (see page 31), next door to the **Trout Lake Community Centre** (see page 216). The **East Vancouver Farmers Market** is held every Saturday during the summer in the community centre parking lot; it's a great market and kids can run around the park afterwards. Also worth checking out is the area known as **Little India**, located along Main from about 49th Avenue to 53rd Avenue. There are great jewelry shops, fabric stores and food shops here, as well as excellent East Indian food and sweets. If you're not familiar with this area, explore it sometime with the kids so they can absorb the South Asian culture.

Science World
1455 Quebec St (at Terminal), Main Street/Science World SkyTrain station
Tel: 443-7443
Hours: Mon. to Fri. 10:00 a.m. to 5:00 p.m.; weekends and holidays 10:00 a.m. to 6:00 p.m.

Prices (for Science World and omnimax): Adults $14.50; kids, seniors and students $10.25; (for Science World only): Adults $11.25; kids, seniors and students $7.50; (for omnimax only): $9.75 per person; children 3 and under free.

North Shore

The **North Shore**, consisting of North Vancouver and West Vancouver, is a forested residential community at the foot of the North Shore mountains. These mountains are, of course, the predominant geographical feature of the Lower Mainland.

If you head over Lions Gate Bridge and turn left on Marine Drive, you'll find yourself in the midst of the municipality of **West Vancouver**, which contains some of the Lower Mainland's most expensive real estate (in particular, the British Properties). There's lots of shopping and many great cafés along Marine Drive, in the quaint and charming neighbourhoods of Ambleside and Dundarave. **Ambleside Park** (see page 35) is excellent for kids and has a playground, water park and in-line skating area, as well as an excellent beach. But, like North Vancouver next door, West Vancouver really shines because of its natural resources. This is a great place for exploring the out-of-doors. **Cypress Provincial Park** (see page 36) at the top of Cypress Bowl Road, off Highway 1 (known as Upper Levels Highway at this point) is popular for skiing or hiking; **Cypress Falls Park** (see page 36), a bit west off Highway 1, has hiking trails and a playground. **Lighthouse Park** (see page 36), at the southern tip of West Vancouver, is a great park for exploring with the kids, with trails, beachcombing and, of course, a lighthouse. Incidentally, Highway 1, which runs through West Vancouver, is the route you'll want to take to **Horseshoe Bay**, where ferries regularly leave for Bowen Island, the Sunshine Coast and Vancouver Island (see page 6). **Bowen Island** is a particularly good day trip for families; it's a short ferry ride and a fun place to explore.

North Vancouver is to the east. Not as expensive as West Van, it's home to many families, which makes for a lot of kid-friendly shops and restaurants, not to mention outdoor spots. To get to North Vancouver, take Lions Gate Bridge from Stanley Park and hang a right at Marine Drive. Alternatively, take the Second Narrows Bridge (another extension of Highway 1). This bridge is accessed from McGill Street if you're coming from East Vancouver. For visitors staying downtown, and for many locals, a far easier way to access North Van is to take the **SeaBus** (see page 103). This way you can avoid the potential traffic on the bridges (while both bridges once satisfied this area's need, increased population has made the routes intolerably slow at times, particularly in the summer when ferry traffic is heavy). Bear in mind that without a car it's difficult to explore areas of North Vancouver beyond the waterfront, although buses do service the area.

The SeaBus is a fun, short ride across the water (those luminous yellow mounds on the North Shore are sulphur) and will let you out at **Lonsdale Quay**, at 123 Carrier Cates Court (985-6261). The quay has an excellent public market and children usually like the fish shop with its live tanks, although they're also taken with the tiny shop that sells dollhouse supplies or distracted by the assortment of other stalls. Sometimes there's someone making balloon animals (for a small donation). Upstairs there's a free ballroom where kids can romp in a space knee-deep in small plastic balls; there are also shops that sell toys and kids' clothing. This public market is not nearly so impressive as **Granville Island**'s but it's a lot less hectic. The atmosphere of the wharf outside the market is great, with a view of downtown Vancouver and of barges butting up against the dock. Musicians often perform here on weekends. Get yourself a dish of steaming clams and enjoy the ambiance while your kids have an ice cream or dance to the live music. If you want to avoid eating at McDonald's (ever so cleverly located near the SeaBus), try the casual eating spots upstairs in the quay.

Aside from the quay itself, most of the waterfront area is industrial and not terribly appealing, but farther east, just off the Second Narrows Bridge is **Maplewood Farm** (see page 46), a very popular spot with kids that gives them the chance to see how a real farm works. Because of its proximity to the mountains, there is more rain in North Vancouver than in Vancouver itself (if such a thing is possible) but this also makes for an amazing rainforest and great nature excursions for families. **Capilano River Regional Park** (see page 33), which spans both North and West Vancouver, contains not only an immense rainforest, but also the **Cleveland Dam**, **Capilano Salmon Hatchery** and **Capilano Suspension Bridge**, all of which are great places for families to explore.

Farther up the canyon you can park and take the Skyride to **Grouse Mountain**, a great year-round area. Noses will be pressed against the window as you make the 10-minute climb to the top of the mountain. (This cable car can get so crowded that faces might be pressed against the window regardless). What a ride! It's a great way to see the surrounding area and kids love the experience. This is a place to go year-round, as there's something different every time you go. Skiing and snowboarding, of course, are popular, and there are clothing and equipment rentals if you've made a spur-of-the-moment trip and are poorly outfitted. You can't bring a sled up here, but make sure your little ones are wearing good ski pants because they won't be able to resist sliding down one of the tiny hills on their bums. There are free sleigh rides at the top (with the purchase of a Skyride ticket), an outdoor skating rink and snowshoe tours of the five-metre-high (16 feet) chainsaw-carved sculptures. In summer, hike the trails, go mountain biking or watch the paragliders. There are a couple of places to eat in the lodge. You can't drive up the mountain as there's no public road, but splurge at least once on a Skyride ticket. It's a real treat. Outdoor enthusiasts prefer making the Grouse Grind (the mountain's noted hiking trail) their route up, but this is an extremely rigorous trail, not one for children. For an outdoor hiking experience that kids *can* enjoy, try **Lynn Canyon Park** (see page 34), **Lynn Headwaters Regional Park** (see page 35) or the **Seymour Demonstration Forest** (see page 35), all excellent places.

The North Shore is excellent for exploring the out-of-doors

Deep Cove, a North Vancouver neighbourhood located off Mount Seymour Parkway, is a lovely, tiny waterfront town with charming shops and cafés, **Cates Park**, **Panorama Park** and **Deep Cove Park** (see pages 34 and 35). Excellent canoe and kayak rentals are available here (see page 50) and the parks have good playgrounds. Deep Cove is at the foot of many hectares of rainforest, accessible via the Baden-Powell trail, an extensive hiking trail that extends all the way into West Vancouver. Kids can usually manage it for the first hour. A portion of the path leads to a fabulous view of Indian Arm.

Grouse Mountain
6400 Nancy Greene Way (at the top of Capilano Rd)
Tel: 984-0661
Hours: Daily 9:00 a.m. to 10:00 p.m. all year
Prices (for Skyride): Adults $15.95; seniors $13.95; youths $9.95; children $5.95; kids under 6 free; families $39.95.

Burnaby

The city of Burnaby is located just east of Vancouver. Burnaby can appear like a big shopping district – which you'll probably love or hate – since one of its star attractions is Metrotown, a huge commercial and business mall. Kingsway, the long diagonal street that bisects Burnaby and East Van, also features shop after shop. Driving along Kingsway from Vancouver is a real pain (a fast, but intense shortcut is 1st Avenue), but the **SkyTrain** (see page 2) does stop at Metrotown, and the stop before Metrotown lets you out at **Central Park** (see page 37), a great park with hiking trails, **Swangard Stadium** and the **Variety Park Playground**. There are a few other excellent parks in the sprawl of Burnaby: **Burnaby Lake Regional Park** (see page 37); **Deer Lake Park** (see page 38), which contains the **Burnaby Art Gallery** (see page 66); **Burnaby Village Museum** (see page 57), which has a *great* carousel); and the **Shadbolt Centre for the Arts**. **Burnaby Mountain Park** (see page 37) is a serene place and a great vantage point from which to see all of downtown Vancouver; the view at night has no equal.

New Westminster

The oldest incorporated city in B.C., New Westminster was once a large fishing and mercantile centre. Located on the north bank of the Fraser River, the city is about 20 km (12 mi) east of Vancouver. Driving here can be an unpleasant challenge (not to be attempted during rush hour), but a trip to New West is a good excuse to take the SkyTrain, which will let you off at **Westminster Quay**, the main attraction in New West. Unfortunately, the SkyTrain doesn't let you off right at the quay. You'll have to choose between climbing up the long flight of stairs (which can be a struggle with kids, especially if you have a stroller) or walking at street level, about three full blocks, a long way around.

The quay runs two km (1.2 mi) along the Fraser River and has a hotel, residential space and offices, with more residential construction in the works, but you'll probably be more interested in the **Westminster Quay Public Market**. This is a small public market by Vancouver standards, but its location on the river makes it an interesting place to visit as there's lots of boating activity constantly going on. Tour the **Russian Foxtrot U-521 Submarine**, the only Russian submarine on display in North America. Or visit the **SS Samson V Maritime Museum**. (Only open on weekends, the museum is free, but donations are welcome.) You can also take a **Paddlewheeler River Tour** (see page 102) or let your kids roam around the **Expo Tugger**, an old tugboat on display on the dock. If you do drive, there is free three-hour validated parking. The market has a few novelty shops and one small toy store. If you're hungry, try **Troll's** upstairs (see page 120). The quay is a great place to watch the tugboats on the river. The two bridges you'll see are the SkyTrain bridge and the Patullo Bridge, the latter being an extension of Highway 99A, which goes south into Washington and north along the west coast of B.C. Besides the quay, **Queen's Park** (see page 38) is worth checking out, as it has a great petting farm and adventure playground.

Westminster Quay Public Market
810 Quayside Dr, at the bottom of 8th St, near New Westminster SkyTrain
  station
Tel: 520-3881
Hours: Daily 9:30 a.m. to 6:30 p.m.

Tri-Cities

The **Tri-Cities** area refers to the cities of **Coquitlam**, **Port Coquitlam** and **Port Moody**, all of which are located east of downtown, separated from Vancouver by Burnaby. Unfortunately the SkyTrain doesn't run out here – either take the bus or drive. Commuters take the **West Coast Express** (see page 106), an excellent train service. If you're based in Vancouver and want to go to parts east in the morning, the train won't work for you during the winter, as it only goes westbound in the mornings and eastbound in the evenings. In summer, however, it does run trains both ways quite frequently; call them for a current schedule.

Coquitlam is a very suburban area with lots of families. There are lots of parks and outdoor spaces; particularly nice is spacious **Mundy Park** (see page 39) which has two tiny lakes and an outdoor pool. There is also an excellent **Aquatic Centre** (see page 89) and good live entertainment at **Place Des Arts** (see page 199). On the outskirts of Coquitlam is **Minnekhada Regional Park** (see page 39), which has hiking trails and good wildlife viewing.

Port Coquitlam, also a suburban community, has a great hiking and cycling trail, the **PoCo Trail**, which runs through the city.

Port Moody is a tiny community located in the Port Moody Arm of the Burrard Inlet and has some lovely beaches lining its shores: **Rocky Point Park** (see page 40), **Town Centre Park** (see page 40) and **Old Orchard Park** (see page 40). On the north side of the arm is **Belcarra Regional Park** (see page 39), which is a bit of a drive, but this is a nice place to swim and explore tidal pools.

Richmond and Steveston

Richmond is a huge sprawl of a city, even larger than Vancouver. Located south of downtown Vancouver, the best way to get there is by driving (there's no SkyTrain and although you can take a bus, it will take you a good hour or more). Try to avoid rush hour, as both sides of the highway tend to get clogged. The best way to get into Richmond from downtown Vancouver is simply, go south. Take Granville Street to 70th Avenue, turn left and continue to Oak Street, then turn right and continue over the Oak Street Bridge, which spans the Fraser River and leads you into the flatlands of Richmond.

And why go to Richmond? Although it's the residing place of choice for many British Columbians, it's not necessarily the tourist spot of choice. There are, for better or worse, an inordinate number of malls stretching along Number 3 Road just west of the Oak Street Bridge. On the other hand, you will find a huge array of Asian-oriented stores here. Around the corner from these is the impressive **Minoru Centre**, which among other things, houses the **Minoru Aquatic Centre** (see page 89), the **Minoru Arenas** (see page 82) and the

Richmond Cultural Centre (see page 40), home to the **Richmond Art Gallery**, **Richmond Arts Centre** and the **Richmond Community Arts Council Museum**.

You won't find rainforest here, but you will find the excellent **Richmond Nature Park** (see page 40). Highway 99 runs right through it. The nature park is one of the last remaining bogs in Richmond, with short and long walks, a variety of vegetation and really interesting Sunday family walks that kids love. East of the park, the land is devoted primarily to farming and you'll find lots of produce stands with excellent fruits and vegetables. If you're driving out here during the day midweek, the traffic is usually light; visiting the Nature Park and getting some fresh produce is actually a quick trip and a great way to experience the real flavour of the area.

Steveston Fishing Village, located in the south part of Richmond (stay on Highway 99, then go west on Steveston Highway), was once a huge fishing and canning centre and is now a sweet little village, fun for an afternoon explore with the kids. The village itself has lots of little shops and restaurants and usually an entertainer is performing outside. Fishing boats pull up to the dock, where they sell catch from their vessels in accordance with area licenses; the prices are good and the fish even better! There are several sites that teach about the history of the area: the **Steveston Museum** (see page 69); the **Britannia Heritage Shipyard** (see page 68), an eight-acre waterfront park with lots of summertime activities; the **Gulf of Georgia Cannery** (see page 68), a national historic site which commemorates west coast fishing; and **London Heritage Farm**, an 1890s farmhouse. Around the perimeter of Richmond and Steveston are flat trails good for walking and cycling with kids.

Surrey

Over three times bigger than Vancouver, Surrey lies southeast of Vancouver and goes all the way from the south shore of the Fraser River down to the southernmost seaside community of White Rock, just minutes from the U.S. border. This is a huge suburban area that's almost impossible to access if you don't have a car. Even if you do take the SkyTrain out here, you'll find yourself walking for miles, it seems, to get from one place to another. Surrey is home to the **Cloverdale Fairgrounds**, which every year hosts the **Cloverdale Rodeo** (see page 245), Canada's second largest rodeo. Worth the trip is the **Rainforest Reptile Refuge** (see page 46) in South Surrey, a great place to see lots and lots of reptiles. If you are in Surrey, check out **Bear Creek Park** (see page 41), which has a superb playground and train ride, or shop at the **Surrey Public Market**, located at 6388 King George Highway (596-8899). **Crescent Beach**, located in South Surrey off Highway 99, is a relaxing spot for swimming, kite flying and clam digging. **White Rock**, close by, also has a nice beach lined with lots of shops and restaurants.

Farther Afield

There are many wonderful areas outside of Vancouver worthy of exploration but impossible to list here. Do keep in mind the **Greater Vancouver Zoological Centre** (see page 45), an hour east of Vancouver, or the **George C. Reifel Migratory Bird Sanctuary** (see page 45) in **Delta**, a great place to run around and see lots of different species of birds. Another great spot is the **Fort Langley National Historic Site** (see page 71), where kids can imagine what it was like to live in Vancouver 120 years ago. Getting to the fort is a bit of a trek, as it's 47 km (28 mi) east of Vancouver, but combine it with a trip to the **Langley Centennial Museum** (see page 72) and the **B.C. Farm Machinery and Agriculture Museum** (see page 70). The town of **Fort Langley** has lots of gift shops, art galleries and restaurants. Kids will love you forever if you take them to **Splashdown Park** (see page 43), off Highway 17 at the south end of Delta, just before the Tsawwassen ferry terminal. It's a wild and wet half-hectare (10-acre) water park that has 13 water slides and other fun stuff.

chapter 3

The Out-of-Doors

"Go play outside!" In a city inundated with rain, this isn't always easy for kids to do. But if you wait for a sunny day, you might wait weeks before you see one (and with kids in the house, you'll go quietly insane in the meantime). The best solution is to go out anyway: dress your kids in good, warm rain gear and sturdy, waterproof shoes or boots, and enjoy Vancouver's beautiful outdoors.

If the rain is getting you down, try a visit to **Stanley Park** (see page 32) or the University Endowment Lands (see **Pacific Spirit Regional Park**, page 31). Spaces like these remind us of the benefits of precipitation; without it we wouldn't have such incredible rainforests. It's great to observe the various mosses and hanging lichens, the multitudes of ferns or the giant banana slugs while meandering down the paths. Vancouver's parks and forests provide excellent settings in which to teach kids about nature. Plus, they're lots of fun!

In summer when the rain subsides (somewhat), Vancouver's out-of-doors really comes to life. There are endless places to go swimming, fishing, boating, bicycling and more. Many of them are listed in this chapter (as well as in other chapters in this book). For even more information, consult one of the many excellent outdoor guidebooks available, in particular Jack Christie's *Day Trips with Kids* (Greystone Books). Another source of information about Vancouver's parks, beaches and golf courses is the Vancouver Board of Parks and Recreation's website, *www.parks.vancouver.bc.ca.*

There are several excellent organizations that teach kids about the out-of-doors, such as **Outward Bound**, the **Sierra Club**, the **Junior Forest Wardens Association of B.C.** and **LIFE – Leadership Initiative For Earth**. For more information about these and other organizations, see page 226.

Additionally, there are numerous community gardens located throughout the Lower Mainland. Getting your own plot is not expensive, and it's a great opportunity to grow vegetables and other plants with your kids (especially for those families who are apartment dwellers). For information on how to obtain a space in a community garden, as well as information on how to compost (another great thing for kids to learn), call **City Farmer** at 685-5832 or access *www.cityfarmer.org/.*

By the way, if your child is interested in ocean life, check out *oceanlink.island.net.* **OceanLink** is a partnership between several B.C. marine organizations; this is an excellent marine science information and interaction website geared to kids. Some of the highlights are Ocean News, Aqua Facts and Ask a Scientist. They also have information on marine life at the Vancouver Aquarium.

P l a c e s   t o   G o

Here you'll find information on parks, beaches and water parks – free public spaces where you can hike, picnic, play, swim and have fun! I also list farms, zoos and nature parks, as well as gardens. These are places where you can go specifically to see something having to do with nature, whether it's zebras at the **Greater Vancouver Zoological Centre** (see page 45) or rhododendrons at the **VanDusen Botanical Garden** (see page 48).

Parks

One of the best things about Vancouver and its environs is the care and attention its various governments put into preserving and maintaining its natural spaces. Even tiny urban parks are well cared for, and it's practically impossible to find any kind of park in the Lower Mainland that isn't clean, safe, well maintained and – most importantly – kid-friendly.

To be included in this book, however, a park had to have something that made it special and particularly suitable for families, whether it was the opportunity for nature exploration or the simple abundance of playground equipment. As a result, you'll find listed both charming urban parks perfect for lovers of slides and swings (like Vancouver's **Tatlow Park**, see page 33) as well as enormous regional or provincial parks with expanses of B.C.'s prized rainforests, great for rural hikes (try **Minnekhada Regional Park** in Coquitlam, page 39). Take time to explore as many of the parks as you can; each one reflects a different facet of Vancouver, including not only its urban spaces and rainforests but also its bogland (**Richmond Nature Park**, page 40) and its extensive Fraser River boating industry (best viewed at Vancouver's **Fraser River Park**, page 30, or **Burnaby Fraser Foreshore Park**, page 37).

Hiking is an excellent activity for kids; and can be as easy or strenuous as you and your family like. It's a great idea to introduce kids to hiking and the forest early on so they begin an appreciation of nature. My only advice is to make it fun. I find it's much more enjoyable to hike with another family; kids don't complain so much when they've got a pal along. Keep hikes short and on level ground until kids are accustomed to walking longer distances. Take frequent breaks and bring along lots of little snacks and drinks. It also doesn't hurt to have some prior knowledge of plantlife so you can point out things to your kids, but it's often just as interesting to poke around dead logs and come across different species of lichens and mosses, then go home and identify them in a book (an excellent book with lots of colour pictures is *Plants of Coastal British Columbia*, Lone Pine Publishing). Or have your child draw pictures of what you see when you get home. The **Western Canada Wilderness Committee** is a grass-roots conservation and research organization dedicated to preserving land in Western Canada. Their store (227 Abbott St. at Water St., tel: 683-8220) has lots of information and maps of trails in various wilderness areas, plus nature guides and books on the environment. This is a good spot to go if you're interested in hiking with your kids or learning more about the plants in particular areas.

Take care if you're going to be hiking at any of the more rural parks on the North Shore, even if you're only planning a 20-minute walk. In the spring when the snow melts, creeks can swell rapidly, making hiking conditions extremely dangerous. Weather can also change quickly, even in summer, so be sure you have warm clothing, a hat, a small first aid kit, a whistle (to scare off bears or call for help) and some extra food and water, and that you and your kids are wearing sturdy shoes. Parks departments are listed below; call the North Vancouver, West Vancouver or Greater Vancouver Regional District number if you're at all unsure about hiking conditions.

Most parks come under the jurisdiction of their particular area's parks board. All other parks (they tend to be larger rural ones) come under the jurisdiction of the Greater Vancouver Regional District (GVRD) or the B.C. Ministry of Environment, Lands and Parks. For more information on the parks listed below, as well as a more complete list of green spaces, call the numbers below or access their websites. Parks are listed alphabetically by region, and individual phone numbers for parks are listed where applicable.

Incidentally, the GVRD offers forest education programs throughout the year, many of which are specifically geared to families. These programs take place at various parks throughout the Lower Mainland. For more information on these programs, call the GVRD number below. Parks departments don't usually offer family programs, but West Vancouver Parks and Recreation has a particularly good one; through the West Vancouver Community Centre it offers a Tiny Trekkers outdoor program for parents and their children from six weeks to five years old. For information on these naturalist walks, call

925-7270. The **Vancouver Natural History Society** also has field trips every weekend of the year for its members; the shorter trips are good for younger members. Call 737-3074 for more information.

B.C. Ministry of Environment, Lands and Parks, 924-2200,
www.elp.gov.bc.ca:80/bcparks/explore/lmaindis.htm
Greater Vancouver Regional District (park information), 432-6350,
www.gvrd.bc.ca/go/todo/pkloc.html
Vancouver Board of Parks and Recreation, 257-8400,
www.parks.vancouver.bc.ca
City of North Vancouver Parks Department, 983-7333
District of North Vancouver Parks Department, 990-3800,
www.district.north-van.bc.ca/parks.htm
West Vancouver Parks and Recreation, 925-7200
Burnaby Parks and Recreation, 294-7450,
www.burnabyparksrec.org/parks/parks.html
New Westminster Parks and Recreation, 527-4567
Coquitlam Leisure and Parks, 927-6969,
www.gov.coquitlam.bc.ca/Parks_Environment/Parks1.htm
Port Coquitlam Parks and Recreation, 927-7900
Port Moody Parks, Recreation and Culture, 469-4555
Richmond Parks and Leisure Services, 276-4383,
www.city.richmond.bc.ca/services/
Surrey Parks and Recreation, 501-5050

Vancouver

Everett Crowley Park
S.E. Marine Dr (at Kerr)
An urban wilderness on the border between Vancouver and Burnaby, this is a great place to take the kids on a nature walk. There are several trails, most of which are short enough for small children, as well as a couple of playgrounds.

Fraser River Park
75th Ave, off S.W. Marine Dr
There's lots of activity on the Fraser River, making this a fun place to walk with the family. Kids can watch the passing tugboats and see planes landing and taking off from Vancouver International Airport. There are lots of birds in the marshy areas, logs and sandy areas to play on and a big grassy area for picnicking.

Hastings Park
North of Hastings St between Nanaimo and Cassiar
Traditionally home to **Playland** and the **Pacific National Exhibition** (1999 will supposedly be its last year here), Hastings Park is being turned into the second largest park in the City of Vancouver. The transformation, which will take

Hastings Park is being turned into the second largest park in the City of Vancouver.

30

another 15 years, will eventually result in a 65-hectare (162-acre) landscape refuge. Different parts of the park will open as progress is made; some smaller areas are now open to the public. The park is also home to the **Hastings Park Racecourse** at Exhibition Park (254-1631), the **Pacific Coliseum** (253-2311) and other auditoriums where concerts and exhibitions are often featured; these are slated to be retained. (For more details about this site, see under East Side in "Neighbourhoods," page 18.)

Jericho Beach Park
West end of Point Grey Rd
The best of everything: a lovely beach with a conveniently located concession stand and a large grassy park with a small lake inhabited by ducks. The park is popular for summertime picnics, and there are great short walks through the trees. This park is a particularly good place for year-round birdwatching; the variety of different habitats all in close proximity make it possible to see a variety of birds within a short period of time. Watch for coots, ducks, herons, bald eagles, red-winged blackbirds and more.

John Hendry Park
Victoria Dr (at 19th Ave)
The park's main feature is **Trout Lake**, a lovely spot surrounded by willow trees. The lake has a small, sandy beach popular with swimmers in the summer (there's a lifeguard), though it's closed off and on throughout the warmer months due to a high coliform count (attributed to bird droppings). The path around the lake is nice for a short stroll, though it can get quite muddy. There's also a covered picnic area, a summer concession stand and the **Trout Lake Community Centre** (see page 216). From May to September, the **East Vancouver Farmers Market** is held in the adjacent parking lot.

Pacific Spirit Regional Park
Bordered by N.W. Marine Dr, S.W. Marine Dr, Camosun St and UBC
Tel: 660-1808
Also known as the University Endowment Lands, Pacific Spirit Regional Park consists of 800 hectares (2,000 acres) of second-growth forest adjacent to the University of British Columbia (UBC). All the trails are safe and well marked, so this is a great place to take kids on long or short walks. Plus, if you are in Vancouver, it's a quick drive to this wilderness spot. This is a good place to practise identifying trees such as tall cedars, Douglas firs and hemlocks, as well as maples, red alders and bitter cherries. Smaller kids like spotting black squirrels or giant banana slugs. Toilets (as well as trail maps) are located at the Park Centre, on the north side of 16th Avenue west of Blanca Street. The main trails are stroller-accessible. This is also a good spot for mountain biking.

Portside Park
Foot of Main St, near Gastown
This small park is a transportation lover's dream. Here your kids can see trains pulling in, seaplanes and helicopters landing, cruise ships departing and cargo being removed from ships at the Port of Vancouver. There is also a nice grassy

area with play equipment. Unfortunately, no swimming is allowed and you shouldn't even let your kids wade in their bare feet; the water is *not* clean.

Queen Elizabeth Park and Bloedel Floral Conservatory

33rd Ave (at Cambie)

Tel: 257-8570

Hours (for conservatory): Mon. to Fri. 9:00 a.m. to 8:00 p.m., Sat. and Sun. 10:00 a.m. to 9:00 p.m. in summer; daily 10:00 a.m. to 5:30 p.m. in winter

Prices (for conservatory): Adults $3.25; seniors $2; kids 6 to 18 $1.60; kids under 5 free

A completely landscaped park at the top of which is the **Bloedel Floral Conservatory**, a huge silver dome containing more than 500 species of tropical and desert plants, as well as pools of koi and 50 species of free-flying tropical birds. Elsewhere in the park are quarry gardens, tennis courts, a roller court area, basketball courts, **Queen Elizabeth Pitch and Putt** (see page 76) and lawn bowling greens. The park boasts a 180-degree view of Vancouver and is a popular spot for weddings; kids love watching the festivities. The park is stroller-accessible and the conservatory has a good gift shop. Also home to **Nat Bailey Stadium**.

Stanley Park

Entrance at the east end of Georgia St, past Denman St. Alternatively, follow Beach Ave along the English Bay side of the West End until you reach the park.

There are some amazing parks in Vancouver, but Stanley Park is the city's treasure. Most of the 405-hectare (1,000-acre) park is forest, with 35.3 km (22 mi.) of clearly marked trails that are generally safe for walking during the day, particularly on weekends. An 8-km (5-mi.) seawall encircles the park, which is great for people with strollers, as well as for bicycle riding and in-line skating (see page 49 for bicycle or in-line skate rentals). While you're in the park, definitely visit the **Vancouver Aquarium** (see page 13), worth a separate trip. Wander around **Lost Lagoon** among swans, ducks and Canada geese. Don't feed them bread, however; it's bad for their digestive tracts. (If your kids really love feeding birds, take them to the **Reifel Bird Sanctuary**, page 45, where you can buy small sacks of birdseed.) The **Lost Lagoon Nature House** has educational materials and offers excellent nature walks throughout the year (call 257-8544 for information). The **Miniature Railway** (see page 106) has eight-minute rides through the evergreens. Steps from it is the **Children's Farmyard** (see page 46). From March to October, **Stanley Park Horse Drawn Tours** (see page 102) has guided one-hour rides around the park. Near English Bay there's a playground at **Second Beach** (see page 42) as well as an oceanside outdoor heated pool, **Second Beach Pool** (see page 90), open during the summer. Another summer venue is the **Lumberman's Arch Water Park**. Also popular are the totem poles at the arch, as well as the gorgeous rose gardens. There are tennis courts, an

Pay parking is in effect throughout all of Stanley Park.

outdoor theatre, a rhododendron garden, **Stanley Park Pitch and Putt** (call 681-8847 for details), and lots and lots of grassy areas to picnic and play Frisbee. Refreshment stands are located throughout the park, as well as four restaurants, the most kid-friendly of which is the **Prospect Point Café** (see page 118). The entrance off Georgia can get pretty crowded, especially on weekends. An alternative route is to take Beach Avenue, which leads to the park, but if you're not familiar with the area, get a map with park details before you set out. Pay parking is in effect throughout and is patrolled regularly, so in the flurry of getting kids unbuckled, don't forget to buy a ticket. You can also take a public bus to the park, and then hop onto the the free **Stanley Park Shuttle Bus**, which stops at 40 locations throughout the park (see page 104.)

Tatlow Park
3rd Ave (at Macdonald)
This is a charming little park with lots of trees shading a lovely playground. A little stream runs through the property, with a couple of bridges for crossing or for throwing sticks into the water. The park ends at Point Grey Road, and if you cross the street you can get down to the ocean; at low tide this is a nice small beach for exploring. (Be careful when crossing, for there's no signal and the cars go by fast. Better yet, cross one block west at the crosswalk or two blocks east at the light.)

Vanier Park
Ogden Ave (at Chestnut)
A big kite-flying spot, this park is right in the midst of a lot of action. Close to **Granville Island** (see page 16) and **Kitsilano Beach** (see page 42), it's also right next to the **Pacific Space Centre** (see page 15), the **Vancouver Museum** (see page 65) and the **Vancouver Maritime Museum** (see page 64). A great spot for a picnic between visits to the museums or just to take a break from riding along the False Creek Seawall.

North Vancouver
Capilano River Regional Park
Capilano Park Rd, just off Capilano Rd and Edgemont Blvd
Hours: Park, dam and hatchery open daily 8:00 a.m. to dusk; suspension bridge open daily 8:30 a.m. to 9:00 p.m. in summer and 9:00 a.m. to 5:00 p.m. in winter
Prices (for suspension bridge): Adults $8.95; seniors $7.50; students $6; children 6 to 12 $3; kids under 6 free; free admission to park, dam and hatchery

A gorgeous forested park, this is a great hiking destination along the shores of the roaring Capilano River. A particularly good family walk is the Coho Loop, which takes about 30 minutes. The canyon walls are steep, so keep hold of your kids' hands. This park also contains the **Cleveland Dam, Capilano Suspension Bridge** and **Capilano Salmon Hatchery**. The **Capilano Suspension Bridge** (985-7474), located at the southern part of the park, hangs 137 metres (450 feet) above the Capilano River. Some adults get a bit panicked when they cross the 70-m (230-ft) steel cable bridge, but kids seem to love it. If you do make your way across, you'll be rewarded with an old-growth forest, in the midst of which is the Living Forest Exhibit, an excellent presentation about the trees and plant life of the West Coast rainforest. There is also a Trading Post Gift Store, Aboriginal carving centre and trails through old growth evergreens. A café and restaurant are close by. (The Capilano Suspension Bridge is a rather pricey excursion, though popular with visitors. Critics favour the Lynn Canyon Suspension Bridge (see below), which is not as grandiose, but it's also not as crowded and it's very, very free.)

A few hundred metres above the bridge (accessible via hiking or driving) is the **Capilano Salmon Hatchery** (666-1790), another great spot for families. It's quite riveting to see the Capilano River rushing by, and when the salmon are going upstream, kids can point to their silver flashes popping up above the water. This facility produces three million salmon a year, helping to supplement the fishing industry, and there are lots of things for kids to see: display aquariums, adult holding ponds and fry-filled juvenile rearing areas. There are below-water-line observation areas, as well as educational displays and nature exhibits. This is certainly an opportunity to show kids different types of salmon as well as their mating and egg-laying habits, but it's also nice just to wander around in one of the most beautiful parts of Vancouver.

The **Cleveland Dam**, located at the top of the park just below **Capilano Lake**, isn't necessarily the most exciting attraction in the world, but it's worth a 15-minute trip if you're at the park. After all, this is where Vancouver gets much of its drinking water, and it's slightly thrilling to stand on the bridge and watch the water going through the dam: 378 million litres (100 million gallons) of drinking water are released here each day, and more than 64 billion litres (17 billion gallons) are stored. The dam spans 195 metres (640 feet) across the canyon.

Cates Park
Off Dollarton Hwy in Deep Cove
A secluded beach with gentle forest walks good for children, as well as nice summer swimming. It's a good getaway from the more hectic beaches of Jericho or Kitsilano. For literary parents: Malcolm Lowry used to live here.

Lynn Canyon Park
Park Rd, past Lynn Valley Rd
Tel: 981-3103
Hours: Daily 10:00 a.m. to 5:00 p.m. from Feb. 2 to Nov. 30; weekends noon to 4:00 p.m. from Dec. 1 to Feb. 1
Unlike Capilano's, the suspension bridge here is free, even if it's not as high up. (It's only suspended a mere 50 metres, or 166 feet, above Lynn Creek.) The park itself is a 90-year-old second-growth Douglas fir and hemlock forest and home to the **Lynn Canyon Ecology Centre**. Inside the centre are displays about ecology, natural history and environmental issues, as well as models, a puzzle table, a puppet theatre and summertime nature programs. There is a snack shop but it's not always open, so bring a picnic lunch.

Lynn Headwaters Regional Park
End of Lynn Valley Rd
Tel: 985-1690 (hiking and trail conditions)
A 250-hectare (617-acre) park with hiking trails, subalpine meadows and incredible views. This is, however, rugged terrain with unpredictable weather, and visitors are asked to check themselves in and out at the park entrance. Wear sturdy shoes and bring extra clothes and a small first aid kit, even if you're only going for the afternoon. There are shorter trails for families, though, and it's an idyllic spot to explore provided you do so sensibly. The visitor centre, the **B.C. Mills House**, has logging and mining artifacts. There are picnic tables.

Mount Seymour Provincial Park
Mount Seymour Rd, off Mount Seymour Pkwy
Mount Seymour is a popular skiing area (for more information, see page 86), but in the summer it's an excellent hiking area and particularly good for families, as there are a variety of hiking trails, ranging from easy to difficult. (A good family hike is the Goldie Lake hike, which takes about an hour.) At the southern part of the park there's a park office on Indian River Road where you can get a free map and interpretive trail booklet. Camping is also available at the park.

Panorama Park and Deep Cove Park
End of Gallant Ave, off Deep Cove Rd
Two parks that run into one another at the edge of picturesque Deep Cove. Canoe and kayak rentals are available (see page 50), plus there's play equipment for kids. The beach is great for swimming.

Seymour Demonstration Forest
North end of Lillooet Rd, past Capilano College
Tel: 432-6286 or 987-1273 (program information)
Hours: Vary widely throughout the year; call for seasonal information

Seymour Demonstration Forest has 11 km of paved, car-free road for bicycling.

A popular spot for bikers and in-line skaters, as there are 11 kilometres (6.8 miles) of paved road with no cars permitted on weekends or after 5:00 p.m. on weekdays. Also good is the fishing at Rice Lake and in the Seymour River, and there are numerous walking trails. This is a big field trip destination for North Van schoolkids, and there are informative interpretive trails that teach visitors about logging and forestry practices. From June to October, there are weekly guided tours open to everyone.

West Vancouver
Ambleside Park
13th St (at Marine Dr)
A beachside park to the west of the Lions Gate Bridge with something for everyone: picnic areas, playground, water park, concession stands. Take a walk on the seawall or swim in the ocean. The park looks out onto Stanley Park and the

bridge, and there is good birdwatching on the artificial island in the tidal slough. For the more active, there is an area for skateboarding, in-line skating and basketball, as well as **Ambleside Pitch and Putt** (see page 76), a fitness circuit, jogging trails, playing fields and a dog park. There's also an art gallery, a fishing pier and a boat launch.

Cypress Falls Park
Off Woodgreen Pl above Upper Levels Hwy, Exit 4
A wilderness park with stands of huge cedar and fir trees. The trail to the lower falls of Cypress Creek is good for small children. There is also a playground and tennis courts.

Cypress Provincial Park
Exit 8 off the Upper Levels Hwy
Website: *www.elp.gov.bc.ca:80/bcparks/explore/parkpgs/cypress.htm*
Like Seymour, Cypress is a popular skiing area (see page 85 for information on **Cypress Bowl**), but this is a gorgeous place to visit year-round and particularly good for hiking, though some of the slopes can be muddy and slippery. There are alpine lakes and forests and amazing views of the Vancouver area. Even if you're not a hiker, come here for a leisurely picnic lunch; there is a nice picnic area that doesn't involve any hiking and still has great views. There's also a year-round chairlift that kids like; on a hot summer day, bring swimsuits and towels, as there's great swimming at **Cabin Lake**.

John Lawson Park
17th St (at Argyle)
Though small, this park is included here because it has an excellent children's playground with cement igloos and innovative lumber and chain structures.

Lighthouse Park
Beacon Lane, off Marine Dr
A 75-hectare (185-acre) mini-forest with old-growth Douglas fir trees, tidal pools, a lighthouse and lots of walks easy enough for children to manage. This is a gorgeous spot no matter what the weather and very popular on weekends. There is no concession stand, so bring lunch and have a picnic at the water's edge. There are lots of tidepools with starfish and sea anemones, but make sure your kids are wearing shoes with good treads so they don't slip on the rocks.

Whytecliff Park
Off Marine Dr, west of Horseshoe Bay
The lovely beach here is popular with scuba divers, but it's also good for swimming or for relaxing on the narrow strip of sand. There's a path of rocks exposed at low tide; you can clamber onto them and reach a tiny island, with great views of the water and islands beyond. There are also change rooms on the beach. Up above, the park has lots of grassy areas, covered picnic tables, tennis courts and a children's playground. The concession stand has some surprisingly good food, like free-range roast chicken and Thai salads, as well as typical fast-food fare.

Burnaby

Barnet Marine Park
Off Barnet Rd, adjacent to Burnaby Mountain Park
A popular summer spot for families, this park is located on the shores of Burrard Inlet. The beach has safe swimming areas, a wharf for fishing, a nonpowered boat launch, trails, a picnic area and concession stands.

Burnaby Fraser Foreshore Park
Fraser Park Dr (at Byrne)
A popular spot for fishing. There is also a paved pathway paralleling the river, which is good for walking with a stroller. Have a picnic and watch the river traffic.

Burnaby Lake Regional Park
Off Hwy 1, near Kensington Ave
Hours: Daily from dawn to dusk; Nature House open 10:00 a.m. to 4:00 p.m. weekends from May to Sept.
This 300-hectare (750-acre) marshland is very different from the masses of beaches and forests in the Lower Mainland. It's also very serene. Look for water lilies, beavers, bugs and diving beetles in the lake. If your kids are quiet enough, you might spot an osprey, grebe, muskrat or turtle feeding among the reeds. (Needless to say, I've never seen them.) The **Nature House** (420-3031) contains displays and offers park maps, information on nature sightings and nature programs. There's also a viewing tower; bring your binoculars.

As the park is right off Highway 1, there's a lot of traffic noise on the part of the trail south of the lake, but with kids in tow, you probably won't be anticipating a quiet walk anyway. Close by is a soccer field and children's playground, as well as the Burnaby Sports Complex, with a skating rink and swimming pool. The lake is part of a bird and wildlife refuge, so no swimming is allowed. However, a lot of rowing is done here; there are no rentals, but if you bring your own canoe, you can launch it near the Nature House or sports complex.

Burnaby Mountain Park
Centennial Way, off Burnaby Mountain Pkwy
The views from this park are amazing. Lots of trails run around the mountain, though many are a bit steep for kids. There is a playground (also located up a steep path), but a favourite summertime activity for kids is to slide down the grassy hill on cardboard. (It's a great tobogganing slope in winter.) There is a series of carved Japanese wood poles that illustrate Ainu mythology and tell of a culture closely connected to water. The restaurant, **Horizons** (299-1155), makes great steaks and alder-grilled seafood but is a better outing for older, quieter children. (They don't have a kids' menu but will serve plain pasta or half orders of chicken wings.)

Central Park
Boundary Rd between Kingsway and Imperial, near the Patterson SkyTrain station
Tel: 294-7450
This 88-hectare (219-acre) park is right on the boundary between Burnaby and

Vancouver. There are lots of trails around the lake, as well as a horseshoe pitch, tennis courts, **Central Park Outdoor Pool** (see page 90), **Central Park Pitch and Putt** (see page 76) and a lawn bowling green. Perhaps the best feature is the **Variety Park Playground**, specifically designed for children with physical disabilities, though all kids are welcome. In the spring and summer the **Vancouver 86ers** (see page 75) play soccer at **Swangard Stadium**, also located here. **La Charcuterie Delicatessen** at Boundary and Kingsway (190 –3665 Kingsway, 439-3354) has excellent sandwiches if you want to pick up a take-out lunch.

Confederation Park
Willingdon Ave north of Hastings
This park has a great playground, water park and the **Eileen Dailly Leisure Pool and Fitness Centre** (see page 88), as well as a running track, tennis courts, a skateboard park and picnic tables. Also popular with kids is the **Burnaby Central Railway** (291-0922; see page 105) on the north side of the park. There is a wooded area wonderful for getaway walks.

Deer Lake Park
Buckingham Ave off Burris St
There are so many things to do in this immediate area: visit the **Burnaby Art Gallery** (see page 66), see a performance at the **Shadbolt Centre for the Arts** (see page 57), ride on the carousel at the **Burnaby Village Museum** (see page 66), walk through **Burnaby Century Gardens** (see page 47) or come to the lake itself and rent a canoe (call **Deer Lake Boat Rentals** at 667-2628). This is also a good spot for fishing and hiking, plus there are lots of shade trees, making it a great spot for a picnic.

Robert Burnaby Park
Off Canada Way at 19th Ave and 1st St
Directly opposite Burnaby Lake, this is a little-known park – surprising, since it's 293 hectares (724 acres) big. There is a playground and lots of grassy areas for kids to play on, but this park's charm lies in the trails that wind through it, surrounded by Douglas firs and western hemlocks, with skunk cabbage in the spring and blackberries in the summer. Also popular in warmer months is the **Robert Burnaby Park Outdoor Pool** (see page 90).

New Westminster
Hume Park
North end of Kelly St, just off Braid
A great water park that also features the **Hume Outdoor Pool** (see page 90), picnic tables, tennis courts, a playground and a concession stand.

Queen's Park
1st St (at 3rd Ave)
Tel: 524-9796 or 526-4811
Hours: Park open year-round; petting farm and pool open May to Aug.
For kids, the centrepiece of this gorgeous park is **Rainbow Playland**, which includes the **Queen's Park Children's Petting Farm** (see page 46) and an

excellent water park. It also features an innovative adventure playground with climbing, swinging and jumping equipment (a section is designed for children with physical disabilities). The park also has a 19th-century rose garden, **Queen's Park Arena** (an ice skating rink; see page 81), the **Queen's Park Bandshell** (with summer performances; see page 56), a gymnasium with family programs (check out their excellent gym sessions for small children) and the **Vagabond Playhouse** (see page 58). Basketball, volleyball, football and softball are also played here; there are several children's sports programs. There is a fitness circuit as well.

Ryall Park
Ewen Ave, in Queensborough
A great water park is the highlight here, with miniature waterfalls, push-button action and more. There is also a playground, playing fields and a picnic area. Ryall Park is home to the **Queensborough Community Centre** (see page 218).

Tri-Cities

Belcarra Regional Park
Bedwell Bay Rd north of Ioco Rd, **Port Moody**
It's a bit of a drive to Belcarra, located across Indian Arm, but you won't regret it once you're here. Extending across 9 km (5.5 mi.) of shoreline, the park includes **Sasamat Lake**, a good swimming spot with very warm water in the summer. There are trails, sheltered caves, tidal pools and lots of places for fishing, hiking, picnicking and beachcombing. Also an excellent playground. It's extremely busy on nice summer weekends, so arrive early in order to find a parking spot.

Como Lake Park
Gatensbury St between Como Lake Ave and Foster Ave, Coquitlam
Even if you're based in Vancouver, this is a really lovely park to venture out to. A pier at the lake is open for fishing only to seniors and children – a great idea! A wood-chip path encircles the lake, and it's a really calm, blissful place. There is also a fenced-in playground, good for toddlers who tend to wander.

Minnekhada Regional Park
Between Oliver Rd and Quarry Rd, **Coquitlam**
This 175-hectare (428-acre) park in the northeast corner of Coquitlam has two large marshy ponds great for walking around; bring your binoculars in the spring and fall so you and your kids can check out the migrating birds. This is one of the parks the Greater Vancouver Regional District uses for family nature programs. (For more information, call the GVRD at 432-6350.) Some people canoe here, but you have to bring your own boat and launch it from the dike that separates the two ponds.

Mundy Park
Bordered by Austin Ave, Mariner Way, Como Lake Ave and Hillcrest St, **Coquitlam**

This park has the **Spani Outdoor Pool** (see page 90), a treat in itself, but there are lots of other great things at Mundy. The playground is really fun and diverse (it's hard to drag my kids away from it), plus there are playing fields, covered picnic tables and hiking trails to two lakes.

Rocky Point Park, Old Orchard Park and Town Centre Park
Off Ioco Rd, **Port Moody**
A number of parks interconnect at the end of Port Moody Arm, including these three major ones, that are great for swimming in the summer because the water is calm, far away from the open ocean. There are in-line skating paths and playgrounds at each park. Rocky Point has the outdoor **Rocky Point Pool** (see page 90), a fishing pier and a boat launch; Town Centre has tennis courts and bike paths. These parks are also nice spots for beachcombing in the winter if you want to get out of the Vancouver area; too bad there are oil refineries along the north shore of Port Moody Arm.

Richmond
Garry Point Park
7th Ave (at Chatham), Steveston
Located on a historic fishing site, this park is close to the **Steveston Fishing Village** (see page 25) and the **Gulf of Georgia Cannery** (see page 68). A scenic park good for walking and picnicking, Garry Point is also popular for kite flying.

Iona Beach Regional Park
Iona Island Causeway, northwest of Vancouver International Airport
The 4-km (2.5-mi.) path is located directly atop one of Vancouver's main sewage outfall pipes, but don't let that deter you from walking and cycling here; it's a great spot for both. The clean beaches here are good for canoeing and kayaking, and this is an excellent spot for watching ducks and sandpipers. Kids like watching planes land at Vancouver International Airport.

Minoru Park
Gilbert Rd (at Granville Ave)
Tel: 276-4107
This very urban park is home to several sports facilities, including the **Minoru Arenas** (an ice skating complex; see page 82) and the **Minoru Aquatic Centre** (see page 89). Lots of organized sports are also played here, among them soccer, football and hockey. The **Richmond Cultural Centre** houses the **Richmond Art Gallery**, **Richmond Arts Centre** and the **Richmond Community Arts Council Museum**. It's close to the big Richmond shopping malls, so if you're compelled to do some major buying and have to take the kids along, you can treat them to swimming or ice skating here afterwards.

Richmond Nature Park
Westminster Hwy (at No. 5 Rd)
Hours: Daily dawn to dusk; Nature House open Mon. to Thurs. 8:30 a.m. to 5:00 p.m., Fri. to Sun. 9:00 a.m. to 5:00 p.m.

This is one of the last remnants of the bogs that used to cover this area. The vegetation here is quite different from the rainforested areas of Stanley Park and Pacific Spirit Regional Park; here you'll find heaths, sphagnum moss, pine trees and a birch forest. Trails wind through the forest, always suitable for kids and sometimes for strollers, if it's not too muddy. The park has multitudes of blueberry bushes. If you visit in the summer when the berries are ripe, you're allowed to eat as much as you want, although people are discouraged from taking home bags of fruit. This is also a good spot to see some of the many bunnies that live here. The downside is the occasional roar of jets overhead. The upside is the park's **Nature House** (273-7015), a hands-on information and activity centre geared to kids. Its staff put on a variety of nature programs, including guided Sunday walks. In the spring and summer, the **Butterfly House** is full of caterpillars and butterflies. Kids inevitably enjoy coming here.

Steveston Park
Moncton St (at No. 1 Rd), Steveston
A good playground, the **Steveston Community Centre** (see page 219) and a Japanese cultural centre are all here. It provides a good play break for the kids after you've explored the **Steveston Fishing Village** (see page 25).

Surrey
Bear Creek Park
88th Ave (at King George Hwy)
This has to be the best playground in Surrey, with lots of different types of equipment. Kids love the **Bear Creek Park Train**, a miniature train that gives short rides through the forest (see page 105). Home to the **Surrey Arts Centre and Theatre** (see page 58).

Tynehead Regional Park
Hwy 1 (at 176th St)
A 260-hectare (642-acre) park of woodlands and meadows at the headwaters of the Serpentine River. The trails are really quiet and provide a good escape; the main trail is stroller-accessible. The **Tynehead Hatchery** at the south end of the park is a big salmon and trout habitat. In fall you can see fish migrating back to the park.

Beaches
Vancouver beaches are staffed by lifeguards from Victoria Day weekend in late May to Labour Day weekend in early September, usually from about 11:30 a.m. to 9:00 p.m. daily (or until the sun sets). At all beaches, kids should swim between the red buoys for maximum lifeguard supervision. Prohibited are dogs, alcohol, inflatable devices in water, fires (barbecues are permitted in containers) and ball playing (except in designated areas). For beach and tide information, call the Vancouver City Parks and Recreation Board's beach information line, at 738-8535, from June to September.

Only the main Vancouver beaches are listed below; they are arranged geographically, starting with Third Beach at Stanley Park and following the curve of

41

English Bay all the way to the beaches near UBC. Beaches not listed here can be found under Parks (see pages 28-41).

Third Beach
West side of Stanley Park, along seawall
A small, relatively quiet beach plus there's a pleasant grassy area above the beach good for picnicking. The water at the beach here is particularly clean, with a low coliform count. There are also washrooms and a concession stand. It's really too far to access by walking along the seawall from English Bay. By car (remember, there's pay parking), enter Stanley Park off Georgia Street, then drive until you see the signs for Third Beach. Better yet, take the free **Stanley Park Shuttle Bus** (see page 104) that goes through the park in the summer.

Second Beach
Southwest side of Stanley Park
Washrooms, concession stands, and a good playground close by. The heated outdoor **Second Beach Pool** (see page 90) is open from May to September. From the beach it's about a 10-minute walk to **Lost Lagoon**, a good place for a short, exploratory walk offering lots of Canada geese, swans and raccoons, plus you can visit the **Lost Lagoon Nature House**. Acessible via car or the **Stanley Park Shuttle Bus** (see page 104), Second Beach is also a short, pleasant walk from **English Bay Beach** (see below).

English Bay Beach
Along Beach Ave from Bute St to Stanley Park
Located in the bustling West End, English Bay is one of the busiest beaches in the Lower Mainland. Shops and restaurants are close by, and the beach has a large water slide (only open at high tide), as well as washrooms and a concession stand. There are usually street performers at night in the summer, and it's a great place for people-watching. Keep in mind that parking can be a nightmare, so don't drive here if you can avoid it. Take the public bus instead. This is a great beach if you're staying downtown and can walk here. (The **Sylvia Hotel** is right across the street; see page 136.)

Sunset Beach
Along Beach Ave from the Burrard Bridge to Bute St
A clean, pleasant beach with washrooms, a concession stand and a small grassy area. Next to the **Vancouver Aquatic Centre** (see page 86) and the mini-ferry dock (see page 102), it's a good place to watch boats going through Burrard Inlet. Parking is nearly impossible; take a mini-ferry from **Vanier Park** or **Granville Island**, or it's 10-minute walk from downtown.

Kitsilano Beach
Arbutus St (at Cornwall)
A lively area popular with 20- to 30-year-olds, featuring concession stands, picnic tables, a playground, washrooms, tennis and basketball courts, and volleyball on the beach. **Kitsilano Pool** (see page 90), an excellent outdoor swimming pool, is open from May to September and includes a small water park. There's a

Starbucks across the street for coffee; other restaurants are close by. The **Vancouver Maritime Museum**, **Vancouver Museum** (for both, see pages 64-65) and **Pacific Space Centre** (see page 15) are within walking distance, as is **Vanier Park** (see page 33).

Locarno Beach
Along N.W. Marine Dr west of Trimble
A wide, sandy beach; at low tide you can walk across miles of wet sand with shallow tidal pools. This is a great spot for family picnics, with lots of room to run around. There are washrooms, picnic tables and a concession stand.

Spanish Banks Beach
Along N.W. Marine Dr, west of Tolmie
A wide, quiet beach with good tidal flats. Spanish Banks is very popular with families looking for a quiet day at the beach, plus there's lots of room to stretch out. It's a nice spot in the evening for a picnic dinner. There are washrooms and two concession stands.

Wreck Beach
Below S.W. Marine Dr, west side of UBC campus, near Gate 6
I almost didn't include this place, mainly because it's a nude beach and some people seem to object to that. However, it's such a gorgeous spot (and not because of the naked bodies) that it's really worth checking out. It's so peaceful and out-of-the-way you'll feel like you're on holiday. Kids can play in the sand, climb the rocks or watch boats going by. If you don't care for the nudity, go in the winter when people are clothed. There is a long flight of stairs leading down to the beach, one reason why it's so sparsely populated, but my four- and six-year-old kids managed them surprisingly well. Also, there's no concession stand, so bring snacks, except in summer, when private vendors do a roaring trade.

Water Parks
Outdoor public water parks are generally open from July to early September, though some are open as early as May. Admission is free. The two best outdoor public water parks in the city are the **Granville Island Water Park** in Sutcliffe Park next to the **False Creek Community Centre** (see page 214) and **Lumberman's Arch Water Park** on the east side of **Stanley Park** (see page 32) adjacent to the seawall. Also see pages 87-90 for a list of swimming pools; many, like **WaterMania** in Richmond or the **Newton Wave Pool** in Surrey (both indoor facilities), offer a diversity of spray and water play. Locations of smaller, outdoor public water parks are listed below, alphabetically by region.

If you want to give your kids a real water experience, check out the following privately owned park:

Splashdown Park
4799 Hwy 17, just before the Tsawwassen ferry terminal
Tel: 943-2251
Hours: Mon. to Thurs. 10:00 a.m. to 4:00 p.m. and Fri. to Sun.

10:00 a.m. to 7:00 p.m. from June 1 to 25; daily10:00 a.m. to 8:00 p.m. June 26 to Sept. 2, weather permitting
Prices: Adults $16; children $11
You might be competing with ferry traffic getting here, but this is a special treat for kids, especially on a very, very hot summer day. This 4-hectare (10-acre) water park has a total of 13 water slides, as well as an arcade, hot tub, video arcade, picnic tables, facilities for basketball, badminton and volleyball, and, of course, food concessions. It gets very crowded on hot summer days. Parking is free.

Vancouver
Chaldecott Park, Wallace St (at King Edward)
Clarke Park, Commercial Dr (at 15th Ave)
Connaught Park, Larch St (at 10th Ave)
Garden Park, Garden Dr (at 3rd Ave)
Grandview Park, Commercial Dr (at Charles)
Maclean Park, Heatley Ave (at Georgia)
Oak Park, 59th Ave (at Oak)
Portside Park, north foot of Main St
Slocan Park, 29th Ave (at Slocan)

North Shore
Ambleside Park, 13th St (at Marine Dr), West Vancouver
Eldon Park, Ruby Ave (at Hillcrest), North Vancouver
Mahon Park, Jones Ave (at 17th St), North Vancouver
Myrtle Park, Strathcona Rd (at Deep Cove Rd), Deep Cove
Viewlynn Park, Viewlynn Dr (at 24th St), North Vancouver

Burnaby
Charles Rummel Park, Government St (at Lozells)
Confederation Park, Willingdon Ave (at Pandora)
Rene Park, Balmoral St (at Sperling)
Suncrest Park, Rumble St (at Joffre)

New Westminster
Hume Park, Kelly St (north of Braid)
Moody Park, 8th St (at 6th Ave)
Queen's Park, 1st St (at 3rd Ave)
Ryall Park, Ewen Ave (at Lawrence)
Sapperton Park, E. Columbia St (at Sherbrooke)

Tri-Cities
Ailsa Park, Ailsa Ave (at Dundonald), Port Moody
Blue Mountain Park, King Albert Ave (at Blue Mountain), Coquitlam
Burns Park, Edgar Ave (at Burns), Coquitlam
Easthill Park, Barnet Hwy (at Union), Port Moody
Panorama Park, Johnston St (north of Panorama), Coquitlam

Farms, Zoos and Nature Parks

The following is a list of places where kids can see domestic and/or wild animals. But keep in mind that all the parks in the Lower Mainland provide potential opportunities to see nature up close. The **Capilano Salmon Hatchery** (see page 34) is particularly good. Excellent spots for birdwatching and wildlife viewing are **Fraser River Park** in Vancouver, **Ambleside Park** in West Vancouver, **Burnaby Lake Regional Park**, **Minnekhada Regional Park** in Coquitlam, the **Richmond Nature Park** and **Tynehead Regional Park** in Surrey (for locations, see Parks, pages 28-41). The **Bloedel Floral Conservatory,** also listed under Parks (see page 32), has koi and tropical birds.

George C. Reifel Migratory Bird Sanctuary
10 km (6.2 mi.) west of Ladner off River Rd on Westham Island, Delta
Tel: 946-6980
Hours: Daily 9:00 a.m. to 4:00 p.m.
Prices: Adults $3.25; seniors and kids 2-14 $1.

Kids always seem to enjoy it here, mainly because there are so many birds (more than 263 species) and lots of room to run around (260 hectares or over 640 acres). This is a wintering area for migratory birds, so you'll see more if you go between October and April, though the place can get hectic on sunny Sundays during that time. The fields of snow geese are startlingly beautiful. May and June are the best months to see ducklings and goslings. There are displays, observation decks and bird blinds. Buy a bag of seeds at the entrance so your kids can feed the birds. You can also get a free map of the grounds, as well as a list of birds currently habitating on the premises. There is a gift shop, picnic tables and washrooms. Dogs are not permitted.

The fields of snow geese are startlingly beautiful.

Greater Vancouver Zoological Centre
5048 264th St, 1 hour east of Vancouver (take Hwy 1 east, then the Aldergrove/U.S. border Exit 73), **Aldergrove**
Tel: 856-6825 or 857-9005
Website: *www.bc-biz.com/vancouverzoo/*
Hours: Daily 8:00 a.m. to dusk year-round
Prices: Adults 16 and up $10.50; seniors and kids 3 to 15 $7.50; kids 2 and under free

There are more than 200 species of exotic and wild animals at this 48-hectare (120-acre) farm, including giraffes, lions, tigers, camels, elephants and hippos, as well as a petting zoo. The Safari Express Train or Happy Hippo Bus Tour is a good way to see the perimeter of the zoo, especially for kids who tire quickly of walking. Better yet, bring a stroller or wagon and walk at your own pace. Stroller rentals are available, but save your money for the gift shop, where there's an array of inexpensive toys. There are concession stands, but since the zoo also has a nice picnic area, many families bring their own lunch and relax under the trees while their kids have fun on the nearby play equipment. On your way back to Vancouver, take a detour to the **Krause Brothers Farm** (6179 248th Street,

856-5757) in the summertime for fresh corn and strawberries. Also nearby are some cut-your-own Christmas tree farms.

Maplewood Farm

405 Seymour River Pl (at Mount Seymour Pkwy), **North Vancouver**
Tel: 929-5610
Hours: Tues. to Sun. 10:00 a.m. to 4:00 p.m.; closed Mondays
Prices: Adults $2; kids $1.50
A lovely 2-hectare (5-acre) park popular with small children, who get to see how a real farm actually works. Maplewood has about 200 domesticated animals and birds, including horses, pigs, sheep, donkeys and ducks. Pet the bunnies, watch the cows being milked or hang out with the goats. Go in the springtime when there are newborn lambs and baby ducks. The farm hosts a number of fun family events throughout the year. See "Calendar of Events" or call for details.

Queen's Park Children's Petting Farm

McBride Blvd between 6th Ave and Royal Ave, **New Westminster**
Tel: 525-0485
Hours: Daily 10:00 a.m. to 5:30 p.m. from May to Aug.
Prices: Admission by donation
There are lots of barnyard animals in this tiny zoo. See page 38 for more information on Queen's Park.

Rainforest Reptile Refuge

1395 176th St (at 16th Ave), **Surrey**
Tel: 538-1711
Website: *www.dynaserve.com/web/reptiles/*
Hours: Tues. to Sun. 10 a.m. to 5:00 p.m.
Prices: Adults $4.95; seniors and students $3.25; kids 3 to 12 $2.50
Pythons, iguanas, Chinese water dragons! Albino pythons, tarantulas, turtles! More than 50 displays of exotic reptiles are located here. The refuge, established in 1986 as a home for unwanted, abused and abandoned animals, is kept warm and humid to simulate the natural rainforest environment. It's staffed entirely by volunteers, who are really helpful with answering questions about the reptiles.

Stanley Park Children's Farmyard

Off Pipeline Rd at the east side of Stanley Park, **Vancouver**
Tel: 257-8530 or 257-8531
Hours: Daily 11:00 a.m. to 4:00 p.m. June to Sept.; weekends only 11:00 a.m. to 4:00 p.m. Oct. to May
Prices: Adults $2.50; kids 2 to 12 $1.25; kids 12 to 17 $1.75; family (2 adults and their children) $5
Pet the bunnies, walk among the goats and chickens, or wander though a room full of snakes and spiders (in cages, of course). The farm is right across from the **Miniature Railway**, and reduced-rate combination tickets are available for both venues (see page 106).

Gardens

Gardens are sometimes more appealing to adults than to children, but Vancouver has some brilliant botanical spaces that introduce kids to a wide variety of plant life they might not otherwise see. Besides, these are outside spaces, so kids can run around freely (as long as they stay out of the flower beds!), an added bonus.

Burnaby Century Gardens

Deer Lake Park, Burke St (at Gilley), **Burnaby**

These gardens are located on the north shore of Deer Lake. Adults will appreciate the 200 varieties of rhododendrons; children often like it, though it's tough competing with the nearby **Burnaby Village Museum** (see page 66).

Dr. Sun Yat-Sen Classical Chinese Garden

578 Carrall St (at Pender), **Vancouver**

Tel: 689-7133

Hours: Daily 10:00 a.m. to 4:30 p.m.

Prices: Adults $6.50; seniors and students $5; kids 5 to 17 $4; kids under 5 free

The first authentic Ming Dynasty garden built outside the People's Republic of China. It's a bit pricey, but this garden is a good spiritual retreat after you've been walking through busy Chinatown. If you can, visit once on your own and take the free adult-oriented tour – it's quite interesting – then bring the kids so you can tell them in your own words how the garden was built. There are fascinating stories behind its architecture; older kids might be interested to learn that it was built without the use of nails or electrical tools. Plus, there's a gift shop at the exit with affordable items for children. Alternatively, visit the free public garden (also a part of Sun Yat-Sen) beside the enclosed garden; young kids particularly enjoy the kid-size black bamboo "forest."

Japanese Friendship Garden

Off Royal Ave (at 4th St) behind City Hall, **New Westminster**

Hours: Daily dawn to dusk

A tribute to New Westminster's sister city, Mariguchi, Japan. There are waterfalls, scenic ponds and a traditional Japanese bridge. It's worth a quick look any time you're in the neighbourhood, but make a point of going in the spring when the garden's 100 ornamental cherry trees are in bloom. Children love the petals that fall like snow.

Nitobe Memorial Garden

West side of UBC campus, near Asian Centre (from Gate 4), **Vancouver**

Tel: 822-6038

Website: *www.hedgerows.com/UBCBotGdn/Gardens/Nitobe2.htm*

Hours: Daily 10:00 a.m. to 6:00 p.m. in summer; Mon. to Fri. 10:00 a.m. to 2:30 p.m. in winter

Prices: Adults $2.50; seniors and students $1.50; kids under 6 free; free admission in winter

A Japanese tea and stroll garden – delicate and tranquil. Even younger ones will like the birds, bridges, tiny waterfalls and the lake full of carp. Not too far from the UBC **Botanical Garden** (see below).

UBC **Botanical Garden**

6804 S.W. Marine Dr, near 16th Ave and Gate 8, UBC, **Vancouver**
Tel: 822-4208
Website: *www.hedgerows.com/UBCBotGdn/VisitUBCBotGdn.htm*
Hours: Daily 10:00 a.m. to 6:00 p.m. from March to Oct.; 10:00 a.m. to 2:30 p.m. from Nov. to Feb.
Prices: Adults $4.50; seniors $2.25; kids under 6 free; free admission in winter
With 28 hectares (70 acres) of plants, there's plenty of space for kids to run around. Bring a stroller if your young ones are not up to walking so you can explore the 400 species of rhododendrons, the Asian Garden, the Alpine Garden, the B.C. Native Garden and the Physick Garden (a medicinal herb garden based on 16th-century designs). Kids especially like the Food Garden, which has dozens of raised beds and almost 200 fruit trees.

VanDusen Botanical Garden

5251 Oak St (at 37th Ave), **Vancouver**
Tel: 878-9274 or 257-8666
Hours: Daily 10:00 a.m. to dusk from April to Sept.; 10:00 a.m. to 4:00 p.m. from Oct. to March
Prices: Adults $5.50; seniors and kids 6 to 18 $2.75; kids under 6 free; family (2 adults and 2 kids) $11 from April to Sept.; adults $2.75; seniors and kids 6 to 18 $1.50; kids under 6 free; family (2 adults and 2 kids) $5.50 from Oct. to March
I'm always surprised at how much my kids like coming here. The garden is different throughout the year, making it easy to have repeat visits. Go in the fall for the heathers and autumn colours, in December and January for the hollies, and in the spring for the glorious bulbs. The highlight for kids is the Elizabethan Maze. This place has easy stroller access; there's also the **Shaughnessy Restaurant** (261-0011), formerly called Sprinklers, but you might not feel comfortable bringing small children here. In December there is the **Festival of Lights** (see "Calendar of Events," page 254).

Things to Do

Here you'll find places to go bicycling, boating, fishing, go-karting, sailing and windsurfing. For information on team sports, golf, skate parks and rinks, snow sports, swimming pools and tennis, see "Sports."

Bicycling

Vancouver is a bicyclist's paradise. The city has so many interconnecting bike routes, it's impossible to list them all here. Both libraries and bookstores carry numerous Vancouver guidebooks for cyclists. For information and maps of cycling trails in Vancouver, contact **Cycling B.C.**, 1367 West Broadway (at Heather), 737-3034.

One popular bike route is around the 9 km (5.5 mi.) Stanley Park seawall, part of the Seaside Bicycle Route which extends all the way from Stanley Park to Spanish Banks. Start at Coal Harbour, at the west end of Georgia Street, then continue around Brockton Point, under Lion's Gate Bridge, past Second and Third Beaches and then on to Lost Lagoon, opposite Coal Harbour. This route is good for kids, as the terrain is flat and bicyclists are only allowed to go in one direction, making for a safe, easy ride, but it's very busy on sunny weekends. A shorter but equally scenic stretch is to start at Kitsilano Beach and ride along the False Creek Seawalk, also part of the Seaside Bicycle Route, on to Granville Island. You can even go as far as Science World (and beyond) before heading back. (Bicyclists can travel in both directions here.) Beginner bicyclists can practice at the stretch of the Seaside Bicycle Route between Jericho Beach and Spanish Banks. Other flat, off-road paths are in **Pacific Spirit Regional Park** (see page 31), on the University Endowment Lands. Also popular with families are the numerous dike trails around Richmond, all of which are flat and easy to ride. There are great bike trails around Steveston, along the west side of Richmond and along the South Arm of the Fraser River.

Remember that all cyclists must wear helmets and obey the same traffic regulations as cars. For GVRD bicycle information, call 432-6375; for bicycle-related concerns, also try the 24-hour **Vancouver City Bicycle Hotline** at 871-6070. For information on maps, safety, laws and routes, access *www.city.vancouver.bc.ca/cycling/*.

The following places, all located near Stanley Park, rent kids' bikes, adult bikes and trailers. Alley Cat and Bayshore also rent in-line skates. (For a list of places that sell bikes, including kids' bikes, tandem bikes, trailers and infant car seats, see page 165.)

Alley Cat Rentals
1779 Robson St (at Denman), near Stanley Park
Tel: 684-5117

Bayshore Bicycles and Rollerblade Rentals
745 Denman St (at Georgia), near Stanley Park
Tel: 682-2453
1601 W. Georgia St at the Westin Bayshore Hotel
Tel: 689-5071

Spokes Bicycle Rental and Espresso Bar
1798 W. Georgia St (at Denman), near Stanley Park
Tel: 688-5141

Boating

Most kids love being out on the water, and boating is a great, relaxing way to spend some family time. Those totally unfamiliar with boating should consider renting a canoe, pedal boat or rowboat on **Deer Lake** (see page 38). If you've got a bit more money and want to explore the outer part of Burrard Inlet, consider renting a small speedboat at Granville Island or Stanely Park for an hour or two; no experience is necessary, though a basic understanding of boating rules and safety will make your trip more relaxing.

The city's bays and inlets are very calm and good for canoeing and kayaking. Lessons are strongly advised for those unfamiliar with boats. Prime kayaking spots are in **False Creek** (rentals are available on Granville Island as well as in other areas; see below) and **Deep Cove**. Note that boats of all kinds must stay at least 300 m (about 1,000 ft) away from swimming beaches. On any boating outing, even if you're only going out for an hour, bring along a few crackers or some sliced apple; kids always seem to get hungry when they're in the middle of a body of water. Sunscreen is very important when boating; it's deceptively breezy. Guard your hat!

The following places rent all manner of crafts for exploring local waters. For sailing rentals and lessons, see page 52.

Adventure Fitness
1510 Duranleau St, on Granville Island, **Vancouver**
Tel: 687-1528
Canoe and kayak rentals and instruction.

Deep Cove Canoe and Kayak Centre
2007 Rockcliff Rd (near Banbury Rd at Naughton), **Deep Cove**
Tel: 929-2268
Rentals, lessons and guided day paddles.

Deer Lake Boat Rentals
Sperling Ave (at Canada Way), **Burnaby**
Tel: 667-2628
Canoe, pedal boat and rowboat rentals.

Ecomarine Ocean Kayak Centre
1668 Duranleau St, on Granville Island, **Vancouver**
Tel: 689-7575 (rentals); 689-7520 (lessons)
Kayaking rentals, sales and lessons.

Granville Island Boat Rentals
1696 Duranleau St, on Granville Island, **Vancouver**
Tel: 682-6287
Speedboat rentals.

Sewell's Marina
6695 Nelson Ave, **Horseshoe Bay**
Tel: 921-FISH (3474)
Speedboat rentals.

Stanley Park Boat Rentals
1525 Coal Harbour Quay (at Denman), **Vancouver**
Tel: 682-6257
Speedboat rentals.

Fishing
There are lots of fishing opportunities in and around the lakes and coasts of Vancouver and the Lower Mainland. Fishing licences are required (though not for ages 16 and under) and can be obtained at most tackle shops. For

information on fishing in B.C., get a copy of the Provincial Sport Fishing Regulations, available at tackle shops.

A lot of fishing in Vancouver is done at **Jericho Beach Park**, **New Brighton Park** and at **Trout Lake** in **John Hendry Park** (for locations, see section on Parks, pages 28-41); in North Vancouver at **Capilano River Regional Park**, **Lynn Headwaters Regional Park**, **Panorama Park** and at the **Seymour Demonstration Forest**; in West Vancouver at Ambleside Beach in **Ambleside Park** and **Horseshoe Bay Park**; in Burnaby at **Barnet Marine Park** and **Burnaby Fraser Foreshore Park**; and in Port Moody at **Belcarra Regional Park**. Another good spot is **Como Lake Park** in Coquitlam; there is a small fishing pier only open to seniors and children – great for grandparent-and-child outings.

Burnaby Fraser Foreshore Park and the pier at Ambleside Beach are my particular favourites; they're easy to get to if you're coming from Vancouver, and they're fun, interesting spots. Small children are not always enamoured of the idea of sitting in the middle of a chunk of wilderness while fishing; they like to watch boats and people. Save the pristine fishing spots for when your kids really start appreciating the gentle tug of young salmon on the rod. Young, beginning anglers can also check out the **Colebrook Trout Farm** (13067 Colebrook, off Hwy 99 past Hwy 10, 594-1865) in Surrey, which rents poles and bait with which to catch trout out of their three tanks – a guaranteed catch. For rental boats and fishing charters, call **Sewell's Marina** in Horseshoe Bay, 921-FISH (3474), or **Uncle's Charters** on Granville Island, 307-4475.

Go-karting

This is an *adventure* and a really fun thing for kids to do. The open-air go-karts ride low on the ground, travelling just over 32 km/h (20 mph) along an almost kilometre-long (half-mile) track similar to a real raceway, with curves, S-bends and straightaways. Kids can ride in a cart alone if they're at least 10 years old and 1.4 m (four-and-a-half feet) tall, but smaller kids can ride in double carts (there are seatbelts) with a parent. A great place to try go-karting is **Richmond Go-Kart Track**, 6631 Sidaway Road (at Westminster Highway) in Richmond (278-6184). They're open seven days a week from noon to 8:30 p.m., weather permitting. (If it's raining, the track closes down.) Prices run at $9 per 12 minutes of carting time, and most people like to take two rides. Another place to keep in mind is **Van Berg's Family Fun Centre**, off Highway 17 (at 52nd Street in Tsawwassen, next door to **Splashdown Park** [943-0483], which offers both single and two-seater go-kart rides (with rules and road conditions similar to the above facility). Van Berg's is open seven days a week, from 11:00 a.m. to 8:00 p.m. (Hours are shorter when school begins; call ahead.) They offer a variety of indoor and outdoor activities, including bumper cars, miniature golf, golf driving cages, a paintball tent, arcade games and batting cages.

Sailing

Sailing classes run mainly during the summer and are open to kids aged seven or eight and up. Most of the following places also rent sailboats.

Jericho Sailing Centre Association
1300 Discovery St (at N.W. Marine Dr), **Vancouver**
Tel: 224-4177

Kitsilano Yacht Club
2401 Point Grey Rd (at Larch), **Vancouver**
Tel: 730-1646

Royal Vancouver Yacht Club
3811 Point Grey Rd (at Alma), **Vancouver**
Tel: 224-1344

windsurfing

Windsurfing is a really difficult activity, best for kids 12 and up. It requires a fair bit of coordination, skill and strength. Windsurfers are required to launch and land their boards between the yellow buoys only at Locarno, Jericho, Kitsilano and English Bay Beaches. Like boaters, they must stay at least 300 m (about 1,000 ft) away from swimming beaches. **Windsure Windsurfing School** (224-0615), part of the **Jericho Sailing Centre Association** (see above), offers lessons, as well as rentals, summer camps and high school programs.

chapter 4

Live Entertainment

Like all art, live entertainment is a matter of individual taste; some kids love music and others adore puppet shows. Most toddlers and kindergartners, however, usually like the kid-oriented shows at the **Massey Theatre** and the **Centennial Theatre Centre** while performances put on by **Ballet British Columbia** and **Bard on the Beach** will be more appropriate for older kids who appreciate ballet or Shakespearean theatre. My particular favourites are the presentations by **Public Dreams**, the **Kiss Project** and the **Axis Theatre Company**, as well as the Saturday Afternoon Kids' Series at the **Vancouver East Cultural Centre**. These companies put on creative, one-of-a-kind shows that are refreshingly non-mainstream while still being suitable for kids.

Vancouver is home to a small but varied number of dance, theatre and musical groups. Listed below are ones particularly good for children, as well as theatres that focus on kids' fare. Admission prices vary widely depending on children's ages and the type of show offered, so call ahead of time to check.

For up-to-date information on events, check the *Georgia Straight*. This free publication comes out every Thursday and has events listings for kids. For free

24-hour information on current children's special events, as well as other cultural events in Vancouver, call 684-ARTS (2787) or access the **Vancouver Cultural Alliance**'s website, *www.culturenet.ca/vcal*. Ticket purchases for live events are usually done through TicketMaster, which can be reached at 280-3311 or 280-4444.

When seeking out live entertainment, be sure to check out "Calendar of Events," page 241, for information on festivals and seasonal activities that feature performances. Information about storytelling events, such as readings at libraries, can be found in "Inside Play" page 93. Finally, keep in mind that community centres often offer different types of storytelling and performances. Look in "Organizations and Services," page 213, for a list of these centres.

Incidentally, if a movie is what you're after, there is a comprehensive list of movie theatres in the *Georgia Straight*. One particularly good venue is the **Ridge Theatre** (738-6311), located at 3131 Arbutus Street (at 16th Avenue). The Ridge has a separate "crying room," where parents with babies and small children can sit and watch the movie without worrying about bothering other theatregoers. This is particularly great if you're a parent with a newborn and can't get or afford a babysitter, plus it's easy to nurse in privacy. And since the Ridge features second-run movies, the admission prices aren't exorbitant – another bonus.

And don't forget the **CN IMAX Theatre** (see page 11) and Science World's **Alcan OMNIMAX Theatre** (see page 18), both of which offer IMAX shows with wraparound digital sound.

Dance, Theatre and Music

Axis Theatre Company
Tel: 669-0631

This innovative company has been producing original theatre entertainment for family audiences for 23 years. It mounts performances at a variety of venues, including the **Surrey Arts Centre Theatre**, the **Waterfront Theatre**, the **Vancouver East Cultural Centre** and **Shadbolt Centre for the Arts**, all listed in this chapter.

Ballet British Columbia
Tel: 732-5003

Although most of its performances, held at the **Queen Elizabeth Theatre** (see page 58), are adult-oriented, once or twice a year Ballet B.C. features shows suitable for kids, providing young ones with a great introduction to the world of ballet.

Bard on the Beach
Ogden Ave (at Chestnut), in Vanier Park, Vancouver
Tel: 739-0559

Classical Shakespearean theatre performed in an open-ended tent in Vanier Park. Good for older kids. Have a pre-theatre picnic dinner at the park, then sit back and enjoy the show. If your child has theatrical aspirations, check out this company's **Young Shakespeareans Summer Workshops** (see "Classes in the Arts," page 197).

Carousel Theatre Company and School
Tel: 669-3410
This company puts on culturally diverse, family-oriented theatrical productions. It performs primarily at the **Waterfront Theatre** (see page 59) on Granville Island.

Centennial Theatre Centre
2300 Lonsdale Ave (at 23rd St), **North Vancouver**
Tel: 984-4484
The September-to-February season at this 718-seat proscenium-arch theatre features six shows, most of them geared toward kids ages three to seven. You'll find a little bit of everything here: magic, theatre, music and puppetry. They bring in both local and national performers, such as Fred Penner or Fred Garbo Inflatable Theatre.

Community Arts Council of Vancouver
837 Davie St (at Hornby), **Vancouver**
Tel: 683-4358
The Community Arts Council is very keen on creating opportunities for people to enjoy and participate in cultural activities. They don't currently have any children's programming happening, but because of their community involvement, it's worth calling them up to see if that changes. There is also an art gallery that features local and emerging artists.

Concerts in the Cove
Gallant Ave, off Deep Cove Rd in Panorama Park, **Deep Cove**
Every Friday evening in July and August different live music is featured here, ranging from blues to classical. Shows start at 7:00 p.m. and take place outside; it's a lovely spot for a family night out.

Gateway Theatre
6500 Gilbert Rd (at Westminster Hwy), **Richmond**
Tel: 270-1812
Four plays are produced annually by the Gateway Theatre, many of which are family-friendly (though largely best for the 10-and-up crowd). In addition, every Christmas the theatre puts on a musical, which is good for kids of all ages. A variety of other dance, theatre and musical performances are staged here throughout the year.

Kids' Koncerts
Orpheum Theatre, Seymour St (at Smithe), **Vancouver**
Tel: 876-3434
Between January and May the **Vancouver Symphony Orchestra** puts on a series of performances at the Orpheum for kids and their families that are appropriate even for three-year-olds. Concerts last about 90 minutes (often requiring a bathroom break) and have included performances by Raffi,

saxophonist Chris Vadala and selections from Mother Goose and "Hansel and Gretel." The theatre is quite beautiful, and even kids are slightly awed by its grandiosity.

The Kiss Project
Tel: 606-6425
In January and February of each year the Kiss Project has performances revolving around dance, theatre and music. There are also shows and workshops for children. These are excellent, innovative presentations; they take place at **Performance Works** (see page 58), on Granville Island.

Kitsilano Showboat Society
2300 Cornwall Ave (at Vine), above the Kitsilano Pool, **Vancouver**
Tel: 734-7332
Hours: Mon., Wed. and Fri. at 7:30 p.m. from June to Aug.
This open-air amphitheatre has been putting on free amateur variety shows in the summer for as long as anyone can remember. This is a nice outing for families on warm summer nights.

Massey Theatre
735 8th Ave (at 6th St), **New Westminster**
Tel: 517-5900
Their children's series runs from September to April and is good for kids even as young as four. Past performers have included Dr. I Wonder's Science Circus, puppeteer Norman Foote and the Uzume Taiko Ensemble.

Mountain Minstrels
Tel: 879-9959
This chamber music group mounts Sunday afternoon concerts throughout the year, usually taking place at the Unitarian Church at 49th Avenue and Oak Street. They provide a great introduction for kids to classical music and the art of listening, with music-accompanied storytelling such as "Puss 'n' Boots" and selections from *Aesop's Fables*.

Music in the Park – The Summer Sunday Review
Queen's Park Bandshell, 1st St (at 3rd Ave), **New Westminster**
Tel: 525-0485
From June to August a variety of bands, singing groups and dancing troupes are featured at this outdoors locale. Shows are free and take place Sundays at 2:00 p.m.

Presentation House Arts Centre
333 Chesterfield Ave (at 3rd St), **North Vancouver**
Tel: 990-3473 or 990-3474 (box office)
A variety of family-oriented programming is performed here throughout the year. Past performances have included a youth performance of *Grease* put on by the Seymour Art Gallery and an original musical based on the myth of Sleeping Beauty. At Christmastime there's always an appropriately themed show popular with kids.

Public Dreams

Tel: 879-8611

This innovative company produces free participatory art events in the community using giant puppets, stilts, lanterns and music. All involve some sort of procession. They have three main yearly events: **Illuminares**, **Circus of Dreams** and the **Parade of Lost Souls**. See pages 247, 249 and 251 for more information. These are not language-dependent, so people of many nationalities can relate to them; a wide variety of cultures is represented in each event. These are magical, inspiring events not to be missed.

Saturday Afternoon Kids' Series

Vancouver East Cultural Centre, 1895 Venables St (at Victoria), **Vancouver**

Tel: 251-1363

Prices: Adults $7; kids $5; group of four $15

An excellent range of kids' performers is featured at the "Cultch" throughout the year. One show might feature the W.P. Puppeteers using shadow puppets and rainmaking rhythms to create a forest environment; another show might host the group Buffalo Spirit with songs, stories and dances of the Great Plains. The theatre is a short walk from Commercial Drive, where there are several kid-friendly restaurants and shops.

Shadbolt Centre for the Arts

6450 Deer Lake Ave (at Canada Way), in Deer Lake Park, Burnaby

Tel: 291-6864 or 421-7699

Website: *www.burnabyparksrec.org/shadbolt/shadbolt.html*

The 150-seat **Studio Theatre** and 300-seat **James Cowan Theatre** host various performances at the centre throughout the year, many of which are family-oriented, such as Centrestage Theatre Company's presentation of *Snow White*.

Theatre Under the Stars

Malkin Bowl, south end of Stanley Park off Stanley Park Drive

Tel: 687-0174

In July and August, family-oriented Broadway musicals are performed in an open-air theatre. There are benches, but they can get uncomfortable, so bring pillows to sit on.

Theatrix Youtheatre Society

Tel: 939-6992

This performing arts school (for kids age four to 14) puts on a few shows of various types every year.

Vancouver TheatreSports League

Tel: 738-7013

This company has a regular gig every week of the year from Wednesday to Saturday at the **Arts Club New Revue Stage** on Granville Island. The family-oriented performances are best for older kids. They also perform at schools and various events, such as the **Spring Break Theatre Festival** (see page 243).

WISE Hall
1882 Adanac St (off Victoria)
Tel: 736-3022
This hall features mainly Celtic music, which is lots of fun. Kids are definitely welcome, though they may pull you to the floor to dance.

Additional Venues
The following is a list of theatres that feature family-oriented performances from time to time, as well as adult-oriented shows often good for older children. Call the numbers listed to see what's on the program. Live concerts are usually shown at **General Motors Place** (see page 12) or **B.C. Place Stadium** (see page 12). Also keep in mind community centres, which sometimes often offer theatrical fare. The **Roundhouse Community Arts and Recreation Centre** (see page 215) has a strong arts focus.

Arts Club Theatres (Main Stage and New Revue Stage)
1585 Johnston St, on Granville Island, **Vancouver**
Tel: 687-1644

Chan Centre for the Performing Arts
6265 Crescent Rd, near Gate 3, UBC, **Vancouver**
Tel: 822-9197

Firehall Arts Centre
280 E. Cordova St (at Gore), **Vancouver**
Tel: 689-0926

Performance Works
1218 Cartwright St, on Granville Island, **Vancouver**
Tel: 606-6425

Queen Elizabeth Theatre and Playhouse
Hamilton St (at Georgia), **Vancouver**
Tel: 665-3050
Home to **Vancouver Opera** (683-0222).

Stanley Theatre
2780 Granville St (at 12th Ave), **Vancouver**
Tel: 736-8423

Surrey Arts Centre Theatre
13750 88th Ave (at King George Ave), **Surrey**
Tel: 501-5566

Vagabond Playhouse
Queen's Park, 1st St (at 3rd Ave), **New Westminster**
Tel: 521-0412 or 521-3055

Vancouver East Cultural Centre
1895 Venables St (at Victoria Dr), **Vancouver**
Tel: 254-9578

Vancouver Playhouse Theatre Company
Hamilton St (at Dunsmuir), **Vancouver**
Tel: 873-3311

Waterfront Theatre
1410 Cartwright St, on Granville Island, **Vancouver**
Tel: 685-6217

Chapter 5

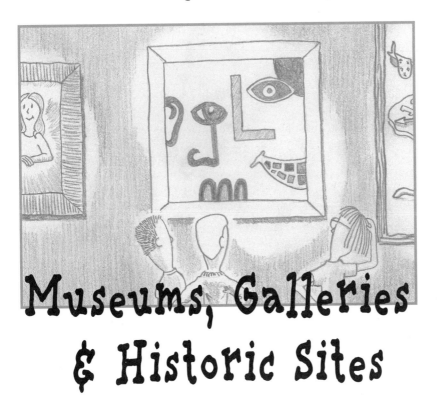

Museums, Galleries & Historic Sites

Kids love art! Most museums and galleries in Vancouver are kid-friendly (although screaming and crying, on the part of the child or adult, will necessitate your quick departure). If you hear of an art opening (and there are lots of them), take your children for an early night out. Or, en route to another destination, check out an art show. You'll find artists and kids have much in common. Check the local papers for gallery openings. *Preview: The Gallery Guide*, has a good list of art shows. It's published five times a year and available free at all galleries. The larger galleries, namely the **Vancouver Art Gallery**, the **Richmond Art Gallery**, the **Surrey Art Gallery** and the **Burnaby Art Gallery** generally provide child-geared programs that relate to their regular exhibitions. The museums listed here also have hands-on activities for children, however. Sadly, smaller galleries don't always have the funds to coordinate child-oriented activities.

This list also includes historic sites, such as the **Gulf of Georgia Cannery** and **Fraser Mill Canadian Railway Station**, museums of a kind that tell of the history of their area.

Vancouver

B.C. Sports Hall of Fame and Museum

Gate A, B.C. Place Stadium (at Robson and Beatty)

Tel: 687-5520

Hours: Daily 10:00 a.m. to 5:00 p.m.

Prices: Adults $6.00; students, seniors and kids $4.00; kids under 5 free

This is a really cool 1,857-square-metre (20,000-square-foot) interactive environment, great for any kid, but fabulous for kids who are into sports. Most popular is the Participation Gallery, where kids can arm wrestle, climb a mock rock face, throw balls in the throwing cage, test their speed on the running track and try out stationary bikes, rowing machines and other interactive games. This is perfect for rainy days and kids with cabin fever. Time travel through the historic galleries and explore sports in B.C. from the 1800s to the present. There are two theatres showing different sports events, and numerous television screens to watch. The Terry Fox Gallery shows his Marathon of Hope route across Canada and the Rick Hanson Gallery shows his Man in Motion journey around the world in a wheelchair. There are also special events throughout the year. It's good for the whole family. The exit is also the entrance, making it easy to keep track of the little ones.

Canadian Craft Museum

639 Hornby St (at Georgia)

Tel: 687-8266

Hours: Mon. to Sat. 10:00 a.m. to 5:00 p.m.; Thurs. 10:00 a.m. to 9 p.m.; Sundays and holidays noon to 5:00 p.m.; closed Tuesdays from Sept. to May

Prices: Adults $6, seniors, students and kids over 12 $4; kids under 12 free; Thurs. evening admission by donation

Good for crafts-oriented kids. Exhibitions are held throughout the year that showcase excellence in Canadian and international craftsmanship and design, both contemporary and historic. Interesting workshops for kids are held from time to time. Christmas is big here, with lots of events revolving around Yuletide crafts. There's a nice museum shop with one-of-a-kind crafts, good for older kids.

Granville Island Sport Fishing Museum, Model Ships Museum, Train Museum

1502 Duranleau St, past the entrance to Granville Island, on the left side

Tel: 683-1939

Website: *www.sportfishingmuseum.bc.ca/fishing/index.html*

Hours: Tues. to Sun. 10:00 a.m. to 5:30 p.m.

Prices: Adults $3.50; students, seniors and kids 6 to 12 $2.50; kids under 6 free

Kids who like boats will love this place. The collection of model ships is quite a good one, and many of the display cases are at a tot's eye level. Older kids with their own rods like the sport fishing lures, though the younger set is more likely to point out the giant clamshell or miniature submarine. Upstairs, the new Train Museum has a great display of moving trains, and the staff are really helpful. Their gift shop has excellent books on boating and fishing.

Old Hastings Mill Store Museum
1575 Alma St (at Point Grey Rd)
Tel: 734-1212
Hours: Mon. to Fri. 11 a.m. to 4:00 p.m., Sat. and Sun. 1:00 p.m. to 4:00 p.m.
from June 1 to Sept. 15; daily 1:00 p.m. to 4:00 p.m. Sept. 16 to May 31
Prices: Admission by donation
This museum is owned and operated by the Native Daughters of British
Columbia. Artifacts from the 1880s provide an interesting introduction to the
history of Vancouver. Kids may be interested only in a quick peek, as the near-
by playground and Jericho Park tend to be far more tempting.

Roedde House Museum
1415 Barclay St (at Broughton)
Tel: 684-7040
Hours: Guided tours Tues. to Fri. at 2 p.m.
Prices (for guided tour): Adults $5; seniors $3; kids under 12 free
This fully restored Victorian home has guided tours (call before coming), lec-
tures, musical evenings and special events. It's more suited to older children, but
there is a Teddy Bears Picnic in the summer (dates vary, call in June to find out),
as well as Christmas crafts for kids. Adults may prefer to leave the kids at home
with a babysitter and attend the autumn salon concert series, which features
classical music and sherry at intermission.

UBC Geological Sciences Museum
Room 106, Earth and Ocean Sciences department, 6333 Stores Rd, UBC
Tel: 822-2449
Hours: Mon. to Fri. 8:30 a.m. to 4:30 p.m.
Prices: Admission by donation
This is not a very big museum but it has various kinds of rocks and crystal sam-
ples that are interesting for school-age kids. Younger ones may like the coloured
gems, but everyone will love the dinosaur skeleton. If you don't want to make a
special trip just to see this museum, combine it with a trip to the UBC **Museum
of Anthropology** (see next entry).

UBC Museum of Anthropology
Opposite Gate 4, 6393 N.W. Marine Dr, UBC
Tel: 822-3825
Hours: Wed. to Sun. 11:00 a.m. to 5:00 p.m., Tues. until 9:00 p.m.
Prices: Adults $6; seniors, students and kids $3.50; kids under 6 free; Tues. 5:00
to 9:00 p.m. free
With its spacious, glass-lined rooms (designed by Canadian architect Arthur
Erickson), its cliffside location overlooking the mountains and the sea, and its
brilliant collection of Northwest Coast art and artifacts, this is a museum to trea-
sure, especially for kids. There is a feeling of spirituality here, especially in the
Great Hall, whose walls soar 15 metres (49 feet) up, enclosing dozens of totem
poles. Check out the canoes and large feast dishes; there are also sculptures by
the well-known Haida artist, Bill Reid. The Koerner Gallery houses a collection

of European ceramics, and there is a wide range of temporary exhibits on the art, history and culture of First Nations and other peoples. Imagination, humour and colour are present in these artifacts, and the museum is a good space for families. The exhibition halls are large enough for younger children to move around without constantly knocking into things. Older kids will enjoy looking through the drawers of exhibition trays in the open storage area. (Over 80 percent of the museum's permanent collection is always on display.) The mask collection is fantastic, though it might scare the pants off some younger kids. Be sure to call or check the newspaper to find out about changing exhibitions; the museum hosts some great things for kids to experience, such as First Nations events with dancers and drummers.

Vancouver Art Gallery
750 Hornby St (at Robson)
Tel: 662-4719 or 662-4700
Hours: Tues. to Sun. 10:00 a.m. to 5:30 p.m., Thurs. until 9:00 p.m.; noon to 5:00 p.m. statutory holidays
Prices: Adults $8; seniors $6; students and kids $4; family (up to five people) $25; members and kids 12 and under free. Thurs. evening 5:00 p.m. to 9:00 p.m. admission by donation ($5 suggested). Admission price includes coat check.
Vancouver's top art gallery, known as the VAG, houses a large permanent collection of paintings by Emily Carr and features permanent and changing shows. Founded in 1931, the VAG is in the former 1910 provincial courthouse, renovated in the 1980s by architect Arthur Erickson. One of the best things about the VAG is that it talks to kids about art in a language they understand. The gallery has a "supersunday" for children, held the third Sunday of every month, that helps kids make interactive connections between art and their own lives. There are hands-on activities, drop-in art-making studios, interpretive performances, guided tours and art demonstrations. Kids are inspired and taught about individual artists and provided with materials to create their own masterpieces. There's an excellent café with a nice outdoor patio (much of the food might be a bit nouvelle for kids), as well as a gallery shop with gift items and innovative children's art supplies and projects.

Vancouver Maritime Museum
1905 Ogden (at Cypress)
Tel: 257-8300
Hours: Tues. to Sat. 10:00 a.m. to 5:00 p.m., Sun. noon to 5:00 p.m.
Prices: Adults $6; seniors and kids over 5 $3; families $14; members and kids under 5 free; seniors free on Tues.
This is the chance for your kids to explore a real ship (in this case, the legendary *St. Roch*). They can clamber up and down the ladders, explore the galley and pretend to swab the decks. The sleeping cabins are quite evocative of ship life, with a pot-bellied stove, bunk beds and clotheslines. At the back of the museum there is a hands-on section where kids can try on captain's garb, see how a boat floats,

or control the movements of a working model of a submersible robot. There are all kinds of drawers to open, containing books, puppets, relics, shells, life jackets, colouring materials and scuba diving gear, as well as "Port in a Box," boxes of items from faraway ports such as Dalian in the People's Republic of China and the port of Sept-Iles in Québec. Use the museum's telescopes to look out over English Bay and find a yacht, a bulk carrier, a container ship or the Point Atkinson Lighthouse. Every day a printout from the **Port of Vancouver** (see page 18) lists the ships currently in the bay, what cargo they're carrying (it may be grains, sulphur, petroleum products, coal or forest products) and where they are from (such as Greece, the Philippines, Liberia, Cyprus, Panama or another far-off place). Permanent exhibits at the museum include large models of ships (some from the 1890s), Inuit stone sculptures and fishing baskets from the Asian–Pacific area. The museum is located in **Vanier Park** (see page 33), around the corner from **Kitsilano Beach** (see page 42), a two-minute walk from the **Vancouver Museum** (see below) and the **Pacific Space Centre** (see page 17).

Vancouver Museum
1100 Chestnut St, in Vanier Park
Tel: 736-4431
Hours: Tues. to Sun. 10:00 a.m. to 5:00 p.m.
Prices: Adults $8; kids 6 and over $5.50; kids under 5 free
This museum explores the heritage of Vancouver. There are all kinds of Northwest Coast artifacts here, as well as displays of relics from the history of the first white settlers to this city. The reconstructed rooms of an early Vancouver home are particularly good. The museum also has an interactive and crafts room related to the exhibitions, and there are special activities for families here on the weekends. There's a nice selection of stuff in the gift shop, from handcrafted First Nations art and jewelry to informative reference books.

The Vancouver Police Centennial Museum
240 E. Cordova St (at Main)
Tel: 665-3346
Hours: Mon. to Fri. 9:00 a.m. to 3:00 p.m.
Prices: Adults 14 and over $5; students, seniors and kids $3
Too-cool 12-year-old boys might think they've seen it all until they check out the morgue and weaponry rooms in this place. It's touted as being the number one police museum in Canada (making you wonder how many police museums there can actually be) and it's easy to understand why. Those curious about crime or police will love it here. There are historical displays of some of Vancouver's best-known crimes and the morgue where Errol Flynn lay after his death. Don't worry – kids under 10 are not allowed in the weaponry or morgue rooms, but there is still a load of paraphernalia for them to look at and lots of mannequins in uniform. This museum is very close to **Chinatown** (see page 14).

North Vancouver
North Vancouver Museum and Archives
209 W. 4th St (at Chesterfield)
Tel: 987-5618
Hours: Tues. to Sun. noon to 5:00 p.m.
Prices: Admission by donation
Community artifacts are emphasized here, but this museum has recently been incorporating kids' activities (including craft making) for each exhibit. In the tugboat exhibit, there is a boat kids can play on, as well as ropes, life jackets and other hands-on stuff. Their collection highlights shipbuilding, early logging and transportation, as well as recreation and community development in the North Shore mountains. This is in the same building as the **Presentation House Gallery**, one of the best contemporary art galleries in the city – have a look when you're at the museum.

West Vancouver
West Vancouver Museum and Archives
680 17th St (at Esquimalt), 2 blocks from Marine Dr
Tel: 925-7295
Hours: Tues. to Sat. noon to 4:30 p.m.
Prices: Adults $1; children $.75; kids under 6 free
Exhibitions vary here and you might find anything from a fire-fighting display to portraits of Squamish Nation ancestors. This museum has a lot of school-oriented programs and occasionally offers drop-in children's activities.

Burnaby
Burnaby Art Gallery
1895 Willingdon Ave (at Lougheed Hwy)
Tel: 291-2242
Hours: Wed. to Sun. noon to 5:00 p.m.
Prices: Free
Hats off to this gallery as they're currently implementing a number of programs that make art more accessible for kids. Beginning in June 2000, the gallery will feature, in conjunction with current exhibitions, self-guided tours for families with things to look for and points to discuss, as well as a children's play area with materials related to what is on display. Look for children's workshops and drop-in programs beginning in 2001. There is free parking underneath the gallery; no café, but you can eat a snack outside on the deck. In addition to utilizing its main space, the gallery features temporary exhibitions all over Burnaby, including those at theatres, shopping malls and abandoned warehouse spaces. Children's activities will soon be occurring in these spaces as well.

Burnaby Village Museum
6501 Deer Lake Ave
Tel: 293-6500 or 293-6501
Website: *www.burnabyparksrec.org/villagemuseum/villagemuseum.html*

Hours: Daily 11:00 a.m. to 4:30 p.m. from May 1 to late Sept.; daily 11:00 a.m. to 4:30 p.m. from Nov. 29 to Dec. 23

Prices: Adults $6.20; students, seniors and disabled $4.35; students 13 to 18 $4.40; kids 6 to 12 $3.75; kids under 6 free

This historical village is about 1.5 hectares (4 acres) in area, with authentically costumed townspeople who welcome visitors into their shops and homes. Your kids may like it best around Christmastime when there's a lot more activity, including a visit from Santa Claus, of course. It's fun to explore the old Chinese herbalist shop (complete with potions and exotic herbs), to visit the village blacksmith or to attend a class in the old schoolhouse. The big attraction is a ride on the 1912 C.W. Parker carousel, which you can go to separately without having to pay for the whole museum.

Gallery at Ceperley House

6344 Deer Lake Ave

Tel: 205-7332

Hours: Tues. to Fri. 10:00 a.m. to 4:30p.m., Sat. and Sun. noon to 5:00 p.m.

Prices: Admission by donation

This gallery features changing shows throughout the year. Upstairs they have an interactive room for kids with paints, pastels and other materials.

Museum of Archaeology and Ethnology at SFU

8602 Academic Quadrangle, SFU at Burnaby Mountain

Tel: 291-3325

Hours: Mon. to Fri. 10:00 a.m. to noon and 1:00 p.m. to 4:00 p.m.

Prices: Admission by donation

The emphasis here is on First Nations culture, with 185 square metres (2,000 square feet) of exhibits that focus on early Native settlements.

New Westminster

Irving House Historic Centre and New Westminster Museum and Archives

302 Royal Ave (at 3rd St)

Tel: 521-7656 or 527-4640

Hours: Tues. to Sun. 1:00 a.m. to 5:00 p.m. May 1 to Sept. 14; 1:00 p.m. to 5:00 p.m. weekends only Sept. 15 to April 30

Prices: Admission by donation

The Irving House is a Victorian dwelling that dates back to 1865; the New Westminster Museum showcases the origins and history of Western Canada's oldest city. This is a particularly good place to bring your kids if you're a New Westminster resident. You'll get a glimpse of items brought by the Royal Engineers, who founded New Westminster in 1859, a lesson in the city's historic May Day celebration and more. The archives are home to historical photographs and information on local people and events. The museum is located kitty-corner to **Tipperary Park**, where there are picnic tables and a lagoon.

Richmond

Britannia Heritage Shipyard
5180 Westwater (at end of Railway Ave), Steveston
Tel: 718-1200
Hours: Tues. to Sat. 10:00 a.m. to 4:00 p.m., Sun. noon to 4:00 p.m. March to Dec.
Prices: Admission by donation
This 3-hectare (8-acre) waterfront park has restored boatyards and canneries. See traditional boat-building techniques, rope making, fancy knot tying and other maritime skills. The best thing about the shipyard is its summer programs for families and kids, in which you can get river tours, learn wood carving and help to restore old boats.

Gulf of Georgia Cannery
12138 4th Ave, **Steveston**
Tel: 664-9009
Hours: Thurs. to Mon. 10:00 a.m. to 5:00 p.m. May 1 to June 30; daily 10:00 a.m. to 5:00 p.m. July 1 to Sept. 7; Thurs. to Mon. 10:00 a.m. to 5:00 p.m. Sept. 8 to Oct. 12
One of the few remaining canneries of the late 1800s, this is a national historic site commemorating the history of the West Coast fishing industry. There are a few hands-on activities for kids, but not too much else. It's worth a look, however, if you're visiting the **Steveston Fishing Village** (see page 25).

London Heritage Farm
6511 Dyke Rd (just west of Gilbert)
Tel: 271-5220
Hours: Sat. and Sun. noon to 4:00 p.m.
This is an 1890s historic farmhouse set on 1.8 hectares (4.6 acres) of lawns and heritage-style herb and flower gardens. There is also a collection of early 20th-century farm equipment, as well as chickens and the Territorial Seeds Ltd. Demonstration garden. This isn't exactly a kid-oriented place, but they do have a few events over Halloween and Christmastime. It's also across the banks of the Fraser River, so you can go beachcombing and have a picnic on the grounds of the farm.

Richmond Cultural Center
180 – 7700 Minoru Gate
Tel: 231-6440 or 231-6457
Hours: Mon. to Fri. 9:30 a.m. to 9:30 p.m., Sat. to Sun. 10:00 a.m. to 5:00 p.m.
Prices: Admission by donation
Here you'll find the **Richmond Art Gallery**, **Richmond Arts Centre** and the **Richmond Museum**. The art gallery shows contemporary work; the museum concentrates more on history, offering kids' activities related to current exhibits. The arts centre has workshops for preschool and school-age groups, ranging from clay, paint and charcoal-based projects to kite and lantern making.

Steveston Museum and Post Office
3811 Moncton St (at 1st Ave)
Tel: 271-6868
Hours: Mon. to Sat. 9:30 a.m. to 1:00 p.m. and 1:30 p.m. to 5:00 p.m.
Prices: Admission by donation
This is a tiny museum in Steveston Village, Canada's largest commercial fishery. Two Steveston parents I spoke with had never thought of this as a museum (it's that small), but it does give you a brief glimpse at old Steveston life. If you need to buy some stamps from its adjoining post office, why not take a look?

Trev Deeley Motorcycle Museum
13500 Verdun Pl, 1 block north of Bridgeport
Tel: 273-5421
Hours: Mon. to Fri. 10:00 a.m. to 4:00 p.m.
Prices: Free admission
This place has over 200 classic and antique motorcycles – perfect for kids (and parents) who like this type of thing.

Coquitlam
Fraser Mill Canadian Railway Station
1011 King Albert Ave (at Blue Mountain)
Hours: Wed to Sun. 10:00 a.m. to noon and 1:00 p.m. to 6:00 p.m. Victoria Day to Labour Day
Prices: Free admission
Located in a corner of **Blue Mountain Park** (a fun site for children; see page 44), this 1891 Canadian Pacific Railway station is good for kids who love trains. It's a pleasant short stop if you're in the park.

Port Moody
Port Moody Station Museum
2734 Murray St
Tel: 939-1648

Hours: Sat. 1:00 p.m. to 5:00 p.m. Sept. to May; Mon. to Sun. 10:00 a.m. to 4:00 p.m. May to Sept.
Prices: Free Admission
A 1907 Canadian Pacific Railway station with lots of hands-on displays relating to life in the early part of this century.

Surrey
Historic Stewart Farm
13723 Crescent Rd (off Hwy 99), near Crescent Beach
Tel: 543-3456
Hours: Tues. to Fri. 10:00 a.m. to 4:00 p.m., Sat. and Sun. noon to 4:00 p.m. mid-Feb. to mid-Dec.; closed mid-Dec. to mid-Feb.
Prices: Admission by donation

This 1880s farm has been restored and furnished to represent what life was like at the turn of the century. Quiet and curious kids will like this place. There is a weaving centre adjacent to the farm that features the art of textile making, and houses a collection of spinning wheels and looms.

Surrey Arts Centre and Theatre
13750 88 Ave (at King George)
Tel: 501-5580 or 501-5566
Hours: Mon. to Wed. and Fri. 9:00 a.m. to 5:00 p.m., Thurs. 9:00 a.m. to 9:00 p.m., Sat. 10:00 a.m. to 5:00 p.m., Sun. noon to 5:00 p.m.
Prices: Free Admission
There are three galleries here, as well as the **Surrey Arts Centre Theatre** (see page 58), which puts on performances for children throughout the year. Two of the galleries feature contemporary art by international and Canadian artists and emerging B.C. artists. Their children's mini-gallery features work either by or for children. There are Art Explorers Tours suitable for kids in preschool and up (to grade 3), and there are family workshops and child-oriented activities. The centre is located in **Bear Creek Park** (see page 41), which has a great playground with a miniature train that gives rides around the park.

Surrey Museum and Archives
6022 176 St (at 60th Ave), in the Surrey Fairgrounds
Tel: 502-6456
Hours: Tues. to Sat. 9:00 a.m. to 4:00 p.m.
Prices: Admission by donation
Surrey's history is traced in various displays here, many of which kids can relate to. Previous exhibitions good for kids were *Construction Toys*, which featured a collection of toys from the past and present, and *Hidden Faces*, which displayed masks made by elementary and secondary school students. (Visitors made their own masks and told stories using the masks as disguises.)

Farther Afield

B.C. Farm Machinery and Agriculture Museum
9131 King St, **Fort Langley**
Tel: 888-2273
Hours: Tues. to Sat. 10:00 a.m. to 4:45 p.m., Sun. 1:00 p.m. to 4:45 p.m. April to Oct.
Prices: Adults $4; students $2; kids 6 to 12 $1; kids under 6 free
Worth a look if your kids like old farm equipment, the museum is also right next door to the **Langley Centennial Museum** (see page 72) and the **Fort Langley National Historic Site** (see page 71).

B.C. Museum of Mining
Hwy 99, at Britannia Beach, 45 minutes' drive north from downtown Vancouver
Tel: 688-8735
Hours: Daily 10:00 a.m. to 4:30 p.m. from May to October; daily 10:00 a.m. to 4:30 during week of spring break; closed rest of the year

Prices: Adults $9.50; students, seniors and children $7.50; kids 5 and under free
Take a train ride underground into a real hard rock mine and to see and experience what early 1900s miners did. There are live demonstrations (though some of them, like the drills, can be quite noisy), as well as the chance for kids to pan for gold. Kids who like bathroom humour (and what kid doesn't?) will appreciate the Honey Wagon, the only underground bathroom they may ever see. This mine was once the largest copper producer in the British Empire; also on the premises is the three-level Mining House, a museum which tells the story of the mine in detail, as well as a 235-ton "super" mine truck. This spot is a bit of a drive from Vancouver, but you can make a day trip of it; there is a village green on-site for picnics, plus cafés close by. The museum is near **Shannon Falls** and **Murrin Lake**. Also nearby is **Porteau Cove**, a lovely pebble beach on the way to Squamish.

Canadian Museum of Flight and Transportation
5333 216th St (at Fraser Hwy), near the airport, **Langley**
Tel: 532-0035
Hours: Daily 10:00 a.m. to 4:00 p.m.
Prices: Adults $4; seniors and kids $3; kids under 6 free; family $10
This collection of fully and partially restored vintage aircraft is so cool kids will want to put their hands all over the planes. Go ahead and let them! Most of the 25 aircraft on display are touchable and there to be explored. There's even a DC-3 kids can go on, when the availability of staff permits. The gift shop sells a variety of aviation-related items.

Delta Museum and Archives
4858 Delta St, **Ladner**
Tel: 946-9322
Hours: Tues. to Sat. 10:00 a.m. to 3:30 p.m., Sun. 2:00 p.m. to 4:00 p.m.
Prices: Admission by donation
This small community museum with three floors of exhibits chronicling daily life in early Delta is housed in a 1912 Tudor-style heritage building. Featured are Victorian period rooms, as well as fishing, farming, archaeology and natural history displays. From time to time they have activities for kids, such as creating family trees with photographs.

Fort Langley National Historic Site
23433 Mavis Ave (off Hwy 1) **Fort Langley**
Tel: 513-4777
Hours: Daily 10:00 a.m. to 5:00 p.m. from March to Nov.; open for prebooked groups of 10 or more from Nov. to March
Prices: Adults $4; seniors $3; kids 6 to 16 $2; kids 5 and under free; family $10.
This 1800s fort houses the original Hudson's Bay Company storehouse and several reconstructed buildings. Costumed guides demonstrate how life was back then. All around the fort there's a log wall that kids can walk on. Kids can also have sack races or pan for gold in long troughs of sand. Three- and four-year olds might get bored easily in this place, but kids seven and older will get more out of it.

Langley Centennial Museum and National Exhibition Centre
9135 King St (at Mavis), **Fort Langley**
Tel : 888-3922
Hours: Daily 10:00 a.m. to 5:00 p.m.
Prices: Adults $4; kids 6 to 16 $2; kids 5 and under free
This museum has special activities throughout the year, including crafts, nature programs, performances and historical demonstrations. This small museum looks at the history of Langley. The National Exhibition Centre has a permanent exhibit of period pioneer rooms and a gallery with First Nations art and artifacts. Travelling exhibits include work by local artists, Swedish sculpture, native masks and Canadian paintings.

c h a p t e r 6

Sports

When asked, some kids might not be able to decide which they like better: playing sports or watching them. This chapter is a guide to both. The first section lists all the professional sports teams in Vancouver, where they play and how to get tickets. The other sections are dedicated to playing amateur sports. This is where to look if your child wants to take swimming lessons or practise baseball swings. You'll also find a list of in-line skate parks, as well as places where your kids can take skiing or snowboarding lessons (get out your chequebook!).

If your kids are sports junkies, they'll love the **B.C. Sports Hall of Fame and Museum** (see page 62) and **Score-Virtual Sportsworld** (Plaza of Nations, 770 Pacific Boulevard, Vancouver, 602-0513). This place bills itself as North America's first "interactive RealSports entertainment facility." It offers a variety of "real" sports, ranging from hockey to rock climbing to motor sports, as well as interactive video games for kids age four and up. Hours are 11:00 a.m. to 11:00 p.m. Monday to Thursday, 10:00 a.m. to midnight Friday to Sunday. What you spend will depend on what you (and your kids) play.

Canucks and Grizzlies fans will like the behind-the-scenes tour at **General Motors Place**. Call 899-7440 for more information. Another good spot is **Hogarth's Sport Chek – The Activity Centre** (3000 Lougheed Highway, at Barnet Highway, in Westwood Mall Shopping Centre, Coquitlam, 944-1100). This is really a sporting goods store (and a great one at that), but there is also a putting green, batting cages, pitching machines, half a tennis court and an indoor driving range; you pay according to what you use. (For more information on where to buy sporting goods, both new and used, look in "Shopping for Kids," pages 139-172.)

If you want to get your child into a league, the best place to call is your local community centre (see page 214). These centres organize a variety of team sports, from soccer to baseball to basketball (not to mention classes in gymnastics, ice skating and more) and also inevitably have information about leagues in their area. If you still need help, call **Sport B.C.** (737-3000), an umbrella group for participatory leagues.

UBC **Community Sports Services** offers a whole slate of sports activities for kids in the summer, including soccer, cycling, fencing, field hockey, racquet sports, badminton and rugby, as well as various camps. For information, call 822-3688.

SportMAPco puts out an excellent map featuring every school, park, ice rink, lacrosse box, track-and-field facility, swimming pool, community centre and hospital in the Greater Vancouver and Lower Mainland. This is a great item for parents who are often driving their children from one playing field to the next. The map is about $5 and is available through **Shoe Strings**, an athletic shop with outlets in Vancouver, North Vancouver, Burnaby, Coquitlam, Richmond and Surrey. Call their downtown Vancouver shop at 668-9622 for more information. Alternatively, call SportMAPco at 931-2496.

For information on bicycling, see page 48; for canoeing and kayaking, page 49; for sailing and windsurfing, page 52. If you need sports-related park information, contact the municipal parks boards, see page 30.

Professional Teams

There are a lot of opportunities to watch professional sports in Vancouver. Keep in mind that all sporting events are packed with people, so keep track of your kids and arrange a meeting point ahead of time in case they get lost. Tickets for all events can be purchased through TicketMaster (280-4400 or 280-4444) or at the gate (though these seats might not be as good and tickets do sell out on occasion). TicketMaster adds a surcharge of a few dollars to every ticket purchased in advance.

B.C. Lions Football Club
B.C. Place Stadium, 777 Pacific Blvd (at Robson), **Vancouver**
Tel: 589-7627
Website: *www.cfl.ca/CFLBC/home.html*
Season: June to Oct.
Prices: Between $15 and $60
Canadian Football League football.

Vancouver Canucks
General Motors Place, 800 Griffiths Way (at Expo Blvd), **Vancouver**
Tel: 899-GOAL (4625)
Website: *http://canucks.hypermart.net/*
Season: Oct. to April
Prices: Range from $30 to $100
National Hockey League hockey.

Vancouver 86ers Soccer Club
Swangard Stadium, Boundary (at Kingsway), in Central Park, **Burnaby**
Tel: 930-2255
Season: May to Sept.
Prices: $8 for general admission (unassigned seats in the uncovered area); $13 to $18 for reserved seats (sheltered from the rain)
A-league soccer.

Vancouver Grizzlies
General Motors Place, 800 Griffiths Way (at Expo Blvd), **Vancouver**
Tel: 899-HOOP (4667)
Website: *www.sportserver.com/SportServer/basketball/nba/van.html*
Season: Nov. to May
Prices: Start at $15 and go up to $250 for floor seats
National Basketball Association basketball.

Baseball/Softball

Young batters can practise in baseball fields in parks. The following are a couple of privately owned batting ranges with pitching machines, good for kids even as young as five. It's best to call in advance to book a batting cage, for these places can get crowded.

The Dugout
110 – 7750 128th St (at 76th Ave), **Surrey**
Tel: 594-8034
Hours: Mon. to Thurs. noon to 9:00 p.m., Fri. noon to 7:00 p.m., Sat. and Sun. 10:00 a.m. to 4:00 p.m.
Prices: $16 for a half hour; $28 for a full hour

North Shore Fun and Fitness
1172 W. 14th St (at Marine Dr), **North Vancouver**
Tel: 983-0909
Hours: Mon. to Fri. 11:00 a.m. to 9:00 p.m., Sat. and Sun. 9:00 a.m. to 6:00 p.m.
Prices: $21.40 per half hour; 20 percent discount Mon. to Fri. if practising is done before 5:00 p.m.

Van Berg's Family Fun Centre
Hwy 17 (at 52nd St), **Tsawwassen**
Tel: 943-0483 (see page 98)

Golf

A particularly favourite golfing activity for kids are pitch and putt courses, which are essentially short golf courses, with the longest hole usually not more than a hundred yards. Golfers only need one club and a putter, available at the courses. Some courses allow young kids to play, but most courses have a minimum age requirement of eight. Games usually cost between $5 and $10; the length of a game depends on the player's skill. Pitch-and-putt courses tend to be open from March or April until the end of October. The **Queen Elizabeth Pitch and Putt** has great views of the city. There is also miniature golf and a golf driving cage at **Van Berg's Family Fun Centre** (see page 98). If you want to whack some balls with your kid, there are a number of good driving ranges located at public golf courses. These are listed after Pitch and Putt Courses below.

Pitch and Putt Courses

Ambleside Par 3 Golf Course
1201 Marine Dr (at 13th St), **West Vancouver**
Tel: 922-3818

Central Park Pitch and Putt
3883 Imperial St (at Boundary), **Burnaby**
Tel: 434-2727

Kensington Park Pitch and Putt
5889 Curtis St (at Holdom), **Burnaby**
Tel: 291-9525

Murdo Frazer Par 3 Golf Course
2700 Pemberton Ave (at Upper Levels Hwy), **North Vancouver**
Tel: 980-8410

Queen Elizabeth Pitch and Putt
33rd Ave (at Cambie), **Vancouver**
Tel: 874-8336

Rupert Park Pitch and Putt
1st Ave (at Rupert), **Vancouver**
Tel: 257-8364

Stanley Park Pitch and Putt
Between Second Beach and Lost Lagoon, Stanley Park, **Vancouver**
Tel: 681-8847

West Richmond Pitch and Putt Golf Course
9771 Pendleton Rd (at Parksville Dr), **Richmond**
Tel: 271-7333

Driving Ranges

Burnaby Mountain Golf Course & Driving Range
7600 Halifax St (at Phillips), **Burnaby**
Tel: 280-7355

Fraserview Golf Course
7800 Vivian Dr (at Lynnbrook), **Vancouver**
Tel: 280-1818

McCleery Golf Course
7188 MacDonald St (at 53rd Ave), **Vancouver**
Tel: 280-1818

Riverway Golf Course & Driving Range
9001 Riverway Pl (at Byrne), **Burnaby**
Tel: 280-4653

University Golf Club
5185 University Blvd (at Blanca), **Vancouver**
Tel: 224-1818

Gymnastics

Gymnastics programs are available for children of all ages. Like dance lessons (see page 199), they help children develop body awareness and confidence, as well as flexibility. Some programs are for newborns and toddlers with an adult caregiver; others focus on gymnastic training for older kids. Overall, they are a great way for kids to exercise within the confines of an indoor space. **Gymboree** is a great program for toddlers to take with their parents; for older kids, **Phoenix Gymnastics Club** is particularly good. For shops that sell leotards and other gym supplies, see page 167.

Club Adagio Rhythmic Gymnastics
5587 Olympic St (at 41st Ave), **Vancouver**
Tel: 261-2752
Their rhythmic gymnastics classes start as young as age four.

Club Aviva
98 Brigantine Dr (at United Blvd), **Coquitlam**
Tel: 526-4464
They offer baby-and-parent programs plus classes for older kids.

Club Elite Rhythmics Inc.
Vancouver and **West Vancouver**
Tel: 327-9448
Their rhythmic gymnastics classes take place at various locations throughout Vancouver and West Vancouver, including some community centres. For ages three to 18.

Gymboree Play Programs
2195 W. 45th Ave (at East Blvd), **Vancouver**, 984-2370
2922 Glen Dr (at Pinetree Way), Coquitlam Centre, **Coquitlam**, 469-2323
Toddler-oriented programs for kids from birth to four years *with* their caregivers.

Omega Gymnastics
125B Glacier St (at United Blvd), **Coquitlam**
Tel: 464-1555
Baby-and-parent programs are offered, as well as classes for older kids.

Phoenix Gymnastics Club
3214 W. 10th Ave (at Trutch), **Vancouver**
Tel: 737-7693
Classes for kids ages three to 12.

Horseback Riding

All of the stables listed here offer year-round riding lessons, but they're not cheap. Lessons tend to cost about $100 for four classes. Kids learn to tack, groom and lead a horse, plus how to ride one, including walking, trotting and cantering. Lessons start as young as age five, but it really depends on your child as to their readiness. Many of the stables also offer trail rides, if your child just wants to see how it feels to be on a horse. (If the child is uncertain, the horse is put on a lead.) Both **JP's Golden Ears Riding Stable** and **Langley 204 Riding Stables** have great trail rides through parks. If it's pouring rain, lessons are either rescheduled or take place in their indoor arenas. For a *taste* of the horseback riding experience, try taking your kids to watch a horse show at **Southlands Riding Club**. They're held from spring to fall at their facilities at 7025 Macdonald Street (at 53rd Ave). Call 263-4817 for more info.

JP's Golden Ears Riding Stable
13175 232nd St, off Hwy 7, **Maple Ridge**
Tel: 463-8761
Besides offering trail rides in Golden Ears Provincial Park, J.P.'s has a huge indoor arena as well as one outdoors.

Langley 204 Riding Stables
543 204th St (at 8th Ave), **Langley**
Tel: 533-7978
Trail rides in Campbell Valley Park, plus lessons. This is considered one of the most respected equestrian parks, with fine-quality horses and great rides.

North Shore Equestrian Center
1301 Lillooet Rd (at Hwy. 1), **North Vancouver**
Tel: 988-5131
Lessons take place at both indoor and outdoor arenas, and the centre is convenient to downtown Vancouver.

Riverside Equestrian Centre
13751 Garden City Rd (at Finn Rd), **Richmond**
Tel: 271-4186
This centre offers lessons in both English and Cantonese, plus it has an enormous indoor complex.

Tamarack Stables
12551 Gilbert Rd (at Steveston Hwy), **Richmond**
Tel: 275-1830
Riding lessons for all levels.

Ice Skating

Many of the rinks below, both public and commercial, are used for ice skating only in the winter; in the summer months the ice is removed and the dry rinks are used for in-line skating, roller hockey, ball hockey or lacrosse. Strips of tickets are available at many skating rinks and can be purchased in advance for a reduced price. Skating and ice hockey lessons, as well as ice time for hockey are also usually offered. Call ahead for times for these activities as well as public skating times.

I would advise lessons for your child unless you're such a good skater that you can lead your child around easily. Prices for lessons vary, but you'll find that lessons at community centres are very reasonable. Do sign up early, as classes tend to fill up.

Dress your kids warmly with mittens, hats and snow pants for the inevitable falls. If they're dressed warmly, they'll have a better time. Bring snacks and a thermos of hot cocoa; if you take a break every 20 minutes or so, they'll also enjoy themselves more. Strollers are usually allowed on the ice. All of the following rinks have skate rentals; many have pro shops as well. Helmets are strongly encouraged and usually provided free of charge. There are usually concession stands open.

If your child likes skating, consider getting them their own skates, along with some for yourself. Having your own pair is much more comfortable and easier than standing in line for rental skates. New ones are fabulous, but I've seen some amazing deals on used skates at secondhand sporting goods stores. For a list of places where you can rent and buy new skating equipment, see page 169; for secondhand skates and supplies, see page 164-165.

During the winter you can find good outdoor skating at **Robson Square** (at Robson and Howe), as well as the rink atop **Grouse Mountain** (see page 22).

Aside from the indoor rinks listed below, there are lots of outdoor spaces for in-line skaters; see the section on In-Line Skating in this chapter, page 83.

Vancouver

Britannia Skating Arena
1661 Napier St (at Commercial)
Tel: 718-5800
This is a popular year-round ice skating rink.

Kerrisdale Cyclone Taylor Arena
5670 E. Blvd (at 41st Ave)
Tel: 257-8121
This rink is for ice skating from September to April; from May to August it's turned into a dry rink for in-line skating and roller hockey.

Killarney Community Centre Ice Rink
6260 Killarney St (at 46th Ave)
Tel: 434-9167
An ice skating rink from September to March, a dry surface from April to August.

Kitsilano Community Centre Ice Rink
2690 Larch St (at 10th Ave)
Tel: 257-6983
A year-round ice skating rink.

Riley Park Arena
50 E. 30th Ave (at Ontario)
Tel: 257-8545 or 257-8643
From September to April this serves as an ice skating rink; it's a dry surface the rest of the year.

Sunset Ice Arena
390 E. 51st Ave (at Prince Edward)
Tel: 718-6517
This is a year-round ice skating rink.

Trout Lake Community Centre Arena
3350 Victoria Dr (at 19th Ave)
Tel: 257-6955
This is an ice skating rink from September to March and a dry surface from April to August.

UBC Thunderbird Winter Sports Centre
Thunderbird Blvd (at Wesbrook Mall), ubc
Tel: 822-6121
This is a year-round ice skating rink.

West End Community Centre Arena
870 Denman St (at Robson)
Tel: 257-8339
This is an ice skating rink from October to April; it's used as a gymnasium in the summer.

North Shore

Ice Sports North Shore
2411 Mount Seymour Pkwy (at Berkeley), **North Vancouver**
Tel: 924-0828
This is an ice skating rink year-round.

Karen Magnussen recCentre
2300 Kirkstone Pl (at Lynn Valley Rd), **North Vancouver**
Tel: 987-7529
This is a year-round ice skating rink.

Lonsdale Arena
123 E. 23rd St (at Lonsdale), **North Vancouver**
Tel: 987-7529
This is an ice skating rink from September to March; it's a dry surface from May to August.

North Shore Winter Club
1325 E. Keith Rd (at Mountain Hwy), **North Vancouver**
Tel: 985-4135
An ice skating rink year-round.

West Vancouver Ice Arena
786 22nd St (at Marine Dr), **West Vancouver**
Tel: 925-7250
This is an ice skating rink from September to April and a dry rink from May to July.

Burnaby
Bill Copeland Sports Centre
3676 Kensington Ave (at Sprott)
Tel: 291-1261 (general inquiries) or 298-0533 (skating schedule)
Website: *www.burnabyparksrec.org/copeland/copeland.html*
This is an ice skating rink from September to April and a dry rink from May to August.

Burnaby Winter Club
4990 Canada Way (at Kensington)
Tel: 299-7788
This ice skating rink is open year-round.

Ice Sports 8 Rinks
6501 Sprott St (at Hwy 1)
Tel: 291-0626
There are eight year-round ice skating rinks here; a dry rink may open in the near future.

Kensington Park Arena
6159 Curtis St (at Holdom)
Tel: 299-8354
There are both ice and dry rinks here year-round.

New Westminster
Moody Park Arena
701 8th Ave (at Canada Way)
Tel: 525-5301
This is a year-round ice skating rink.

Queen's Park Arena
1st St (at 3rd Ave)
Tel: 524-9796
This is an ice skating rink from September to April and a dry surface from May to August.

Tri-Cities

Coquitlam Sports Arena
633 Poirier St (at Foster), **Coquitlam**
Tel: 927-6969
This is a year-round ice skating rink.

Planet Ice
2300 Rocket Way (at Port Mann Bridge), **Coquitlam**
Tel: 941-9911
There are four ice skating rinks here, open year-round.

Port Coquitlam Recreation Centre Arena
2150 Wilson Ave (at Kingsway), **Port Coquitlam**
Tel: 927-7933
This is an ice skating rink from September to March and a dry surface from April to August.

Port Moody Arena
300 Ioco Rd (at Ungless), **Port Moody**
Tel: 469-4565
This is an ice skating rink from September to April; it's closed May to August.

Richmond

Minoru Arenas
7551 Minoru Gate (at Granville Ave)
Tel: 278-9704 or 276-4383 (public skating schedules)
There is ice skating from September to March; the rink is closed from April to August.

Richmond Ice Centre
14140 Triangle Rd (at No. 6 Rd)
Tel: 448-5366 or 276-4383 (public skating schedules)
This is a year-round ice skating rink.

Surrey

Cloverdale Arena
6090 176th St (at 60th Ave)
Tel: 502-6410
This is an ice skating rink from September to April; it's open for in-line skating some of the rest of the year.

Ladner Leisure Centre Arena
4600 Clarence Taylor Cres (at Hwy 17), Delta
Tel: 946-0211
This is an ice skating rink from September to March; it's open for lacrosse the rest of the year.

Newton Arena
7120 136B St (at 72nd Ave)

Tel: 501-5044

This is an ice skating rink from September to June; in-line skating occurs July to August.

North Surrey Arena
10375 135th St (at 104th Ave)
Tel: 502-6300
Both a dry rink and an ice skating rink are open year-round.

South Surrey Arena
2199 148th St (at 16th Ave)
Tel: 502-6200
This is a year-round ice skating rink.

Stardust Skating Centers
10240 135th St, near Surrey Central SkyTrain station
Tel: 584-6630 or 584-4312 (skating information)
These are year-round dry rinks.

Indoor Rock Climbing

Indoor rock climbing is very popular in Vancouver, perhaps because it's a great chance for climbers to practise when the weather prohibits them from climbing the nearby mountains safely. The activity is also very popular with kids, though since it involves some balance and concentration, it's best for kids six and older. The facilities listed here provide a wall for rock climbing that simulates a mountain's rocky crags and crevices. Instructors teach or assist participants (depending on their level of skill) to climb the "rock." This is a popular birthday party for 10- to 12-year-olds, and even my five-year-old son enjoys it for short periods. **Score-Virtual Sportsworld** (see page 99) also has rock climbing facilities.

Cliffhanger Indoor Rock Climbing Centre
106 W. 1st Ave (at Manitoba), **Vancouver**
Tel: 874-2400

The Edge Climbing Centre
1485 Welch St (at Philip), **North Vancouver**
Tel: 984-9080

Rock House Indoor Climbing Centre
3771 Jacombs Rd (at Cambie), **Richmond**
Tel: 276-0012

Vertical Reality Climbing Gym
7728 128th St (at 76th Ave), **Surrey**
Tel: 594-0664

In-Line Skating

Skate parks are listed below; in-line skaters can also try the Seaside Bicycle Route which goes from Stanley Park to Spanish Banks. A portion of the parking lot at Sunset Beach (Beach Avenue at Burrard Bridge) is usually cordoned off for in-line skate practice. The Granville Island Water Park is also a good place to practice during the water park's off-season; there are lots of slopes and smooth surfaces. On rainy days, check out the various indoor rinks (see page 83).

For skate rentals, see "The Out-of-Doors" under Bicycling, page 49. To buy new or secondhand skates, see "Shopping for Kids" under Sporting Goods, page 163.

Ambleside Park, 13th St (at Marine Dr), **West Vancouver**
China Creek Park, Broadway and Clark Dr, **Vancouver**
Clarke Park, 14th Ave (at Commercial), **Vancouver**
Confederation Park, Willingdon Ave north of Hastings, **Burnaby**
Ladner Leisure Centre, Hwy 17 (at Ladner Trunk Rd), **Delta**
Pinnacle Skate Park, Poirier St (at Foster), **Coquitlam**
Skateboard Park, River Rd (at Lynas Lane), **Richmond**
Seylynn Park, Mountain Hwy (at Main), **North Vancouver**
Town Centre Park, Pinetree Way between Guildford and Pathan, **Coquitlam**
William Griffin Park, Fell Ave (at Upper Levels Hwy), **North Vancouver**

Martial Arts

The martial arts are a great way for kids to let off energy in a positive way; they're great exercise and build self-confidence and self-discipline. There are so many martial arts schools in the Vancouver area that it's almost impossible to determine the best. This list is merely a partial guide to some of the better martial arts schools in various municipalities. One of Vancouver's top martial arts schools, also its oldest, is **Divine Winds Martial Arts**. Classes at all facilities start as young as age four or five for boys and girls. For further help with martial arts associations in your area, call **Sport B.C.** at 737-3000. For stores that sell martial arts outfits and supplies, see page 167.

Aikido with Ki
Classes at Sea Island Elementary, 1891 Wellington Cres, **Richmond**
Tel: 261-3136

Champions Karate Academy
125 E. 1st St (at Lonsdale), **North Vancouver**
Tel: 983-3799

Divine Winds Martial Arts
4266 Hastings St (at Madison), **Burnaby**
Tel: 622-4524

Kee's Tae Kwon Do
1760 Kingsway (at Commercial), **Vancouver**
Tel: 873-5355

Kel Lee's Academy of Martial Arts
2916 Graveley St (at Renfrew), **Vancouver**
Tel: 255-5344

Oriental Martial Arts College
5665 Kingsway (at Imperial), **Burnaby**
Tel: 430-2307
Specializes in students with attention deficit disorder (ADD).

Port Moody Karate
2507 St. Johns St (at Kyle), **Port Moody**
Tel: 939-8441

Sirota's Alchymy
5640 Hollybridge Way (at River Rd), **Richmond**
Tel: 244-8842

Sun Hang Do Martial Arts
3665 Kingsway (at Boundary), **Vancouver**, 437-0065
1046 Austin (at Marmont), **Coquitlam**, 931-3311
10034 King George Hwy (at 100th Ave), **Surrey**, 930-5141

Snow Sports

Vancouver is blessed with being right next to some amazing mountain ranges, all of which offer excellent snowboarding, downhill skiing and cross-country skiing, usually until as late as May of each year. The following places all offer facilities, lessons and equipment rentals and are all within easy reach of Vancouver. All-season tires or chains are recommended for roads. There are additional ski resorts outside the Lower Mainland. For shops that sell new and secondhand supplies for snowboarding and skiing, see "Shopping for Kids" (page 163).

Skiing doesn't come cheap; between equipment rentals, lift tickets, lessons for the kids, transportation and food, you can easily drop a couple of hundred bucks for a family of four for just one day. Shop around for deals on lessons. You can go tobogganing at Cypress and Mount Seymour, but not at Grouse.

Cypress Bowl
Cypress Bowl Rd, above Upper Levels Hwy, **West Vancouver**
Tel: 926-5612
This is the North Shore's largest downhill ski resort and has great long slopes for advanced skiers. There are shorter ones for small kids as well.

Grouse Mountain
Nancy Greene Way, above Capilano Rd, North Vancouver
Tel: 984-0661
Website: *www.grousemtn.com*
The slopes aren't very big here, but they're usually just fine for kids who don't require advanced-skiing conditions. This place is only a half hour's drive from downtown Vancouver, though you do have to take the pricey Skyride (see page 22) to get up to it. Note that you can't bring toboggans onto the Skyride. You can see Grouse's ski runs lit up at night from most parts of the Lower Mainland.

Mount Seymour
Mount Seymour Rd, above Mount Seymour Pkwy, **North Vancouver**
Tel: 986-2261
This is also close to downtown Vancouver, about a 30- to 40-minute drive. The ski schools tend to be inexpensive here, and there's a good tobogganing area just off the parking lot.

Swimming

I am constantly impressed by the swimming pools in Vancouver. Most of them are located at community centres and reflect the same care and thought that go into the centres themselves. They're clean, well-kept and community-oriented and offer a huge array of swimming lessons and programs, from baby-and-parent play to family swim times. Lessons are offered to all ages and levels. Indoor pools are usually open year-round and tend to offer more facilities: toddler pools, wave pools, steam rooms or fitness equipment. Outdoor pools are only open in the summer, and although lessons are offered, these pools tend more to be places to have fun, swim laps, or just hang out and soak up the sun.

Call ahead to find out public swim schedules; there are often designated times for baby-and-parent play or family swims. Prices vary depending on the facility, but they are usually no more than a few dollars a person except for the more elaborate pools. Community pools run by the Vancouver Board of Parks and Recreation offer swim "strips," a strip of tickets you buy in advance for a reduced price.

Prices for lessons vary quite a bit as well, depending on where you take them. I've always been pleased by the classes provided at the UBC **Aquatic Centre**, especially for toddlers. When my kids got older, however, it seemed as if the classes got bigger and swimmers spent a lot of time by the side of the pool. Now I take them to **Aquaventures Swim Centre**; it's expensive, but the classes are small, the teachers are excellent, and the kids seem to learn quickly. My feeling is that whatever it takes, whether you can afford lessons or simply teach them yourself, all kids should learn to swim well. Not only is it fun, but it's really important for kids to be safe near a body of water and know how to handle themselves.

Aside from swimsuits and towels, bring plastic bags for wet suits and shampoo for washing hair when you're done. Many people bring blow-dryers so they're kids don't go out into the (often cold) air with wet hair; some pools have hand driers situated at head level. A lot of kids are happier swimming with goggles on; it enables them to see more clearly underwater and the chlorine doesn't sting their eyes. For places to buy swimming equipment, see page 163.

If you've got tiny ones, keep in mind that the **Vancouver Aquatic Centre** has an excellent toddler pool with a gently sloped entry (instead of steps), perfect for parents with babies and toddlers. It's a shallow pool, so even nonswimming parents will feel safe. (Lifeguards are on duty at all pools, by the way.)

Indoor Pools

Two excellent pools that go above and beyond the realm of an indoor swimming pool are **WaterMania** in Richmond and the **Newton Wave Pool** in Surrey; both have all kinds of water play, wave action and more. **Ladner Leisure Centre** in Delta is also exceptional, with its swimming pools, slides, lessons and water play.

Vancouver

Aquaventures Swim Centre
1630 W. 5th Ave (at Fir)
Tel: 736-7946

Britannia Swimming Pool
1661 Napier St (at Commercial)
Tel: 718-5800

Jericho Hill Centre Pool
4196 W. 4th Ave (at N.W. Marine Dr)
Tel: 874-6464

Kensington Pool
5175 Dumfries St (at 18th Ave)
Tel: 718-6200

Kerrisdale Pool
5851 W. Blvd (at 41st Ave)
Tel: 257-8105

Killarney Pool
6260 Killarney St (at 49th Ave)
Tel: 434-9167

Lord Byng Pool
3990 W. 14th Ave (at Wallace)
Tel: 222-6090

Percy Norman-Riley Park Pool
30 E. 30th Ave (at Main)
Tel: 257-8680

Renfrew Pool
2929 E. 22nd Ave (at Rupert)
Tel: 257-8393

Stan Strongе Pool
700 West 59th Ave (at Cambie)
Tel: 321-3231

Templeton Pool
700 Templeton Dr (at Adanac)
Tel: 718-6252

UBC Aquatic Centre
6121 University Blvd, next to bus loop, UBC
Tel: 822-4522 or 822-4521

Vancouver Aquatic Centre
1050 Beach Ave (at Thurlow),
Tel: 665-3424

North Shore

Karen Magnussen Wave Pool
2300 Kirkstone Pl (at Lynn Valley Rd), **North Vancouver**
Tel: 987-7529

Lonsdale Recreation Centre
123 E. 23rd St (at Lonsdale), **North Vancouver**
Tel: 987-7529

Ron Andrews recCentre
931 Lytton St (at Mount Seymour Pkwy), **North Vancouver**
Tel: 987-7529

West Vancouver Aquatic Centre
776 22nd St (at Marine Dr), **West Vancouver**
Tel: 925-7210

William Griffin recCentre
851 W. Queens Rd (at Westview), **North Vancouver**
Tel: 987-7529

Burnaby

Bonsor Recreation Complex Pool
6550 Bonsor Ave (at Central Blvd)
Tel: 439-1860

C. G. Brown Memorial Pool
3702 Kensington Ave (at Sprott)
Tel: 299-9374 or 298-0533 (swimming schedule)

Eileen Dailly Leisure Pool and Fitness Centre
240 Willingdon Ave (at Triumph)
Tel: 298-SWIM (7946)

New Westminster

Canada Games Pool and Fitness Centre
65 E. 6th Ave (at McBride)
Tel: 526-4281

Tri-Cities

Chimo Indoor Swimming Pool
620 Poirier St (at Foster), **Coquitlam**

Tel: 933-6027

City Centre Aquatic Centre
1210 Pinetree Way (at Guildford), **Coquitlam**
Tel: 927-6999

Hyde Creek Indoor Pool
1379 Laurier Ave (at Coast Meridian), **Port Coquitlam**
Tel: 927-7946

Richmond
Minoru Aquatic Centre
7560 Minoru Gate (at Granville Ave)
Tel: 278-3178 or 276-4383

Richmond Aquatic Centre
14200 Triangle Rd (at No. 6 Rd)
Tel: 448-5353

WaterMania
14300 Entertainment Blvd (at Steveston Hwy)
Tel: 448-5353

Surrey
Ladner Leisure Centre
4600 Clarence Taylor Cres (at Hwy 17), **Delta**
Tel: 946-0211

Newton Wave Pool
13730 72nd Ave (at 138th St)
Tel: 501-5540

North Surrey Pool
10275 135th St (at 104th Ave)
Tel: 502-6300

Outdoor Pools

Outdoor pools, all of which are run by the parks boards, are generally open from Victoria Day to Labour Day. Fees are no more than a few dollars per person, and in most cases books of 10 tickets can be purchased at a discount. Since they're only open a portion of the year, outdoor pools don't usually have separate phone numbers. Call the appropriate local parks board (see page 30) for more information.

All the pools, except UBC, are located near parks and concession stands. The Kitsilano Pool is in a particularly beautiful setting on English Bay. This pool is quite large, with a sloped entry and long swimming lanes; it's also right next to Kitsilano Beach. The Student Union Building near the UBC pool has a cafeteria that is open most of the year and vending machines. For a day of even more outdoor water fun, check out the privately run **Splashdown Park** (see page 43).

Vancouver

Kitsilano Pool, Cornwall Ave. (at Vine)
Maple Grove Pool, Yew St. (at S.W. Marine Dr)
Mount Pleasant Pool, Ontario St (at 16th Ave)
New Brighton Pool, McGill St, west of the Second Narrows Bridge
Second Beach Pool, Stanley Park (at Beach Ave)
Sunset Pool, E. 51st Ave (at Main)
UBC **Aquatic Centre**, 6121 University Blvd, next to bus loop, 822-4522 or 822-4521

Burnaby

Central Park Outdoor Pool, Boundary Rd (at Kingsway)
Kensington Outdoor Pool, Kensington Ave (at Hastings)
McPherson Outdoor Pool, Rumble St (at Royal Oak)
Robert Burnaby Park Outdoor Pool, 12th Ave (at 2nd St)

New Westminster

Hume Outdoor Pool, Kelly St (at Braid)
Kiwanis Outdoor Pool, 10th St (at 7th Ave)

Tri-Cities

Centennial Outdoor Pool, Shaughnessy St (at Barnet Hwy),
Port Coquitlam
Eagle Ridge Pool, Lansdowne Dr (at Guildford), **Coquitlam**
Robert Hope Outdoor Pool, Lamprey Dr. (at Humber Cres),
Port Coquitlam
Rochester Pool, Rochester Ave (at Marmont), **Coquitlam**
Rocky Point Pool, Murray St (at Moody), **Port Moody**
Spani Pool, Hillcrest St (at Foster), **Coquitlam**
Westhill Pool, Westhilll Pl (at Glenayre), **Port Moody**

Richmond

South Arm Outdoor Pool, South Arm Pl (at Williams)
Steveston Pool, 4151 Moncton St (at No. 1 Rd)

Surrey

Bear Creek Pool, 88th Ave (at King George Hwy)
Greenaway Pool, 60th Ave (at 180th St)
Hjorth Road Pool, 148th St (at 100th Ave)
Holly Pool, 148th St (at 107th Ave)
Kennedy Pool, Holt Rd (at 88th Ave)
Kwantlen Pool, 104th Ave (at Old Yale)
Port Kells Pool, 88th Ave (at 192nd St), west of Hwy 1
Sunnyside Pool, 26th Ave (at 154th St)
Unwin Pool, 133rd St (at 68th Ave)

Tennis

There are more than 200 free tennis courts in public parks throughout the Lower Mainland. Call your local parks board (see page 30) for a complete list of parks with courts. For the most part courts operate on a first-come, first-served basis, with a maximum 30 minutes of play if others are waiting. Rubber-soled shoes must be worn. Tennis lessons are offered by the following community centres in Vancouver (see page 214 for a complete list of centres).

Douglas Park Community Centre
810 W. 22nd Ave (at Heather)
Tel: 257-8130

Dunbar Community Centre
4747 Dunbar St (at 33rd Ave)
Tel: 222-6060

False Creek Community Centre
1318 Cartwright St, on Granville Island
Tel: 257-8195

Killarney Community Centre
6260 Killarney St (at 49th Ave)
Tel: 434-9167

Trout Lake Community Centre
3350 Victoria Dr (at 19th Ave)
Tel: 257-6955

chapter 7

Inside
Play

What to do, what to do . . . It's hard to find activities to keep kids occupied, especially in a city that gets rain day after day (or week after week). Luckily there are lots of indoor activities in the Lower Mainland that give kids the opportunity to run around and let off excess energy.

A word of warning. Some of the places listed here (arcades, indoor playgrounds, laser tag and paintball) are *loud*. Frankly, I can't think of one good reason to go to an ear-splitting arcade or frenzied indoor playground. Oh yeah – kids love them. But if you live in Vancouver, chances are your children will get invited to more than one party at one of these popular locales, so hey, let them go then. (Besides, all you have to do is drop them off – and run.) In the meantime, if your kids are going stir crazy, there are less hectic places to work off some steam (while salvaging your ears, not to mention your sanity), namely indoor gyms, indoor rock climbing centres (see page 83), indoor swimming pools and indoor skating rinks (see page 79). Community centres also often have open gym times for toddlers and older kids, available on a drop-in basis (see page 214). If you're desperate to entertain a baby or toddler, consider the numerous

Family Places located around Vancouver (see page 219). For quiet time, find out about story times at any of the local libraries (see page 222).

Arcades

All the places listed here, except **Digital U**, have a multitude of video games, as well as air hockey, sports games, pinball games and more. Arcades are particularly appealing to kids seven and up (especially boys), who will ask you for large sums of money to satisfy their arcade habit (they seem to drop 20 bucks here in an hour easily). All the machines require quantities of change, but the owners of these venues thoughtfully provide change machines. They're also all located at or near malls (so they're easy to get to on public transit), which is a handy thing if you need to give your son an incentive when you want to take him shopping for school clothes. **Digital U** is essentially a coffee shop that rents computer time by the hour; they also have Nintendo, Playstation and various PC games for those unlucky kids who don't have such systems at home. Prices run from $9 to $11 per hour.

Circuit Circus

1496 Cartwright St, in the Kids Only Market on Granville Island, Tel: 608-6699, **Vancouver**

4800 Kingsway (at McKay), in Metrotown Centre, Tel: 439-7765, **Burnaby**

4247 Lougheed Hwy (at Austin), in Lougheed Mall, Tel: 299-1763, **Burnaby**

Digital U Computing Centers

1595 W. Broadway (at Fir)

Tel: 731-1011

Johnny Zee's Amusements

6200 McKay Ave (at Kingsway), in Station Square in Metrotown, **Burnaby**

Tel: 433-6472

Lester's Family Amusement Centre

6400 Kingsway (at Gilley), **Burnaby**

Tel: 431-0477 or 438-1366

Bowling Lanes

For a while it there looked like bowling was becoming passé (not that it was ever very fashionable). But someone from the National Bowling Association must have realized that kids were a hot ticket because suddenly bowling has gotten a lot more kid-friendly. Nearly all the bowling lanes here offer bumper bowl, in which the gutter is blocked off, more or less ensuring at least one good crash (great for four-year-olds, as well as some parents I know). Call ahead to find out when bumper bowl is offered. Bowling is also less serious than it used to be, although you still have to wear the stupid shoes (at some lanes kids are allowed to wear socks if shoes in their size are not available). Most places offer glow-in-the-dark bowling in the evenings, where the regular lights are turned off, the music is turned on, and the black lights, strobe lights and disco lights go into action.

If you haven't taken the kids bowling, try it at least once. It's inexpensive, something both kids and adults enjoy, and let's face it, kids love knocking things down (actually, so do I). A family of four should expect to spend less than $20 for one game (which lasts about 30 to 40 minutes), including shoe rental. Although I've seen three- and four-year-olds bowl successfully, most kids in this age group don't have the strength to get the ball down the lane, so this is a better activity for the five-and-up crowd. Snacks and drinks are usually available at the snack bar, but don't count on being able to get a healthy lunch, so eat before you go.

Vancouver

Commodore Lanes & Billiards
838 Granville St (at Robson)
Tel: 681-1531

Grandview Bowling Lanes
2195 Commercial Dr (at Grandview Hwy)
Tel: 253-2747

Town 'n Country Bowl & Billiards
745 S.E. Marine Dr (at Fraser)
Tel: 325-2695

Varsity–Ridge 5 Pin Bowling Centre
2120 W. 15th Ave (at Arbutus)
Tel: 738-5412

North Vancouver

North Shore Bowl
141 W. 3 St (at Lonsdale)
Tel: 985-1212

Thunderbird Bowling Centre
120 W. 16th St (at Lonsdale)
Tel: 988-2473

West Vancouver

Park Royal Bowling Lanes
1080 Park Royal South (at Taylor Way), in Park Royal Shopping Centre
Tel: 925-0005

Burnaby

Brentwood Lanes Bowling Center
5502 Lougheed Hwy (at Holdom)
Tel: 299-9381

Hastings Bowling Lanes
4437 E. Hastings St (at Willingdon)
Tel: 298-2811

Middlegate Lanes
7155 Kingsway (at Edmonds), in Middlegate Mall
Tel: 522-3654

Old Orchard Lanes
4429 Kingsway (at Willingdon)
Tel: 434-7644

New Westminster
Lucky Strike Lanes
1205 6th Ave (at 12th St)
Tel: 526-6622

Tri-Cities
Maillardville Lanes
933 Brunette Ave (at Lougheed Hwy), **Coquitlam**
Tel: 526-7610

Port Coquitlam Bowladrome
2263 McAllister Ave (at Shaughnessy), **Port Coquitlam**
Tel: 942-5244

Port Moody Lanes
3150 St Johns St (at Moray), **Port Moody**
Tel: 461-2481

Richmond
Lois Lane's Bowling & Billiards
23200 Gilley Rd (at Westminster Hwy)
Tel: 540-8182

The Zone Bowling Center
14711 Steveston Hwy (at No. 6 Rd)
Tel: 271-2695

Surrey
Clover Lanes
5814 176A St (at 60th Ave)
Tel: 574-4601

Dell Lanes
10576 King George Hwy (at 105A Ave), in Dell Shopping Centre
Tel: 581-8230

Scottsdale Lanes
12033 84th Ave (at Scott Rd)
Tel: 596-3924

Ceramics Studios

A fairly new concept (meaning they weren't around when I was a kid), ceramics studios are places where kids (and adults) can choose an unfired ceramic piece (containers, figurines, dishware and more) and paint it. Brushes, paints, sponges and stencils are supplied; all kids need is their imagination. The piece is then glazed and fired and ready to be picked up in a couple of days. (Remembering to pick it up is the only tricky part.) Prices vary from place to place, depending on what type of piece you pick and how long you take to paint it, but for something like a coffee mug, you might expect to pay around $20, including the mug, the glazing and the firing. This activity is best for kids five and up and it's a great birthday party for the six- to ten-year-old age range (see page 183), but all kids seem to love these places. A friend brought his five-year-old son to **Crankpots**; he glopped some paint on a ceramic pot and had a blast. His artistic 13-year-old sister very meticulously painted a beautiful plate as a birthday present for her mum. This *is* an activity that requires sitting down for at least half an hour and is not the best place to take toddlers who are unable to resist picking fragile items off shelves and throwing them on the floor.

Color My Pots
2668 W. 4th Ave (at Stephens), **Vancouver**
Tel: 731-2286

Crankpots
1184 Denman St (at Comox), Tel: 688-8541, **Vancouver**
555 W. 12th Ave (at Cambie), in City Square, Tel: 871-0302 **Vancouver**
1735 Marine Dr (at 17th St), Tel: 922-5092, **North Vancouver**

Just Kiln Time
1864 W. 1st Ave (at Cypress), **Vancouver**
Tel: 732-7995

Paint and Fire Café/All Fired Up
3436 W. Broadway (at Waterloo), **Vancouver**
Tel: 739-8868

Picasso's Pottery Bar
3495 North Rd (at Cameron St), **Burnaby**
Tel: 444-4410

Indoor Playgrounds

All of the places listed here (except **Score-Virtual Sports World**) are brightly-coloured indoor spaces full of mazes, slides, ladders, games, arcades, climbing equipment and more. There is a huge amount of visual, aural and tactile stimulation (so overwhelming that children often enter the place happy and leave a hysterical mess). Weekends are particularly intense, but if you take your kids during the week these places are a lot quieter and just as much fun. Prices vary depending on age and what facilities are used, but expect to spend $5 to $8 per child for admission; arcade games, train rides, laser tag and food are extra. By the way, kids have to remove their shoes before entering the play area, but are required to wear socks (which is important to remember if it's summer and your child wears sandals everyday). **Score-Virtual Sports World** focuses on games and sports-oriented activities and does not have mazes, ball pits or the like, but it can still get intensely crowded here on weekends. Another interactive sports venue is the **B.C. Sports Hall of Fame and Museum** (see page 62). **Van Berg's Family Fun Center** has a variety of indoor and outdoor activities, including bumper cars, arcade games, paintball and more; see page 51 for more information.

Adventure Zone and Circuit Circus
1496 Cartwright St, in the Kids Only Market, on Granville Island, **Vancouver**
Tel: 608-6699
The Adventure Zone is a four-level indoor playground with a spiral slide, web climber, ball room and lots of tunnels and crawl spaces. Kids have to be three feet tall to go in without an adult. **Circuit Circus**, right next to it, has arcade-type games for kids. (See under "Arcades" in this chapter for other **Circuit Circus** locations.) There is also a snack bar with sandwiches, cookies and juices. (For Granville Island parking and transit information, see page 102.)

Bonkers
5300 No. 3 Rd (at Alderbridge Way), in Lansdowne Mall, **Richmond**
Tel: 278-7529
A huge indoor playground with a climbing and ball pit area, a toddler area, a games and arcade room and snack bar. Bring earplugs for the grown-ups in your party. There's lots of parking in the mall; for better or worse, Bonkers is located next door to **Toys "R" Us** (see page 156).

Crash Crawly's Adventure Fun Centre
1300 Woolridge St (at Lougheed Hwy), **Coquitlam**
Tel: 526-1551
If you can handle *this* place, **Bonkers** will seem tame in comparison. The enormous indoor playground has ball pits, tunnels, slides, a miniature train, a toddlers' play area and a concession stand. If that's not enough, there's also laser tag, a car circuit and a miniature train. Lots of parking here, but the place is a bit tough to find, so look at a map beforehand.

The Gator Pit
2003 Park Royal South (at Taylor Way), in Park Royal Shopping Centre, **West Vancouver**
Tel: 925-0707
This is an indoor four-level jungle-themed structure of mazes, tunnels, slides, tubes and two ball pits. A good break if you've been shopping with the kids; there's free mall parking.

Jolly Genie's Pizza and Play Park
9898 Government Pl (at North Rd), **Burnaby**
Tel: 421-8408

Here you'll find climbing equipment, a ball pit, toddler area, token-operated rides (eight tokens are included in the $4.95 price tag) and arcade games. Besides pizza, they have sandwiches, hot dogs and lasagna.

Kid City
19888 Langley By-Pass, **Langley**
Tel: 532-8989
This indoor playground is a bit out of the way (it's east of Surrey) but it's a huge treat for kids. There are 13,000 square feet of games, ball pits, web bridges, obstacle courses and more.

Playdium
4700 Kingsway (at McKay), in Eaton Centre, **Burnaby**
Tel: 433-PLAY (7529)
There are over 200 interactive games and attractions here; kids can fight, shoot, race a car and more. There's also a neat IMAX ride film where kids get strapped into seats and bump along in sync with the motion of the film.

Score-Virtual Sports World
770 Pacific Blvd S., at the foot of Cambie Street Bridge, in the Plaza of Nations, **Vancouver**
Tel: 602-0513
Hours: Mon. to Thurs. 11:00 a.m. to 11:00 p.m., Fri. and Sat. 10:00 a.m. to midnight
This facility boasts 27,000 square feet of virtual reality sports with over 100 attractions and sports and games, including hockey, soccer, water skiing, lacrosse, football, motor sports and indoor rock climbing. Most of the activities are better for kids four and up as they require some level of skill. Pre-purchased tokens are used for all the games; expect to spend $20 in an hour.

Laser Tag Arenas

A definition for those unfamiliar with this game: laser tag is played in a large indoor space, its purpose being to "shoot" light beams at an opponent using special "laser" guns. The kids are outfitted in special vests and if they're "hit," their guns are deactivated for several seconds. A computer at the front office keeps tally of who gets the most hits. Each game consists of about 20 people and kids play against whoever happens to be there at the same time. Games, which last about 15 minutes, tend to cost around $6 to $7 per person, and since most kids like to play about two or three rounds, the cost can get a bit steep, especially if you bring siblings or friends. While the game carries violent connotations, be aware that no one is ever actually hurt. I find that kids who are taught to be gentle and respectful toward one another still like to let off steam once in a while, and laser tag can be a good outlet for that. Not surprisingly, boys tend to prefer this game more than girls do. Although I've seen kids as young as five years old in a game, it's really better for the seven-and-up crowd. The interiors of these places, which are dark and rigged up with theatrical smoke, black lights, moving spotlights, ramps and mazes, can be somewhat scary. It's a good idea to go in and play a game with your child until they're comfortable. All the venues listed here have snack bars with hot dogs, pop and other fast foods. Laser tag is also available at **Crash Crawly's Adventure Fun Centre** (see page 98); they have a much smaller laser tag area suitable for younger kids.

Laserdome
143 W. 16th St (at Lonsdale), **North Vancouver**
Tel: 985-6033

Planet Lazer
100 Braid St (at E. Columbia), Tel: 525-8255, **New Westminster**
7391 Elmbridge Way (at Westminster Hwy), Tel: 448-9999, **Richmond**

Paintball Fields

This is a team-oriented game, much like laser tag, but players hit each other with paint instead of light beams. Participants are outfitted in coveralls, face masks and visors and given paintball guns that shoot tiny balls. When the balls hit someone (or something), they break open and splatter the victim with paint. Unlike laser tag, this game can hurt; one paintball devotee I know has bruises up and down his legs from the impact of the paintballs. An excellent paintball field is **Tsawwassen Paintball Games** (501-9966) in Delta, at 4799 Hwy 17, just before the Tsawwassen Ferry terminal in Splashdown Park. They charge $25 per person, which includes an all-day field pass and 100 paintballs. Only kids 12 and over are allowed, and most of them like to play for about three hours. There is a concession stand that provides hot dogs and other fast food. Technically, this is not an inside activity since the game takes place on an outdoor field, but parts of the field are covered areas and most kids don't seem to mind a bit of rain when they play, as long as it's not pouring. **Van Berg's Family Fun Center** also has a paintball tent, as well as lots of other activities; see page 51 for more information.

c h a p t e r 8

Get Up
and Go!

Most kids love anything having to do with transportation. Lucky for them, Vancouver is full of cars, boats, buses, trains and more. A number of airplane, seaplane and helicopter companies offer sightseeing trips to Saltspring Island and the Gulf Islands, as well as trips to downtown Victoria. For a list of companies, see page 106. Also not cheap is the **Skyride** to **Grouse Mountain**, but it's a great thrill for kids (see page 22). Cheaper alternatives include a trip on the **SkyTrain** (see page 2), a ride on the **SeaBus** (see page 103) or a mini-ferry ride to Granville Island (see page 102), all of which young children adore. For a complete discussion of Greater Vancouver's public transit system, see "Getting Around," page 2. For boat rentals, see page 50. Also consider a horse-drawn tour through Stanley Park; **Stanley Park Horse Drawn Tours** (681-5115) offers narrated rides from March to October. By the way, a good transportation lookout is **Portside Park**, at the foot of Main Street near Gastown (see "The Out-of-Doors," page 31). There kids can see cruise ships docking, helicopters landing and trains pulling into the station, as well as cargo ships being loaded and unloaded.

Boat Rides and Tours

Boat rides are so much fun for kids (unless they're prone to seasickness). Take a mini-ferry for a quick, 10-minute ride or splurge on a three-hour cruise along the Fraser River. Either way, boats are a great way to see the surrounding area.

Aquabus
False Creek, **Vancouver**
Tel: 689-5858
Prices: Adults $2; kids 3 to 12 and seniors $1; kids 2 and under free
This fleet of little rainbow-coloured ferryboats offers commuter service around False Creek. The boats link two downtown locations with Granville Island, Stamp's Landing and Science World. A sweet ride popular with tourists and locals, this is also a clear favourite with young children. If you're downtown, hop on one of the little boats at the foot of Hornby or Davie Street and arrive in style at **Granville Island** (see page 16) or **Science World** (see page 18), two other kid favourites. All Aquabuses take bicycles, but the one between the Hornby Street dock and Granville Island is particularly easy to board with a bike. The company also offers 25-minute mini-cruises of False Creek. It also has a converted fishing boat used for 45-minute cruises of English Bay and False Creek, accommodating up to 21 passengers.

Bowen Island
(BC Ferries)
Tel: 1-888-223-3779 (BC Ferries information and reservations)
Prices: Adults $5.75; kids 5 to 11 $3; kids under 5 free; cars (including driver but not passengers) $18.25. All prices are for round-trip fares.
The 20-minute ferry ride from Horseshoe Bay to Bowen Island is a fun adventure for kids, especially those who have never been on a ferry before. Once you get to the island there's lots to do, including exploring the local parks, having a picnic, or hanging out at Snug Cove, where there are restaurants and shops. On Sundays in the summer there's a terrific crafts market. Since it's such a short distance from Vancouver this is an easy day trip. Ferries depart roughly every hour; note that they don't run between 12:05 p.m. and 2:30 p.m.

False Creek Ferries
False Creek, **Vancouver**
Tel: 684-7781
Prices: Adults: $2 to $5; kids 3 to 12 $1 to $3; kids under 3 free
Like Aquabus, False Creek Ferries has little boats that ferry passengers to various parts of False Creek. These ones travel between the downtown **Vancouver Aquatic Centre** (see page 86) and **Granville Island** (see page 16), and also go to the **Maritime Museum** (see page 64) and **Science World** (see page 18).

The Fraser River Connection
800 Quayside Dr (at 8th St), near the New Westminster SkyTrain station, **New Westminster**
Tel: 525-4465

Website: *www.vancouverpaddlewheeler.com*
Prices: Vary widely depending on cruise; Fraser River Exploration Cruise: Adults
$37.95; students and seniors $33.95; kids 6 to 12 $11.95; kids 5 and under free
Paddlewheeler cruises along the Fraser River; trips take between three and seven
hours. The best cruise for kids is the Fraser River Exploration Cruise, which
takes three hours and comes with a buffet lunch.

Harbour Cruises
Depart from Coal Harbour, **Vancouver**
Tel: 687-9558
Prices: Adults $18; kids 12 to 17 $5; kids 5 to 11 $6; kids 4 and under free
Daily one-and-a-half-hour rides around Vancouver's waterfront in a paddle-
wheeler.

SeaBus
Links downtown **Vancouver** and Lonsdale Quay, **North Vancouver**
Tel: 521-0400
Website: *www.bctransit.com/seabus/*
The SeaBus offers commuter passage between Lonsdale Quay in North
Vancouver and the SeaBus terminal at the refurbished Canadian Pacific Railway
station downtown. Part of B.C. Transit, it operates in the same way as a bus. One-
way passage takes 12 minutes and is a great thrill for young kids, especially since
they get a train station on one side and a quay on the other. On the trip you'll see
the operations of the **Port of Vancouver** (see page 18), as well as the North Shore
mountains, Stanley Park and the two bridges to the North Shore – Lions Gate to
the west and Second Narrows to the east.

Starline Tours
810 Quayside Dr (at 8th St), **New Westminster**
Tel: 522-3506 or 272-9187
Hours: April to Oct.
Prices: Vary according to cruise; trip to Steveston: Adults $41.95; students,
seniors and kids (13 to 18) $36.95; kids 5 to 12 $25.95
These are narrated boat tours that depart from Westminster Quay and go to
Steveston, Pitt Lake or Harrison Lake. They also have a boat that takes voyagers
to see the **Benson & Hedges Symphony of Fire** (see page 247). Harrison Lake
is a 10-hour trip and rather long for kids, but I've seen a lot of kids on the six-
hour trip to Pitt Lake; the Steveston trip takes only about five and a half hours.
The boats go rain or shine; there is a covered area inside the boat. At all locations there is a 90-minute stop, often with a complimentary lunch and the
chance to explore the town of Steveston, to stop at the Harrison Hot Springs
Hotel, or to go swimming in Pitt Lake. This is certainly a pricey adventure, but
great for visitors and residents who want to see the Fraser River – an underex-
plored area of the Lower Mainland.

Bus Tours

When it comes to kids, the best bus tours are *short* ones; the **Stanley Park Shuttle Bus** and the **Vancouver Trolley Tour Bus** are about all young ones can handle. Longer bus tours are included here mainly because they're so popular with visitors. They are a good way to see a lot of the area in one go, but are definitely not suitable for younger kids; those over 12 may not mind seeing the lay of the land.

Gray Line of Vancouver
Tel: 879-3363
This is a large sightseeing outfit that offers tours of Vancouver, Victoria, Whistler and Squamish. There is pickup and return service to all downtown hotels.

Landsea Tours
Tel: 669-2277 or 225-7272
Daily tours of Vancouver and Victoria are offered; they also have pickup and return service from all downtown hotels.

Pacific Coach Lines
Tel: 662-7575
Website: *www.pacificcoach.com*
In addition to its intercity service, Pacific offers a full range of sightseeing tours.

Stanley Park Shuttle Bus
Tel: 257-8438
Website: *www.parks.vancouver.bc.ca*
Hours: Daily 9:30 a.m. to 6:00 p.m. from May to Sept.
The Vancouver Board of Parks and Recreation offers this free shuttle bus service that loops around the park, making regular stops along the way. It operates on a 15-minute schedule, stopping at 40 of the most popular sights in Stanley Park. Pick it up outside the Vancouver Aquarium (see page 13), across from Coal Harbour.

Vancouver Trolley Tour Bus
Tel: 451-5581
Website: *www.vancouvertrolley.com*
Hours: Daily 9:00 a.m. to 4:00 p.m. in the summer
Prices: Adults $18; kids 4 to 12 $10; kids under 4 free
Tours of the city are given on classic turn-of-the-century trolleys. Visitors can jump off and reboard at any of the 15 stops as often as they like for one price. Like the Stanley Park Shuttle Bus, the Vancouver Trolley is good because if your kids get antsy, you can just get off at any time.

Westcoast City and Nature Sightseeing
Tel: 451-1600
Website: *www.vancouversightseeing.com*

This outfit offers sightseeing trips within Vancouver and to Grouse Mountain, Whistler and Victoria, as well as Native culture tours.

Train Rides

I don't think I've ever met a child who doesn't like train rides. The only down-side is that since adults have to ride with them, you have to squeeze yourself into the tiny cars. Older kids (10 and up) may appreciate the other, scenic train rides mentioned here. These are much longer and can be a great one-on-one experi-ence for an adult and a child.

Bear Creek Park Train

88th Ave and King George Hwy, **Surrey**

Tel: 501-1232

Ten-minute train rides go through the park every day from 10:00 a.m. to sun-set; the train is near a good playground (see separate entry on Bear Creek Park on page 41) and the **Surrey Arts Centre and Theatre** (see page 58).

British Columbia Scenic Rail Tours

Depart from BC Rail station, 1131 W. 1st St (at Pemberton),

North Vancouver

Tel: 984-5246

Website: *www.bcrail/com/bcrpass*

Prices: Adults $45 and up; kids 5 to 11 $12.50 and up; kids under 5 free

BC Rail offers three great rail tours: the **Royal Hudson Steam Train**, the **Cariboo Prospector Passenger Train** and the **Whistler Explorer Scenic Train**. The Whistler Explorer is a day trip from Whistler to Kelly Lake and back. The Cariboo Prospector is a day trip with stops at Whistler, Lillooet, 100 Mile House, Williams Lake, Quesnel and Prince George. The Royal Hudson is a two-hour trip from North Vancouver to Squamish. The return trip can be made via **Harbour Cruises'** *MV Britannia*. Prices aren't cheap, but the trips are phenomenally beautiful. BC Rail has a number of other travel packages as well.

Burnaby Central Railway

Penzance Dr (at Willingdon Ave), Confederation Park, **Burnaby**

Tel: 291-0922

Hours: Sat., Sun. and holidays 11:00 a.m. to 5:00 p.m. from Easter to Thanksgiving

Prices: Adults, seniors and kids 3 and up $2; kids 2 and under free

One of the area's best mini-train rides, this real steam train runs along a 1,676-m (5,500-ft) track beside a restored turn-of-the-century village. Note that it's closed in the winter. There is a concession stand and picnic tables close by, plus **Confederation Park** (see page 38) has a playground, hiking trails and a skate park.

Downtown Vancouver Historic Railway
Just north of 6th Ave (at Moberly), **Vancouver**
Tel: 325-9990
Hours: Weekends and holidays 1:00 p.m. to 5:00 p.m. from June to Sept.
Prices: Adults $2; seniors (over 65) and kids under 13 $1
The B.C. Electric Railway once ran all the way to Steveston; today its refurbished car goes on a shorter run, starting from its station at the entrance to Granville Island, stopping at the Leg-in-Boot station at Moberly and 6th and then running as far as Ontario Street. It's a short trip but one that kids like. Electric trains of this type used to go all the way to Chilliwack before cars and buses came along. Prices include the return trip, which can be done another day if you're heading off to Granville Island or beyond.

SkyTrain
Links downtown **Vancouver** and **Surrey**
Tel: 521-0400
Website: *www.bctransit.com/skytrain/*
An automated light-rail transit (LRT) system operated by B.C. Transit that has 20 station stops between Vancouver and Surrey. This is a great way to travel between Vancouver, New Westminster, Burnaby and Surrey without the hassle of driving, and the 28.8-km (18-mi.) route has panoramic views along the elevated portion. Plus, it's a cheap, fun trip for kids. Avoid taking a leisure trip during rush hour; it is a commuter route and will be quite crowded then.

Stanley Park Miniature Railway
Off Pipeline Rd in Stanley Park, **Vancouver**
Tel: 257-8350
A charming eight-minute ride on a tiny train through a small wilderness section of **Stanley Park** (see page 32). Look for skunks, raccoons, peacocks and squirrels.

West Coast Express
Tel: 683-RAIL (7245) or 689-3641
Website: *www.mcs.net/~dsdawdy/Canpass/wcx/wcx.html* (unofficial site)
This is a commuter train service that runs Monday to Friday 10 times a day from Coquitlam, Port Coquitlam and Port Moody to Vancouver. In the winter, the train runs only westbound in the morning and only eastbound in the evening, and it is always full of commuters, but if you happen to be going in that direction, it's a good way to get to and from the Tri-Cities area.

Airplane, Seaplane and Helicopter Trips

A number of outfits offer transportation to Saltspring and the Gulf Islands, as well as to downtown Victoria. Many of these also have sightseeing trips. These aren't cheap (a one-way adult fare from downtown to Victoria runs about $85 to $90; kids up to 12 are usually half price), but they're good if you want to get to the islands fast or have the financial luxury to show your kids what Vancouver looks like from above.

Altair Aviation 465-5414
Baxter Aviation 683-6525
Coast Western Airlines 684-8768
Harbour Air Seaplanes 688-1277
Helijet Airways 273-1414
KD Air Corporation 688-9957
North Vancouver Air 278-1608
Sea Air Seaplanes .... 273-8900 or 1-800-447-3247
Vancouver Helicopters 270-1484
West Coast Air 899-8692

c h a p t e r 9

where to Eat
with kids

What restaurants are good for kids? Contrary to popular belief, Happy Meals and Disney-themed toys are not prerequisites for eating out with children. What is essential is a restaurant staff that is welcoming to kids, i.e., the maître d' shouldn't shudder when you and your family walk through the door. (Come to think of it, for a restaurant to be kid-friendly, there shouldn't be a *maître d'*.) There should also be *something* on the menu that kids like. Even if you want to expand your seven-year-old's culinary palate, offering him a choice between foie gras with lentil cream sauce and pheasant roasted on a bed of braised endive just isn't going to make anybody happy.

Listed here are some restaurants that offer kids' menus, a sure sign that children are welcome. However, this chapter goes beyond pasta with tomato sauce and chicken strips with fries. Because families in Vancouver come from a wide range of cultural backgrounds, I've tried to reflect this in my restaurant selections. If the food is not familiar to you, you might be squeamish at the thought of taking your kids to any new, exotic or out-of-the-way places, but if you give it a shot, you might be surprised at how easy – and delicious – it can be.

Exposing your kids to different types of cuisine is a really good way to introduce them to the world at large, and encourages curiosity and open-mindedness. Let your kids see how Chinese dragging noodles are made or take them out for Ethiopian food that they can eat with their fingers, not a fork. Frankly, nearly all restaurants offer some type of food that is appealing to kids, whether it's Italian pasta, Chinese noodles or Thai chicken on a skewer. Hotel restaurants, with a few exceptions, usually offer kids' menus; see page 131, for a review of some of these.

Here are a few observations I've made when dining out with kids. Be realistic about what you're expecting from your children. My own two kids have gone through stages in their lives when it was simply impossible to take them out to eat. (When my daughter was 18 months old, she refused to sit in a high chair. She either threw her food on the floor or ran around the restaurant, banging on people's chairs with a spoon. As my newborn son was simultaneously colicky, we abandoned restaurants until we all got a bit older and wiser.)

I'm a big advocate of bringing along things to occupy kids. Colouring books and sticker books are great items, as well as favourite small toys – nothing that's going to take over the table. Even keeping a small notebook and pen in your purse is great for a distraction if the service is slow. Another tactic is to come early. If you arrive just as the restaurant is opening for dinner, the servers tend to be fresh and enthusiastic, take more time with kids than they might normally, and you won't be worrying about bothering other diners. (My daughter did once ask me why so many of the restaurants we go to are always empty.)

There are, of course, multitudes of restaurants in Vancouver, so the following list is just a sampling of some of the better ones for kids. Restaurants here are arranged according to category; the municipalities in which they are located are highlighted in bold for easier reference. If you're worried about money (and who isn't?), be reassured that many of these restaurants are extremely inexpensive, and the kids' meals at them are often less than their fast food equivalents. Kids' meals, including a drink, tend to be less than five dollars.

Price ratings are based on dinner for one adult with one nonalcoholic drink, taxes and tip. Lunch usually costs 25 percent less. Normally people tip 10 to 15% of the bill (calculated on the before-tax amount), depending on the level of service. I try to tip on the high side when dining out with kids, particularly if the staff has been super-accommodating. A rating of Inexpensive/Moderate or some similar split means there are some food items that would fit in the former category, some in the latter. Fast food restaurants are not included here, mainly because their menus are commonly known and their loud, colourful signage will certainly make you aware of their presence.

Inexpensive – Less than $15
Moderate – $15 to $25
Expensive – More than $25

Cafés and Restaurants

Benny's Bagels
1780 Davie (at Denman), in the West End, **Vancouver**, 685-7600
2505 W. Broadway (at Larch), in Kitsilano, **Vancouver**, 731-9730
5728 University Blvd (at Acadia), UBC, **Vancouver**, 222-7815
3365 Cambie (at 17th Ave), **Vancouver**, 872-1111
1375 Adanac (at Clark), **East Vancouver**, 718-5777
Hours: Vary by location
Prices: Inexpensive
Some of the best bagels in town, as well as juices and sandwiches. A good place to go when your child is desperate for a snack. Get yourself a cup of coffee at the same time and you'll all feel better.

Bert's Restaurant
2904 Main (at 13th Ave), **East Vancouver**
Tel: 876-1236
Hours: Mon. to Thurs. 6:00 a.m. to 9:00 p.m., Fri. to Sat. 6:00 a.m. to 10:00 p.m., Sun. 9:00 a.m. to 9:00 p.m.
Prices: Inexpensive/Moderate
If the grandparents are in town and think even **Milestone's** (see page 116) is too pretentious, Bert's will make them feel at home. When I came with my children, a stony-faced woman said, "Sit anywhere you like," but a friendly young wait-ress took our order and brought crayons and extra paper placemats to colour. This is a no-frills family diner where you can feed the kids without going broke. The adult menu has daily specials such as baby beef liver with onions and gravy, plus a regular assortment of pasta, seafood, sandwiches, Greek dishes, a "Calorie Counter's Corner" and senior citizen specials. Kids are offered standard items such as spaghetti and burgers ($3.95 each), as well as mashed potatoes with veg-gies and gravy for $2.95. The kids' menu states: "If you are nice boys and girls, Bert will treat you with a dish of ice cream." (My kids weren't being particular-ly nice that day, but the waitress brought dessert anyway.) There is a full bar and beer on tap, but this is not the place to find a decent glass of wine, nor any par-ticularly memorable food. Cream pies and fruit pies à la mode round out the menu.

Boathouse Restaurant
1795 Beach Ave (at Denman), in the West End, **Vancouver**, 669-2225
6695 Nelson Ave (at Bay St), **Horseshoe Bay**, 921-8188
900 Quayside Dr (at Begbie), in the Inn at the Quay, **New Westminster**, 525-3474
8331 River Rd (at Sea Island Way), **Richmond**, 273-7014
Hours: Vary by location
Prices: Moderate/Expensive
Okay, this isn't Le Crocodile, but the Boathouse is a good place when you want to "go out for dinner" and have the kids in tow. At the Denman location, there is a casual bistro downstairs, with tapas, salads, burgers, sandwiches, oysters and

111

other relatively inexpensive entrées. The upstairs restaurant is more formal, but I tend to prefer it with my kids, as I find the downstairs a bit barlike. Depending on the location, the adult menu may have items such as fresh fennel and blue cheese salad, a seafood hot pot, Australian rack of lamb or grilled vegetarian fettucine. Specials have included fresh lobster or oven-roasted, sesame-crusted fresh halibut. The kids' menu is a reasonable $4.95, including a drink, and offers the choice of fish-and-chips, pasta with tomato or alfredo sauce, chicken strips, grilled chicken breast, hamburger or a grilled cheese sandwich. Kids can colour their menu with crayons. When I've gone to the Denman location, the staff have been really nice, the views great, and we've all been happy, but some parents have reported inconsistent food and service at the other locations.

Bread Garden Bakery and Café
812 Bute St (at Robson), **Vancouver**, 688-3213
1040 Denman St (at Comox), in West End, **Vancouver**, 685-2996
1109 Hamilton (at Helmcken), in Yaletown, **Vancouver**, 689-9500
1880 W. 1st Ave (at Burrard), in Kitsilano, **Vancouver**, 738-6684
2996 Granville (at 14th Ave), **Vancouver**, 736-6465
333 Brooksbank Ave, in Park and Tilford Centre, **North Vancouver**, 983-8483
550 Park Royal N., in Park Royal Shopping Centre, **West Vancouver**, 925-0181
4575 Central Blvd (at Bonsor), in Metrotown Centre, **Burnaby**, 435-5177
2991 Lougheed Hwy, in Pinetree Shopping Centre, **Coquitlam**, 945-9494
8380 Lansdowne Rd. (at Cooney), **Richmond**, 273-5888
2270 152nd St, between 102nd and 104th Avenues, in Guildford Town Centre, **Surrey**, 589-8859
Hours: Vary by location
Prices: Inexpensive
A cafeteria-style bakery and café. The food is not exceptional (it's pre-made and kept warm or reheated when you order), but this is a good place to pop into to get a quick bite en route to another destination. There's enough variety here to please kids and adults: pastas, sandwiches, salads, desserts, et cetera. A few of the Bread Gardens, including the 1st Avenue location, have refrigerated sections with prepackaged food to go – good when you're going on a picnic.

Bridges Restaurant
1696 Duranleau St, Granville Island waterfront, **Vancouver**
Tel: 687-4400
Hours: Mon. to Fri. 11:00 a.m. to 10:00 p.m., Sat. 10:30 a.m. to 10:30 p.m.
Sun. 10:00 a.m. to 10:00 p.m.; open later in the summer
Prices: Moderate/Expensive
This is a hopping spot on summer weekends, so if you come at 7:00 p.m. on a Friday night in July, don't expect to be seated right away. (Reservations are only taken in nonsummer months.) Come early after a day on Granville Island, try to get a table on the sunny deck and enjoy a meal with the kids while you watch

the mini-ferries chug through False Creek. The upstairs restaurant is more elegant and not so suitable for small children. Adults can order Caesar salad, calamari with cilantro aioli or one of the excellent pizzas, such as one with smoked salmon, cream cheese and capers. The kids' menu includes standard items, such as pasta and chicken fingers. The staff is friendly and used to boisterous crowds, so you'll feel right at home here with your children.

Café Deux Soleil

2096 Commercial Dr (at 6th Ave), **East Vancouver**
Tel: 254-1195
Hours: Daily 8:00 a.m. to 10:00 or 11:00 p.m.
Prices: Inexpensive
This funky café has a warm, welcoming atmosphere with all the flavour of Commercial Drive and is popular with both families and the twentysomething crowd. Order breakfasts, soups, veggie burgers or sandwiches from the counter before finding yourself a table. (Mind the lumpy seats!) There are kids' choices as well, like French toast or peanut butter sandwiches. To one side of the room is a slightly elevated stage (music is often performed at night) where children can romp and play with the toys. This is a *great* spot to bring smaller children, though it's crowded on weekends and often harder to find a table then. Thumbs up to the owners, who play a good mix of prerecorded music. The live evening performances are also fun, but the volume level at night can be a bit too much for small ears.

Calhoun's

3035 W. Broadway (at Balaclava), in Kitsilano, **Vancouver**
Tel: 737-7062
Hours: Open 24 hours
Prices: Inexpensive
This is a sunny, cheery spot for Kits parents who've been shopping at nearby **Kidsbooks**, the **Toybox** or for clothes at **Timeké** or (see "Shopping", page 139). Since you order the premade dishes from the counter, your food comes up fast, though the reheated portions can be a bit on the dry side. Still, they've put some thought into the variety of choices offered. From shepherd's pie to Thai noodle salad, there's something for everyone, including a good selection of salads, quiches and pastas. Finicky kids will often go for the fruit salad, quesadilla or penne with cheese. There are high chairs and booster seats, a changing table in the bathroom, and the noise level is loud enough to feel totally comfortable with children but not so overwhelming you can't hear yourself talk. Desserts are yummy, the coffee is good, beer and wine are available, and the fenced-in outside patio is great on a sunny day. What else? The café is open 24 hours, so if you're planning an early morning drive to the Okanagan, stop here first for muffins or breakfast burritos.

Earl's

1185 Robson St (at Bute), **Vancouver**, 669-0020

1601 W. Broadway (at Fir), **Vancouver**, 736-5663

901 W. Broadway (at Laurel), **Vancouver**, 734-5995

303 Marine Dr (at Capilano), **North Vancouver**, 984-4341

4361 Kingsway (at Boundary), **Burnaby**, 432-7329

3850 Lougheed Hwy (at Boundary), **Burnaby**, 205-5025

2850 Shaughnessy St (at Lougheed Hwy), **Port Coquitlam**, 941-1733

5300 No. 3 Rd (at Alderbridge Way), **Richmond**, 303-9702

7236 120th St (at 72nd Ave), **Surrey**, 501-2233

10160 152nd St (at 101st Ave), **Surrey**, 584-0840

7380 King George Hwy (at 72nd Ave), **Surrey**, 591-3500

Hours: Daily approx. 11:30 a.m. to 11:00 p.m. or midnight, depending on the location

Prices: Moderate

Earl's is the place to take your kids when you want a good meal and are tired of going to coffee shops where children are served lunch in cardboard boats. The food is fresh and interesting, with lots of choices – appetizers to salads, fresh fish, pizzas, pastas and more. I've been here at least a dozen times, and the staff are always super nice to my kids (there must be an employee policy to that effect). Twice the waitresses have brought my kids into the kitchen to "help" make ice cream sundaes. There are choices kids will like, such as cheese pizza. My kids inevitably split an order of chicken strips and fries, and I usually favour the spicy Thai chicken salad or one of the fresh salmon specials with a glass of Mission Hill Chardonnay. Kids might like the calamari, if you don't tell them what it is. The restaurants have fun decor, such as old posters and papier-mâché animals.

Hard Rock Café

686 W. Hastings St (at Granville), **Vancouver**

Tel: 687-7625

Hours: Mon. to Fri. 11:00 a.m. to 10:00 p.m. or midnight, Sat. and Sun. noon to 10:00 p.m. or midnight; closing hours depend on crowd and time of year

Prices: Moderate

If you've been to one Hard Rock Café, you've been to them all. This place is still popular with tourists and hard to beat for older kids who think the rock memorabilia decor is really cool. The food is not fabulous and service can be slow, but there is a kids' menu and it's a fun place if you've never been.

Harry's Off Commercial

1716 Charles (at Commercial), **East Vancouver**

Tel: 253-1789

Hours: Daily 9:00 a.m. to 11:00 p.m.

Prices: Inexpensive

A bright, friendly café with a largely gay and lesbian clientele. Although the food selection is limited to mostly sandwiches and a few cooked items, such as burritos or shepherd's pie, the service is prompt and the owners are very friendly. Best

114

of all, there's a small area with toys so you can linger a few minutes over a cup of coffee and the daily paper while the kids occupy themselves. There's also a pool table.

Humpty's Family Restaurant
5000 Steveston Hwy (at No. 5 Rd), in Ironwood Plaza, **Richmond**
Tel: 271-3381
Hours: Open 24 hours
Prices: Inexpensive
This place has a huge menu with excellent prices, making it a good Richmond dining spot. Even the kids can eat for just a few bucks a head, but go Fridays between 5:00 and 9:00 p.m., when they'll dine for free. If you live in Vancouver, check this place out if you're heading to the **Richmond Nature Park** (see page 40); the restaurant is a few minutes south of the park off Hwy 99. Humpty's is also close to **Steveston Fishing Village** (see page 25).

Joey Tomato's Kitchen
2850 Shaughnessy St (at Kingsway), **Port Coquitlam**
Tel: 552-9111
Hours: Sun. to Thurs. 11:00 a.m. to 11:00 p.m., Fri. to Sat. 11:00 a.m. to midnight
Prices: Moderate
You can't miss the three-foot-wide replicated tomatoes embedded in the outside walls of Joey's. Bellinis, martinis and other drink specials are featured, but don't let the pub-type atmosphere dissuade you from coming here with children. Entrées include Pizza Margherita (made in the wood-fired oven) or the Cavatappi Michelangelo (chicken breast with sun-dried tomatoes, garlic and peas). You can also get Italian paninis (sandwiches) for $9. No entrée is more than $12.98; most are in the $10 range. The bambinos' menu has pizza, macaroni and cheese, or chicken fingers and fries, all for $5.99 each.

The Keg
1122 Alberni St (at Thurlow), **Vancouver**, 685-4388
595 Hornby St (at Dunsmuir), **Vancouver**, 687-4044
1499 Anderson St, on Granville Island, **Vancouver**, 685-4735
132 W. Esplanade Ave (at Chesterfield), **North Vancouver**, 984-3534
2656 Eastbrook Pkwy (at Hwy 1), **Burnaby**, 294-4626
800 Columbia St (at 8th Ave), **New Westminster**, 524-1381
2968 Christmas Way (at Westwood), **Port Coquitlam**, 464-1626
11151 No. 5 Rd. (at Steveston Hwy), **Richmond**, 272-1399
15146 100th Ave (at 152nd St), **Surrey**, 583-6700
Hours: Vary by location
Prices: Moderate
This is a steak-and-salad joint good for those who are craving the same. You won't have any problems bringing your kids here; the menu is standard but decent, the staff friendly, and there's a kids' menu as well. Beyond that, it's nothing too special.

The Lazy Gourmet
1605 W. 5th Ave (at Fir), **Vancouver**
Tel: 734-2507
Hours: Mon. to Thurs. 11:30 a.m. to 11:00 p.m., Fri. 11:30 a.m. to midnight, Sat. 10:30 a.m. to 3:00 p.m. and 5:30 p.m. to midnight, Sun. 10:30 a.m. to 3:00 p.m. and 5:30 p.m. to midnight; take-out counter open Mon. to Fri. 7:00 a.m. to 6:00 p.m., Sat. and Sun. 8:00 a.m. to 5:00 p.m.
Prices: Moderate
I confess the Lazy Gourmet is at the top of my list when it comes to eating out with my kids. Why? Because both my kids and I get to eat food we actually like. I can start my meal with the exquisite roasted garlic (served with chèvre and sliced pears) and move on to a market salad or fresh fish special, my son gets to eat cheese pizza, and my daughter adores the macaroni and cheese (the best either of us has ever had). The french fries (served with a garlic aïoli) are excellent.

This place might appear to be for adults only: its sparse design, high ceilings and nice table settings don't seem conducive to small children. Lunchtime does attract more of a business crowd, but do take your kids for an early dinner or for the brunch on Saturday or Sunday. You'll be glad you did. The staff is extremely welcoming to kids and always bring them some fun toy to play with (and I mean *fun*, like a neat puzzle or small game). It's not the cheapest meal in town but it's original, well-made food. Booster seats are available. The take-out counter is open throughout the day and a good place to grab a bagel, coffee or juice when you're running around.

Lugz
2525 Main St (at Broadway), **East Vancouver**
Tel: 873-6766
Hours: Mon. to Sat. 6:30 a.m. to 11:00 p.m., Sun. 9:00 a.m. to 11:00 p.m.
Prices: Inexpensive
A hip coffee bar with comfy chairs and Seattle's Best Coffee. There's no children's menu, but there are enough simple choices to please both kids and parents who want a light bite: bagels, milkshakes, yogurt, ham-and-cheese sandwiches, bagels with peanut butter. The music is good and there are toys for kids to play with.

Milestone's Restaurant
1145 Robson St (at Thurlow St), **Vancouver**, 682-4477
1210 Denman (at Beach Ave), in the West End, **Vancouver**, 662-3431
1109 Hamilton (at Helmcken), in Yaletown, **Vancouver**, 684-9111
2966 W. 4th Ave (at Balaclava), in Kitsilano, **Vancouver**, 734-8616
1096 Park Royal S. (at Taylor Way), in Park Royal Shopping Centre, **West Vancouver**, 925-9825
4420 Lougheed Hwy (at Rosser), **Burnaby**, 291-7393
200 – 5951 No. 3 Rd. (at Westminster Hwy), in London Plaza, **Richmond**, 273-4111
Domestic Terminal Building, Level 3, Vancouver International Airport, **Richmond**, 303-3221

116

Hours: Vary by location, but generally open Mon.to Fri. 11:00 a.m. to 10:30 p.m., Sat. 9:30 or 10:00 a.m. to midnight, Sun. 9:00 or 10:00 a.m. to 10:00 or 11:00 p.m.

Prices: Moderate

For a restaurant chain, this place really delivers. There is the usual assortment of grilled fish, meats, pastas and seafood – always good and occasionally exceptional. Each Milestone's has its own character. Some are more barlike, selling groovy martinis to the after-work business crowd, but all of them are good for kids. Their children's menu has standard items such as pasta or chicken fingers ($3.95 each), and the staff are always pleasant and efficient. The Denman location is good for families, for it's right at English Bay; same with the Park Royal location, with its proximity to the beach.

Moxie's Restaurant

2991 Lougheed Hwy (at Pinetree), in Pinetree Village, **Coquitlam**, 552-2562
Hours: Mon. to Wed. 10:00 a.m. to 11:00 p.m., Thurs. to Fri. 10:00 a.m. to midnight, Sat. 9:00 a.m. to midnight, Sun. 9:00 a.m. to 11:00 p.m.

610 6th St (at 6th Ave), in Royal City Centre, **New Westminster**, 521-1600
Hours: Mon. to Thurs. and Sat. 10:00 a.m. to 11 p.m., Fri. 10:00 a.m. to midnight, Sun. 10:00 a.m. to 10:00 p.m.

Prices: Inexpensive/Moderate

Standard-looking coffee shop decor with food along the lines of Earl's or Milestone's. Moxie's has an interesting and varied selection of soups, appetizers and entrées, with largely Mexican and Southwestern influences. There are over 100 items, including Smokin' BBQ Ribs, the Santa Fe Chicken Sandwich or the Caribbean Grilled Chicken Salad. The kids' menu, which ranges from $4 to $5, includes the standard burgers, pasta or chicken fingers, as well as barbecue wings or a soup-and-sandwich combo. Kids' meals come with Beetle Juice (a house special combo fruit juice) and Moxie's "famous" Erupting Volcano dessert. Their weekend brunch also has special items for kids. (A big favourite is the cinnamon bun French toast.) There are crayons to colour with and often balloons to take home.

Planet Hollywood

969 Robson St (at Burrard), **Vancouver**
Tel: 688-7827
Hours: Sun. to Thur. 11:00 a.m. to 11:00 p.m., Fri. to Sat. 11:00 a.m. to 1:00 a.m.
Prices: Moderate

Teenagers love it here, particularly boys (and dads), who get to see Pamela Anderson's *Baywatch* bathing suit and other showbiz memorabilia. The number of television screens here is overwhelming, and the whole restaurant is a big scene you'll either love or hate. Food here is California-style, with Italian and Asian influences, and includes salads, pasta, pizza, fajitas and burgers. Because of the noise level and touristy atmosphere, kids are definitely welcome, though go for lunch or an early dinner and avoid the late-night twentysomething meat market ambience of this place.

The Prospect Point Café
North end of Stanley Park, **Vancouver**
Tel: 669-2737
Hours: Daily 11:30 a.m. to 5:00 p.m.; open for dinner Fridays and Saturdays at 5:00 p.m.
Prices: Moderate
This tourist-oriented restaurant has been renovated in recent years, and prices have unfortunately gone up as a result. It's still a good spot to bring friends who want to see the city. The café is located at picturesque Prospect Point, with a view from the restaurant of the Lions Gate Bridge. Overfed raccoons delight kids with their begging. The adult menu emphasizes salmon dishes, and kids can choose from burgers, hot dogs, pasta, chicken strips and fish-and-chips. There's outdoor seating in the summer and a gift shop and small sidewalk café, both of which open at 9:30 a.m.

The Red Onion Restaurant
2028 W. 41st Ave (at Arbutus), in Kerrisdale, **Vancouver**
Tel: 263-0833
Hours: Mon. to Sat. 8:30 a.m. to 11:00 pm, Sun. 11:00 a.m. to 9:00 p.m.
Prices: Inexpensive
A Vancouver fixture since 1985, the Red Onion is an unpretentious restaurant with excellent prices and great service. Its food, though basic, is quite good, and the place is big with families. Hot dogs are their specialty (and possibly the best you'll ever have), charbroiled with fried onions, tomato, a mustard-based sauce and a custom-made bun. (Kids' versions are toned down.) There are also soups and salads, vegetarian selections and an excellent chicken sandwich. The small-fry menu features hot dogs, burgers, peanut butter-and-jelly sandwiches and cheddar cheese melts, with prices in the $3 to $4 range. Desserts, made from scratch, include everything from cinnamon buns to pecan pie. A welcome alternative to the McDonald's across the street.

Sodas Diner
375 Water St (at Cordova), in Gastown, **Vancouver**, 683-7632
Hours: Daily 10:30 a.m. to 10 p.m.
4497 Dunbar St (at 29th Ave), **Vancouver**, 222-9922
Hours: Mon. to Thurs. noon to 9:00 p.m., Fri. 11:00 a.m. to 10:00 p.m., Sat. 10:00 a.m. to 10:00 p.m., Sun. 10:00 a.m. to 9:00 p.m.
Prices: Inexpensive
A clean-cut fifties-style joint with a menu to match. Kids can pick from their favourites: hot dogs, hamburgers, chicken fingers or grilled cheese sandwiches, all with fries for $3.75. The rest of the menu includes blue plate specials such as chili, as well as burgers, appetizers, a daily soup, a daily fresh pasta, sodas, shakes and beer on tap. At the Dunbar location, the jukebox really works, and kids love the pint-size stools at the lowered counter. Crayons are provided and the staff really seem to love kids. There's also an enclosed outside patio for sunny weather. Their other location has the same 1950s theme and attracts more of a tourist

and lunchtime business crowd, but kids love the Archie comics sitting at each table.

Sophie's Cosmic Café

2095 W. 4th Ave (at Arbutus), in Kitsilano, **Vancouver**

Tel: 732-6810

Hours: Daily 8:00 a.m. to 9:00 p.m.

Prices: Inexpensive/ Moderate

If your kids seem to gravitate toward the wacky (and what kid doesn't?), they'll love Sophie's. Nearly every inch of wall space in this café is covered in some sort of kitschy memorabilia, from old lunchboxes to classic Coca-Cola bottles. If that's not enough to amuse them, there's a corner full of toys to explore. There's no kids' menu but plenty to appeal to everyone, from eggs made a dozen ways to burgers served with tons of curly fries. It *is* a tiny place and there's not much space between tables, so it's not the best spot for a stroller or if you've got a kid who wants to run around. Sophie's is a popular spot for weekend brunch. Don't go then unless you want to queue up with your kids in the inevitable pouring rain. There's an outside patio that is nice in clear weather.

T.G.I. Friday's

803 Thurlow (at Robson), **Vancouver**

Tel: 682-6422

Hours: Sun. to Thurs. 11:00 a.m. to 11:00 p.m., Fri. to Sat. 11:00 a.m. to 1:00 a.m.

Prices: Moderate

If you've been shopping on Robson Street with the kids, they're probably bored and hungry. Treat them to T.G.I. Friday's for lunch, and they might forgive you for dragging them in and out of stores. Friday's has over 100 items, from basic American burgers to exotic salads. There are also more than 300 alcoholic and nonalcoholic drinks. The decor is fun but be prepared – this place is loud, loud, loud.

The Tomahawk

1550 Philip Ave (at Marine Dr), **North Vancouver**

Tel: 988-2612

Hours: Sun. to Thurs. 8:00 a.m. to 9:00 p.m., Fri. to Sat. 8:00 a.m. to 10:00 p.m.

Prices: Inexpensive/Moderate

This North Van institution has been around for 70-plus years serving huge portions of food amidst North Shore and West Coast Native artifacts. Their breakfasts are fantastic, with sides like Yukon-style bacon and Klondike (thick-cut) toast, but also try it for lunch, when you can get meat loaf, rainbow trout or oysters on toast. The kids' menu (with crayons for colouring) has items like the Pale Face Delight (a grilled cheese sandwich) and other standards, such as burgers and chicken strips, all in the $5 range.

Tomato Fresh Food Café
3305 Cambie St (at 17th Ave), **Vancouver**
Tel: 874-6020
Hours: Daily 9:00 a.m. to 10:00 p.m.
Prices: Moderate
A nice neighbourhood café, the Tomato serves up healthy cuisine that's appealing to both grown-ups and kids. The adult menu includes items such as vegetarian chili, spicy lamb sausages, Tuscan chicken with mashed potatoes or Cajun prawns with corn risotto. The "fresh sheet" lists the daily special, plus there's an assortment of fresh-squeezed juices and wines by the bottle and glass. The kids' menu features peanut butter-and-banana or grilled cheese sandwiches, "tomato pasta" or a chicken-and-zucchini quesadilla, with prices ranging from $3.50 to $5.95. Kids can also get milkshakes, root beer and floats. Desserts include Rice Krispies squares, brownies, fruit crisp and more. Sometimes the food here is disappointing and it's slightly overpriced, but it's a healthy alternative to other places, and the decor is cheery, with its checkered floor, red and yellow walls and rotating art exhibits. They also have a take-out counter – nice if you're going to the beach and want a picnic lunch.

Troll's Seafood
6408 Bay (at Royal), in Horseshoe Bay, **West Vancouver**, 921-7755
Hours: Daily 6:00 a.m. to 8:00 p.m.
810 Quayside Dr. (at 8th St), in Westminster Quay Public Market, **New Westminster**, 515-0507
Hours: Mon. to Thurs. 11:00 a.m. to 9:00 p.m., Fri. to Sat. 9:30 a.m. to 10:00 p.m., Sun. 9:30 a.m. to 9:00 p.m.
Prices: Moderate
A family-oriented restaurant, Troll's has great fish-and-chips as well as burgers, pasta and dinner entrées. The Horseshoe Bay Troll's is a popular family spot to eat lunch before boarding the ferry, plus it's across the street from a small park with play equipment. The New West locale is a relaxing lunch or dinner spot after playing on the Quay, plus it has a good view of the Fraser River, so kids can watch the barges and other boats. Servers are friendly, there's a kids' menu, and food is very reasonably priced.

Family Restaurants

Family restaurants have inexpensive choices, and their kids' food tends to be healthier than that of their fast food counterparts. All of these restaurants have kids' menus, of course, as well as colouring materials, booster seats, high chairs and staffs used to dealing with children. The food is not exceptionally good, though it's usually perfectly acceptable. All these restaurants are in the Inexpensive/Moderate range.

ABC Country Restaurant
2350 Boundary Rd (at Lougheed Hwy), **Burnaby**, 293-1242
6500 Hastings St (at Kensington), **Burnaby**, 291-8444
2773 Barnet Hwy (at Landsdowne), **Coquitlam**, 464-9131
100 Schoolhouse St (at Lougheed Hwy), **Coquitlam**, 526-2272
3580 No. 3 Rd. (at Cambie), **Richmond**, 276-9222
7380 King George Hwy (at 72nd Ave), **Surrey**, 596-2997
15373 Fraser Hwy (at 88th Ave), **Surrey**, 583-3228
8080 120th St (at 80th Ave), **Surrey**, 591-7087
2160 King George Hwy (at 24th Ave), **Surrey**, 531-2635
19219 No. 10 Hwy (at 192nd St), **Surrey**, 576-7770
Hours: Vary by location, but generally open daily 7:00 or 8:00 a.m. to 10:00 or 11:00 p.m.

Knight and Day Restaurant
3684 Lougheed Hwy (at Boundary), **Vancouver**, 299-7701
2601 Westview Dr, off Hwy 1, **North Vancouver**, 983-3083
5075 Kingsway, between Royal Oak and Nelson, **Burnaby**, 435-8818
2635 Barnet Hwy (at Lansdowne), **Coquitlam**, 942-1337
3631 No. 3 Rd. (at Cambie), **Richmond**, 244-8858
9677 King George Hwy (at 96th St), **Surrey**, 588-7575
Hours: Open 24 hours except some locations that close Sunday at midnight, then open again at 6:00 a.m. Monday

Red Robin
752 Thurlow St (at Alberni), in the Carlyle, **Vancouver**, 662-8288
1001 W. Broadway (at Oak), **Vancouver**, 733-6494
801 Marine Dr (at Fell), **North Vancouver**, 984-4464
112 – 4640 Kingsway (at Sussex), in Metrotown Centre, **Burnaby**, 439-7696
9628 Cameron St (at Ericson), **Burnaby**, 421-7266
3000 Lougheed Hwy, between Christmas and Westwood, **Coquitlam**, 941-8650
10237 152nd St (at 102A Ave), in Guildford Town Centre, **Surrey**, 930-2415
Hours: Vary by location, but generally open daily 11:00 a.m. to 10:00 p.m. or midnight

Ricky's Family Restaurants
111 Dunsmuir (at Beatty), at the Stadium SkyTrain station, **Vancouver**, 602-9233
3434 Lougheed Hwy, between Rupert and Boundary, **Vancouver**, 253-2027
4820 Kingsway, in Metrotown Centre, **Burnaby**, 451-3400
Hours: Vary by location

White Spot

1616 W. Georgia St (at Cardero), **Vancouver**, 681-8034

580 W. Georgia St (at Seymour), **Vancouver**, 662-3066

2518 W. Broadway (at Larch), **Vancouver**, 731-2434

2850 Cambie St (at 13th Ave), **Vancouver**, 873-1252

5367 W. Blvd (at 37th Ave), **Vancouver**, 266-1288

650 W. 41st Ave (at Cambie), in Oakridge Centre, **Vancouver**, 261-2820

1041 S.W. Marine Dr (at Oak), in the Coast Vancouver Airport Hotel, **Vancouver**, 263-6667

1476 Kingsway (at Knight), **East Vancouver**, 874-2825

1126 S.E. Marine Dr (at Ross), **East Vancouver**, 325-8911

2205 Lonsdale Ave (at 23rd St), **North Vancouver**, 987-0024

333 Brooksbank (at Cotton), **North Vancouver**, 988-4199

752 Taylor Way (at Marine Dr), **West Vancouver**, 922-4520

4129 Lougheed Hwy (at Gillmore), **Burnaby**, 299-4423

4075 North Rd. (at Lougheed Hwy), **Burnaby**, 421-4620

5550 Kingsway (at MacPherson Ave), **Burnaby**, 434-6668

3025 Lougheed Hwy (at Westwood St), **Coquitlam**, 942-9224

5880 No. 3 Rd (at Ackroyd), **Richmond**, 273-3699

6551 No. 3 Rd (at Westminster Hwy), **Richmond**, 278-3911

10181 152nd St (at 100th Ave), **Surrey**, 585-2223

13580 102nd Ave (at King George Hwy), **Surrey**, 581-2511

Hours: Vary by location, but generally open Mon. to Fri. 6:30 a.m. to 11:00 p.m., Sat. and Sun. until 10:00 p.m.

Home of the legendary kid's meal served in a cardboard pirate ship, complete with a chocolate coin treasure.

Chinese

Floata Seafood Restaurant

180 Keefer St (at Columbia), in Chinatown, **Vancouver**, 602-0368

Hours: Daily 7:30 a.m. to 3 p.m. for dim sum, 5:00 p.m. to 10:00 p.m. for dinner

4380 No. 3 Rd. (at Cambie), in Parker Place, **Richmond**, 270-8889

Hours: Daily 9:00 a.m. to 10:30 p.m.

Prices: Inexpensive/Moderate

The cavernous Chinatown location seats 1,000, and the noise level is high enough to make any family feel comfortable. Dim sum, yummy steamed or fried stuffed Chinese dumplings, is the order of the day, but you can also order larger dishes. The Richmond location tends to have better food.

Hon's Wun-Tun House

1339 Robson St (at Denman), **Vancouver**, 685-0871

268 Keefer St (at Gore), in Chinatown, **Vancouver**, 688-0871

288 Pender St (at Gore), in Chinatown, **Vancouver**, 681-8842

408 6th St (at 4th Ave), **New Westminster**, 520-6661

310 – 3025 Lougheed Hwy (at Westwood), **Coquitlam**, 468-0871

101 – 4600 No. 3 Rd. (at Cambie), **Richmond**, 273-0871

Hours: Vary by location
Prices: Inexpensive
Most Chinese restaurants are super for kids – they tend to be quick, cheap, delicious and full of families. Hon's is one of the best along these lines, serving up reliably great-tasting dishes, among them noodles, dumplings, and traditional meat and seafood entrées. They also have an excellent vegetarian selection. If you haven't taken your kids out for Chinese food before, try bringing them here. Chances are there's something they'll like, whether it's fried rice or Shanghai noodles with chicken (better than Campbell's chicken noodle soup). The noise level is comfortably high, and the staff doesn't get perturbed if you make a mess – easy to do if your son is experimenting with chopsticks for the first time. They've got booster seats and high chairs (and forks!). Most of the time a stroller can be accommodated.

Kam Gok Yuen
142 E. Pender St (at Main), in Chinatown, **Vancouver**
Tel: 683-3822
Prices: Inexpensive
This is a great place to stop when you've been exploring Chinatown with the kids and suddenly realize you're starving. This is a no-frills place – simple chairs, little artwork, no atmosphere – but the food is great and not expensive. There's no kids' menu, but the portions are large enough that you can easily share. Try not to overorder. They have excellent congee, a sort of rice porridge with meat, or order one of the barbecued ducks hanging in the window. They're incredibly tasty and succulent.

Pink Pearl
1132 E. Hastings St (at Clark), Vancouver
Tel: 253-4316
Hours: Daily 9:00 a.m. to 10:00 p.m.; dim sum stops at 3:00 p.m.
Prices: Moderate
Carts of dim sum start rolling up to your table as soon as you sit down, which is great when you're really hungry. This is one of the best places for dim sum in the city and extremely popular with families, even those with two- and three-year-old kids. The seafood tanks are popular with kids, and they also like seeing the carts roll by, especially the one with dishes of Jell-O dotted with paper umbrellas or the one with its own portable grill that fries rolled up rice noodles. If your kids don't care for dim sum (though pot stickers and barbecued pork buns are often well received), you can order other dishes off the menu. (I usually end up ordering a plate of beef fried rice for my own finicky eaters.) The staff are really friendly with kids, while still being efficient, so you can eat a good meal and get out quickly if need be. The dim sum starts at 9:00 a.m. and stops at 3:00 p.m., so be sure to arrive within those hours if you want dumplings. The restaurant seats nearly 700 (with a noise level to match), but there is enough space to park a stroller among the masses of round tables.

123

Shao-Lin Noodle Restaurant
548 W. Broadway (at Cambie), **Vancouver**
Tel: 873-1816
Hours: Wed. to Mon. 11:00 a.m. to 10:00 p.m., Tues. 11:00 a.m. to 3:00 p.m.
Prices: Inexpensive
There are so many tasty noodle restaurants in Vancouver, it's impossible to include them all here. This one is particularly great for kids, however, because they get a front seat on the action. Through a sheet of glass they can see the chefs making and cooking noodles of every variety, whether thick or thin, pushing or dragging. Dishes are generous and good for sharing; any kid who likes pasta will love it here.

English

The Diner
4556 W. 10th Ave (at Sasamat), **Vancouver**
Tel: 224-1912
Hours: Mon. to Sat. 9:30 a.m. to 8:30 p.m., Sun. 11:30 a.m. to 7:30 p.m.
Prices: Inexpensive
English restaurants are not known for their friendly attitude to children (a statement I can make with confidence, having spent three months in London with an infant and a two-year-old). This British import, however, is much more welcoming to families. From the English knickknacks to the pictures and postcards on the wall to the stacks of papers piled on a back table, you'll feel as if you're eating at Granny's house. Stella, who runs the Diner, plays the part perfectly, joking and laughing with customers, particularly the kids, and fussing to make sure everyone's coffee is refilled. The food is relatively mediocre, but with lots of comfort items: devilled-egg sandwiches, steak-and-kidney pie, fish-and-chips and more. Half orders are available for kids under 12. There's no Guinness on tap for adults, though. (It really *is* just like Granny's.)

King's Fare Fish and Chips
1320 W. 73rd Ave (at Hudson), **Vancouver**
Tel: 266-3474
Hours: Sun. to Wed. 4:00 p.m. to 8:00 p.m., Thurs. 4:00 p.m. to 9:00 p.m., Fri. to Sat. 11:30 a.m. to 9:00 p.m.
Prices: Inexpensive/Moderate
What kid doesn't love fish-and-chips? King's Fare makes some of the best, from cod to halibut to oysters. The children's meal comes with one piece of fish, chips, as well as a beverage or sundae. If your kids *don't* love fish, they can get chicken nuggets.

Ethiopian
Nyala
2930 W. 4th (at Bayswater), in Kitsilano, **Vancouver**
Tel: 731-7899
Website: *www.nyala.com*

Hours: Daily 5:00 p.m. to 10:00 p.m. or later
Prices: Inexpensive/Moderate
This is a fun place for kids and the food is good. The dishes are simple stews made of meats or vegetables, most of which are mild enough for children's mouths. Kids (and parents) get a kick out of the fact that they don't have to use a fork. Pieces of spongy bread (*injera*) are used to pick up food. This is a funky place and a nice change from other restaurants, plus the staff is always super friendly. Plus, they offer smaller, kids' portions. Do try this place.

Greek

Kalamata Greek Tavern
478 W. Broadway (at Cambie), **Vancouver**
Tel: 872-7050
Hours: Tues. to Sun. 5:00 p.m. to 10:00 p.m.; closed Mondays
Prices: Moderate
This place serves excellent Greek food. Try the *avgolemeno* (chicken, rice, egg and lemon soup) or go directly for the grilled loin lamb chops with olive oil, fresh garlic and oregano. (You get about six and they're really succulent.) All the main courses come with Greek salad, roast potatoes, tzatziki and pita bread. There is no kids' menu but they do have a kids' souvlaki for $7.95, which is pricey but the portion is generous, making good leftovers for school lunches. Kids might also like the *keftethes*, a huge plate of meatballs for only $5.50. The baclava is homemade and some of the best I've ever had, but children usually prefer the chocolate ice cream with a raspberry centre. The waitresses all wear beepers, which quietly go off when food is ready. As a result, the service is prompt as well as friendly. Kalamata is a small place and fills up quickly. Make a reservation or come early on weekends; it tends to be quieter on Tuesday and Wednesday nights. Too bad it's no longer open for lunch.

Stepho's Souvlaki Greek Taverna
1124 Davie St (at Thurlow), **Vancouver**
Tel: 683-2555
Hours: Daily 11:30 to about midnight
Prices: Inexpensive/Moderate
That lineup you see on Davie Street at dinnertime is people waiting to get into Stepho's. It's that good. The portions are huge and the service is great; their calamari and souvlaki are particularly tasty. There is no kids' menu, but the meals are big enough to share. Lunch is quieter, but if you do want to go for dinner, get there when it opens, before it gets packed.

Indian

Ashiana Tandoori
1440 Kingsway (at Knight St), **East Vancouver**
Tel: 874-5060
Hours: Mon. 5:00 p.m. to 10:00 p.m., Tues. to Sun. 11:30 a.m. to 10:30 p.m.
Prices: Moderate

This is one of Vancouver's best Indian restaurants, but be sure to specify "mild" when ordering dishes for your children. The staff is really friendly but service can be slow, so order some naan while you're waiting or bring a colouring book for the kids. The owners have kids so this is a very family-friendly place, plus the curries and tandoori chicken are excellent.

Italian

Anton's Pasta Bar
4260 E. Hastings (at Madison), **Burnaby**
Tel: 299-6636
Hours: Mon. to Thurs. 11:30 a.m. to 10:30 p.m., Fri. and Sat. 11:30 a.m. to 11:00 p.m., Sun. 4:00 p.m. to 10:00 p.m.
Prices: Inexpensive/ Moderate
Anton's has been here for years, and it's popular with the SFU crowd as well as families. Most pasta dishes are $12.95, and they're large enough to feed two or even three people (though the minimum charge per person is $10, not including children). If you want *penne alla silana* and your kids want spaghetti and meatballs, don't worry; they can get a half order. Lineups start at around 5:00 or 6:00 p.m., and earlier on weekends, so get here early if you don't want to wait in line, as they don't take reservations. Despite the fact that it gets hectic, the waitresses are really fast and attentive. (I got extra napkins without having to ask.) Kids can colour their menu, and there's a fabulous tiramisu for dessert – if you have room left for another huge portion of food.

Chianti Café and Restaurant
1850 W. 4th Ave (at Burrard), in Kitsilano, **Vancouver**
Tel: 738-8411
Hours: Mon. to Sat. 11:30 a.m. to 10:30 p.m. or so; Sun. 3:00 p.m. to 10:00 p.m. or so
Prices: Inexpensive/Moderate
Unlike the East Side, the West Side is lacking in good family-run Italian restaurants. Chianti is certainly not the exception (food can range from mediocre to pretty good), but this is a fine place to have a cheap, hearty plate of pasta and enjoy a relatively stress-free meal with your children. The kids' menu is good value: for $3.95 kids get their choice of spaghetti in tomato sauce, tortellini in *panna* or ravioli with meat sauce, all with pop or juice and ice cream. Adults can choose from a variety of pasta dishes, as well as veal, chicken and seafood. There's a coffee can full of crayons for colouring the menus and the staff are really friendly with kids. (Once my two walked off with free Chianti T-shirts.) Chianti's Pasta Shop next door sells fresh uncooked pasta and ready-to-heat sauces.

The Old Spaghetti Factory
53 Water St (at Abbott), in Gastown, **Vancouver**, 684-1288
50 8th St (at Carnarvon), **New Westminster**, 524-9788
Hours: Mon. to Thurs. 11:30 a.m. to 10:00 p.m., Fri. 11:30 a.m. to 11 p.m.,

Sat. 11:30 a.m. to 11 p.m., Sun. 11:30 a.m. to 9:00 p.m.

Prices: Moderate

The Gastown restaurant is a very popular spot with tourists, probably because of its location and longevity but also because it's a good place to relax with kids after a day of exploring the city. The pasta choices are numerous, and there's a kids' menu. Both locations are huge, with the one in Gastown bordering on cavernous, and the noise level can get pretty high during peak hours.

Romano's Macaroni Grill
1523 Davie St (at Nicola), in the West End, **Vancouver**
Tel: 689-4334
Prices: Moderate/Expensive

Come at night if you want to hear the servers singing opera between waiting on tables. (Come at lunch if you don't.) Romano's is housed in a heritage building (the former home of the owner of B.C. Sugar) and is very popular with groups and families. Kids will like the giant bowl of crayons at the entrance, and parents may or may not like the jugs of mediocre red and white house wine on each table. (You only pay for what you drink.) The menu has items such as panini, pizza, chicken, veal and pasta. "Family Recipes" include bruschetta, *pizza vegetale* and *capellini al pomodoro*. The kids' menu includes a choice of macaroni and cheese, pizza, chicken strips, chicken breast, farfalle or grilled cheese sandwiches. Prices for kids 12 and under are $6.99 for dinner and $4.95 for lunch, including a drink. Above age 12, the price goes up a dollar per year until the age of 16, when kids pay full price. There are also pre-set menus for parties of eight or more – one of the reasons this is a popular place for groups. The food here is okay, but Anton's is much better and cheaper, if you don't mind the drive to Burnaby. For those staying downtown who like dinner theatre, this is a fun place to check out.

Japanese

Fukuroku Sushi
4260 No. 3 Rd. (at Cambie), **Richmond**
Tel: 273-0622
Hours: Daily 11:30 a.m. to 2:00 a.m.
Prices: Moderate

What a great idea! A Japanese restaurant with a children's play area! The food here is really good. There's sashimi, robata, noodles and rice bowls, and the sushi is fresh and delicious. Sit at the bar, where you can select sushi displayed on boats floating in a canal around the bar, or get one of the coveted tables separated from the playroom by a sheet of glass, so you can see your kids playing on the climbing equipment or building at the Duplo table. (This play area is practically soundproof, so you don't have to hear the accompanying high-pitched shrills.) If your kids don't care for sushi, have them try the chicken karrage (fried chicken) or the yakitori (chicken on a skewer). Rice bowls are other simple options. The only problem can be getting your children to take a break from playing and come and eat their meal, but this is an excellent spot if you want to have some adult conversation with kids around. There are juices, sake, a full bar and yummy desserts such as plum Jell-O, grasshopper pie or *akafuku* (sweet rice cake covered with red bean paste).

Mexican

Las Margaritas
1999 W. 4th Ave (at Maple), in Kitsilano), **Vancouver**
Tel: 734-7117
Hours: Sun. to Thurs. 11:30 a.m. to 10:00 p.m., Sat. 11:30 a.m. to 11:00 p.m.
Prices: Moderate
If you don't mind generic Mexican food, this is the place for you, particularly if you've got kids. They're really kid-friendly here, with a tot-size menu and colouring materials. Kids also like the fun decor, and the patio is pleasant on a sunny day. This place can get a bit hectic on Friday nights when the after-work crowd comes in for margaritas; taste one and you'll see why they're so popular.

Tio Pepe's Restaurante Mexicano
1134 Commercial Dr (at Napier), **East Vancouver**
Tel: 254-8999
Hours: Mon. to Sat. 5:00 p.m. to 10:00 p.m., Sun. 4:00 p.m. to 9:00 p.m.
Prices: Inexpensive/Moderate
This is Vancouver's only Yucatecan restaurant (around since 1988). It's a small place and the tables are close together, so don't bring any kids who can't sit still, for there's no room to run around. Also, there's no kids' menu. So why come? The food here is delicious and authentic, and there is enough variety for kids to find something on the main menu they like. There are standard Mexican items such as tacos, ceviche and burritos, as well as Yucatecan fare such as a very tart and refreshing nopales cactus salad or the *cochinita pibil* (baked pork with Yucatecan spices and wrapped in banana leaves). Kids often order à la carte, preferring flautas, rice and beans, or cheese quesadillas.

The staff is really nice and the atmosphere is friendly. The service can be a bit slow; bring a colouring book or a toy if you think your child will get antsy. Otherwise, just come early before the crowds settle in. If you have room left after eating, treat everyone to the Mexican hot chocolate; it's intensely good, particularly on a cold winter night. Tio Pepe's does take-out and has free delivery in the area.

Topanga Café
2904 W. 4th Ave (at Macdonald), in Kitsilano, **Vancouver**
Tel: 733-3713 or 733-3021
Hours: Mon. to Sat. 11:30 a.m. to 11:00 p.m.; closed Sundays
Prices: Moderate
A small but friendly Mexican restaurant, this is a relatively easy place to take kids. Young ones are encouraged to colour the menus; multitudes of adult-decorated versions are framed on the walls. Standard Mexican fare is featured here: tacos, burritos, enchiladas, chile rellenos. Eggplant filling is available for vegetarians.

There's no kids' menu, but children can get quesadillas or burgers, and most of the items on the menu are mild enough for their palates. Desserts include chocolate cake, cheesecake and sweet empanadas. Food here can be rather pricey (lunches range from $8.85 to $14.95); go for the daily specials or order à la carte. This is a nice place to go after a day at Kits Beach or Jericho Beach Park. If you are going for dinner, arrive early; the café gets pretty full in the evenings and you might have to wait for a table.

Thai

Thai House
1116 Robson St (at Thurlow), **Vancouver**, 683-3383
1103 Denman St (at Comox), in the West End, **Vancouver**, 685-8989
1766 W. 7th Ave (at Burrard) in Kitsilano, **Vancouver**, 737-0088
180 W. Esplanade (at Chesterfield), **North Vancouver**, 987-9911
4940 No. 3 Rd. (at Alderbridge), **Richmond**, 278-7373
4600 Kingsway (at McKay), **Burnaby**, 438-2288
Prices: Moderate
Believe it or not, Thai food and children really do work well together. For those not accustomed, introduce your kids to the beef, pork or chicken satay (meat on a skewer), the pad Thai noodles (a sweetish flat rice noodle) or chicken fried rice. Kids also tend to like Mee Krob, a sweet, crispy rice vermicelli. Thai House has no kids' menu, but portions are big enough to share; just make sure you don't order something too spicy for kids. They offer free delivery.

Vegetarian

Thankfully, nowadays most restaurants have some vegetarian choices. Particularly good for nonmeat eaters are **Café Deux Soleil**, **The Red Onion Restaurant**, the **Tomato Fresh Food Café**, **Hon's Wun Tun House**, **Nyala**, **Ashiana Tandoori**, **Anton's Pasta Bar** and **Topanga Café** (see listings in this chapter). Or try the following spot:

Naam
2724 W. 4th Ave (at Macdonald), in Kitsilano, **Vancouver**
Tel: 738-7151
Hours: Open 24 hours
Prices: Inexpensive
A Kitsilano fixture, the Naam is a vegetarian restaurant with an assortment of veggie burgers, stir-fries, noodles, sandwiches and salads. Good here is the Naam Burger, their special organic tofu, beet, walnut and "multi-ingredient" burger. Get miso gravy on the side to go with your fries; also good is the fruit smoothie. There is a kids' veggie burger with fries for $4.95, though children often choose something else from the menu, such as a quesadilla or veggie burrito. There's a good selection of herb teas, fresh juices, beer and wine, and nice desserts, such as apple crisp or walnut carob cake. You can get take-out or buy a loaf of Naam bread at the counter; it makes great toast.

Chapter 10

Where to Stay with Kids

In planning a holiday with children, picking a hotel can be one of the hardest things to do. It should suit your family's needs, be in a price range you can afford, and be a relaxing place to come back to at the end of the day. When visiting Vancouver, most families like to stay downtown, where they can be close to Stanley Park, Robson Street and other attractions. Downtown is expensive, however, and there are many worthwhile alternatives. The North Shore is a good location if you plan on doing a lot of skiing or family hikes in the area. Burnaby, Richmond and Coquitlam give you more for your money, and they're all a short drive into Vancouver.

Listed below are hotels in a variety of locations and price ranges. These hotels were chosen based on their kid-friendliness, as well as their cleanliness, safety and location. If only one location of a chain is listed, this is due to its particular kid-friendliness or convenient location. Many offer kitchens or kitchenettes, great for saving money since you don't have to go out for every meal, plus it's very easy to heat bottles for babies or make grilled cheese sandwiches for starving six-year-olds. For more information on hotels, booking and travel in

B.C., call Super, Natural British Columbia's one-call accommodation and reservation service, at 663-6000 or 1-800-663-6000. The toll-free service is available seven days a week. For more information on accommodation in Vancouver, check out the websites listed in the introduction (see page xiii).

Price ratings below are based on standard accommodations for a family of four in July. (As with restaurants, a rating of Inexpensive/Moderate means that the rate you pay depends on what room you choose.) Bear in mind that these prices are for the high season (July and August), and rates are quite a bit lower in non-summer months. Call to check out prices ahead of time; they can fluctuate not only according to season, but also according to availability or special promotions. Price ratings do *not* include the hefty 17 percent taxes normally added to a hotel bill (10 percent Provincial Room Tax and 7 percent Goods and Services Tax). If you're not a Canadian resident you can get a rebate on the GST amount (see "Introduction," page xi). Incidentally, downtown hotels tend to charge a lot for parking; they usually tell you how much up front, but if they don't, make sure you ask so you don't find any surprises on your bill.

Inexpensive – $50 to $125

Moderate – $126 to $200

Expensive – $201 to $300

Very Expensive – More than $300

Best Western Chelsea Inn

725 Brunette Ave (at Lougheed Hwy), **Coquitlam**

Tel: 525-7777

Prices: Inexpensive

This is a simple, pleasant hotel in Coquitlam, right across the river from Surrey. Rooms with stoves and refrigerators are available; cribs and cots are an additional $10 per night. The outdoor pool is open in the summer, and there is a restaurant downstairs where kids can split portions. There are also laundry facilities. If the kids are tired of visiting relatives or driving into Vancouver to see the sights, treat them to a half day at **Crash Crawly's Adventure Fun Centre** (see page 98) just down the street.

Canyon Court Motel

1748 Capilano Rd (at Marine Dr), **North Vancouver**

Tel: 988-3181

Prices: Inexpensive

A no-frills motel that is still clean, safe and popular with families. It has an outdoor heated pool and two movie channels. There is no restaurant on the premises, but there are three restaurants two blocks away, one of which is **Earl's** (see page 114).

Comfort Inn Airport

3031 No. 3 Rd. (at Sea Island Way), **Richmond**

Tel: 278-5161

Prices: Inexpensive

Comfort Inns are never fancy, but they're always clean and friendly. Kids aren't charged for, so the rate is extremely reasonable. This one has an outdoor pool and a restaurant on the premises. It's right near the airport and a good place to stay if your flight gets in late, the kids are tired, and you don't want to drive into Vancouver.

Delta Pacific Resort and Conference Centre
10251 St. Edwards Dr, off Hwy 99, **Richmond**
Tel: 278-9611 or 1-800-268-1133
Website: *www.deltapacific.bc.ca*
Prices: Moderate
Don't let the highway or airport proximity deter you from staying here. This 5.6-hectare (14-acre) resort offers lots of recreation and activities, providing an excellent break when you've been doing too many day trips with the kids. There are two outdoor pools as well as an indoor pool with a 68-metre (225-foot) water slide – *very* popular with kids. Plus they have a supervised Children's Creative Centre, where you can drop your child off any day of the week from 9:00 a.m. to 9:00 p.m. (for a meagre $3 charge per day). The centre has games, puzzles, painting activities, video games, movies, swimming and an outdoor jungle gym. While the kids are playing, parents can swim or use the whirlpool or sauna, plus there are four indoor tennis courts, two squash courts, a fully equipped fitness room and a massage therapy clinic. The hotel has four restaurants (kids six and under eat free) and 24-hour room service. For all this, room rates are extremely reasonable, especially compared with downtown Vancouver, only 20 minutes away.

Executive Inn
4201 Lougheed Hwy (at Willingdon), **Burnaby**
Tel: 298-2010
Prices: Inexpensive/Moderate
This is *not* just a place for business travellers. This all-suite hotel is perfect for families who are looking for a nice hotel at a reasonable price. All rooms have a small kitchen, and there's an outside pool and whirlpool plus a restaurant. It's about a 15-minute drive to downtown Vancouver, and there's a shuttle service to Metrotown Centre.

The Four Seasons Hotel
791 W. Georgia St (at Howe), **Vancouver**
Tel: 689-9333, 1-800-268-6282 (in Canada), 1-800-332-3442 (in U.S.)
Website: *www.fshr.com*
Prices: Very Expensive
This is *the* place to stay when you're in Vancouver. That is, if you can afford it. Both kids and adults are totally pampered at this top downtown hotel. Kids will love the milk and cookies sent up upon arrival, as well as the colouring books and tot-size robes. If you've left anything at home, don't worry. The hotel has everything from diapers to baby toys, playpens to strollers, stuffed animals to kids' movies. They've thought of every detail, from socket covers to stepstools in the bathroom. The hotel is located on the second floor of the Pacific Centre

Shopping Mall (an odd but convenient location for such an elegant place), so you can also find anything you need at nearby shops. (In fact, the only thing you really need to bring is your wallet.) There are two excellent restaurants in the hotel: the **Chartwell** and the **Garden Terrace**. The former is a bit stuffy for kids, but both it and the Garden Terrace have kids' menus. Children's food is also available from the 24-hour room service. There is an indoor/outdoor pool (welcome to kids), a health club, twice-daily housekeeping, a complimentary town car if you need a lift to a downtown location and other extras, such as hair dryers and plush robes.

The Greenbrier Hotel
1393 Robson St (at Broughton), **Vancouver**
Tel: 683-4558
Prices: Moderate
If you don't require luxury, you'll be pleased by what the Greenbrier has to offer. All rooms are simple, bordering on spartan, but the real plus for families is that they come with complete kitchens, making each more of an apartment than a hotel room. Parking is free, a rarity in downtown, and the hotel is centrally located on Robson Street, close to attractions.

Holiday Inn
1110 Howe St (at Helmcken), **Vancouver**
Tel: 684-2151
Prices: Moderate
This is a simple, clean downtown hotel for a reasonable price. There is an indoor pool, restaurant and lounge. Kids 12 and under eat free when with parents. On the third floor there's a kids' activity centre with games, puzzles and video games. There are a couple of other Holiday Inns in Vancouver, but this one is the most centrally located.

Hotel Vancouver
900 W. Georgia St (at Burrard), **Vancouver**
Tel: 684-3131 or 1-800-441-1414
Prices: Very Expensive
Located in a gorgeous old building with a distinguishable green copper roof, the Hotel Vancouver unfortunately seems to be catering a lot to tours and conventions in recent years. But it's such a lovely place to stay that you probably won't mind the occasional swarms of people filtering through the lobby. In addition to the health club (with its glass-roofed swimming pool, whirlpool and small wading pool for kids), the hotel offers mini-bars in the rooms, as well as movie and video game rentals. On arrival, kids get colouring books and crayons. Babysitting, laundry and other services are available. **Griffin's**, one of the hotel's restaurants, has a kids' menu, plus kids five and under eat free. Its Sunday brunch is pricey but good, with everything from calamari and panfried trout to eggs, bacon, sausages, rack of lamb and roast pork.

Lonsdale Quay Hotel
123 Carrie Cates Court (at Lonsdale), in Lonsdale Quay, **North Vancouver**
Tel: 986-6111 or 1-800-836-6111
Prices: Expensive
This is a simple, cheery place to stay. Pop downstairs to the public market in the morning and grab a muffin and coffee, or maybe a glorious towering basket of strawberries. It's only a 15-minute SeaBus ride to downtown Vancouver, so you can explore the city, then get away from it when you've had enough. The hotel is close to the North Shore mountains, and it's easy to get to places like **Lighthouse Park** (see page 36) or **Maplewood Farm** (see page 46). Rooms here are basic but clean, and although you won't be treated like royalty, the staff is friendly and helpful. Try to get a south-facing room so you can get a view of downtown Vancouver.

Marriott Residence Inn
1234 Hornby St (at Davie), **Vancouver**
Tel: 688-1234 or 1-800-331-3131
Prices: Moderate
This Marriott has particularly spacious rooms – great for families. Even better, all units come with kitchens or kitchenettes. There's even a free grocery shopping service (a real plus when I arrived with two cranky kids and needed milk for my son and aspirin for me). There's also a pool, a whirlpool, cribs and playpens, and a complimentary continental breakfast. Aside from these things, it's a clean, nicely kept hotel in the midst of the city and a good alternative to some of the pricier hotels downtown.

Ramada Guildford Inn
10410 158th St (at 104th Ave), **Surrey**
Tel: 930-4700
Prices: Inexpensive/Moderate
For those staying in Surrey this is a good location, as it's close to Highway 1 and a half-hour drive from Vancouver. There is an outdoor heated pool, a fitness area, room service and a restaurant with a kids' menu. It's down the road from Guildford Town Centre, a large shopping centre, and near **Tynehead Regional Park** (see page 41).

Stay 'n Save Inn
3777 Henning Dr (at Boundary), **Burnaby**
Tel: 473-5000 or 1-800-663-0298
Prices: Inexpensive
Right on the border between Vancouver and Burnaby, this is a simple hotel with large rooms. Kitchen units are available for an additional $10 per night. Off the Lougheed Highway, it's not far from **Central Park** (see page 37) and **Burnaby Lake Park** (see page 37). It's also not far from downtown Vancouver and right near the Second Narrows Bridge, so North Vancouver is close, too. Local calls are free, and there is a family restaurant with a kids' menu.

135

Sylvia Hotel
1154 Gilford St (at Beach), **Vancouver**
Tel: 681-9321
Prices: Inexpensive/Moderate
An ivy-covered brick building across from **English Bay Beach** (see page 42), the landmark Sylvia Hotel is more charming outside than in. The rooms are a bit shabby and the staff can err on the curt side, but the location (a block from Stanley Park) and excellent prices still make this a good spot for families. Some of the units come with kitchen facilities, and one-bedroom suites are available. There is room service, and a restaurant and lounge are located on the main floor. Cribs and rollaway cots can be obtained for a small fee. The hotel is popular, so book your room well in advance, particularly if you're coming in the summer or if you want a cheerier south-facing room. If you do stay here, go to **Book Warehouse** (see page 160) and pick up a copy of *Mister Got to Go*, a children's book written by Lois Simmie about a real cat at the Sylvia Hotel. It's a fun story that the kids will really enjoy.

2400 Motel
2400 Kingsway (at 33rd Ave), **Vancouver**
Tel: 434-2464 or 1-888-833-2400
Prices: Inexpensive
This fifties-style motel is located on traffic-heavy Kingsway, but it's still a good choice for families. The units are scattered on 1.4 hectares (3.5 acres) of well-kept, landscaped grounds. Request a unit toward the back so kids can run around safely. There are a number of rooms to choose from, ranging from a standard room with two double beds to larger one- and two-bedroom units with kitchens (complete with dishes, pots, pans and utensils). Nonsmoking rooms are available, rollaway beds and cribs are available for a small fee, and – best yet – there's no charge for parking. Central to both Burnaby and Vancouver.

Westin Bayshore
1601 W. Georgia St (at Denman), **Vancouver**
Tel: 682-2377 or 1-800-WESTIN-1 (1-800-937-8461)
Prices: Moderate
This resort-style hotel is located on Coal Harbour, between downtown and Stanley Park. There are city, mountain or harbour views, 1.6 hectares (4 acres) of landscaped gardens, a health club, and outdoor and indoor pools. It's a great spot for travellers wanting to avoid the glut of downtown high-rises while still being in the midst of the action. The Westin Kids Club provides everything you need for kids: cribs, high chairs, mini-refrigerators, kids' movies, bottle warmers, potty seats, safety kits… the list goes on. Kids can even dial the free Story Line speed dial on the room's desk phone and choose from 10 bedtime stories. The hotel has other amenities you'd expect from a Westin: 24-hour room service, nonsmoking rooms, babysitting, laundry services and an on-call doctor and dentist. Bicycle rentals or half-day fishing trips can be arranged. They even provide jogging maps of Stanley Park if you're so inclined. (Yes, they have jogging strollers.) The Westin

is not as lavishly decorated as the Four Seasons, but it's also not as expensive, making it easier to spend your money elsewhere.

YWCA

733 Beatty St (at Georgia), **Vancouver**
Tel: 895-5830
Prices: Inexpensive/Moderate

As one would expect, this is basic, clean accommodation, though it's definitely more upscale than most YWCAs. Families can choose from different rooms, such as a unit with two double beds or another with five single beds. All rooms have refrigerators, cribs are free, plus there are communal kitchens, television lounges and laundry facilities. It's right at the edge of downtown and a five-minute walk to the Stadium SkyTrain station. Since the YWCA is a nonprofit organization, they don't charge GST, so guests are only charged the 10 percent Provincial Room Tax, making it a good deal for Canadian residents. There is a YMCA at 955 Burrard Street (at Barclay, 681-0221), which doesn't have as many amenities but is less expensive.

Shopping for kids

Here you'll find nearly everything kids need (or want), from school clothes to musical instruments to candy shops. Out of necessity I've had to limit this list to some of the best stores, based on the quality and availability of kids' merchandise in them, so many stores that do sell merchandise for kids in the Greater Vancouver area aren't mentioned here. Although department stores are not listed, keep in mind Vancouver's outlet for **The Bay**, which carries reasonably-priced children's clothing, toys and more. The downtown location of **The Bay**, which has another 10 locations in the Lower Mainland, is at Georgia and Granville (681-6211). There are six **Sears** department stores in and around Vancouver; the closest to the downtown core is the one in North Vancouver, at 943 Marine Drive (985-7722).

Some of the best shopping values can be found at **Army & Navy**, at 27 West Hastings (682-6644); they sell everything from baby shoes to fishing tackle. A second **Army & Navy** store is at 502 Columbia Street in New Westminster (526-4661); it's not as good, but the area is safer. Many of the shops listed below are located in Greater Vancouver's many malls, which are too numerous to list here. Keep in mind that both the Oakridge Centre mall

(263-3422), at 650 West 41st Avenue in Vancouver, and the Eaton Centre mall (431-8770) at 4700 Kingsway in Metrotown in Burnaby, have **Jellybean Centres** on their premises, places where staff will watch your kids while you're at the mall, for around six dollars an hour (depending on the child's age). Kids can play with toys, make crafts, play in the ball room and romp on the equipment while you go off and spend money. For party supplies, see page 186; for pharmacies, see page 238. For baby furnishings, equipment, and clothing, see "For Parents of Babies," page 205.

Clothing — New
Most stores that sell new kids' clothing tend to be expensive, although the quality is usually excellent. Pass hand-me-downs to friends or relatives, or recoup some of the money you spent by selling clothes to a children's clothing consignment shop (see page 148); better yet, donate them to charity (see page 148), where they'll be put to great use.

Vancouver
Amrit Fashions
#102-6569 Main St (at 49th Ave)
Tel: 327-1481
Southasian clothing for adults and kids; there are other excellent clothing shops for kids in the 6500 block of Main.

Aunt Em's
1494 Cartwright St, in the Kids Only Market on Granville Island
Tel: 682-2116
Charming higher-end clothes for newborns and up to age 12; some French designer items.

BJ&L
555 W. 12th Ave (at Cambie), in City Square
Tel: 876-3755
Clothes and shoes for newborns and up to age seven; *the* place for a child-size Harley Davidson jacket or pair of Doc Martens.

Bratz
2828 Granville St (at 13th Ave)
Tel: 734-4344
Designer kids' clothes; hair styling also available.

Dionne Imports Ltd.
293 E. Pender St (at Gore)
Tel: 681-5522
Inexpensive casual wear for children of all ages.

The Everything Wet Store
1496 Cartwright St, in the Kids Only Market on Granville Island
Tel: 685-5445
Raincoats, boots, bathing suits, sandals and other water-related beach gear.

The GAP Kids
1125 Robson (at Thurlow), Tel: 683-09062134
W. 41st Ave (at West Blvd), Tel: 269-2550
777 Dunsmuir St (at Howe), in Pacific Centre, Tel: 688-5574650
W. 41st Ave (at Cambie), in Oakridge Centre, Tel: 269-2550
Expensive but functional cotton clothing for newborns to adults.

Gymboree
650 W. 41st Ave (at Cambie), in Oakridge Centre
Tel: 261-6929
Sturdy, colourful cotton clothing for newborns to young teens.

Hazel & Co. Maternity & Kids
3190 Cambie St (at 16th Ave)
Tel: 730-8689
Trendy designer clothes for newborns to teens; a great maternity section and gifts and toys.

Isola Bella
5692 Yew St (at 41st Ave)
Tel: 266-8808
Predominantly French and Italian fashions for newborn to size 16; great shoes.

Jacob Jr.
777 Dunsmuir St (at Howe), in Pacific Centre, Tel: 683-4110
650 W. 41st Ave (at Cambie), in Oakridge Centre, Tel: 261-1918
Jacob-designed clothes for ages three to adult; classic, casual and trendy without being funky.

Kiddie Castle Children's Wear
1744 Renfrew St (at 1st Ave)
Tel: 253-6854
From newborn to size 10, both casual and dressy fashions.

Kids Expressions
3095 W. Broadway (at Macdonald)
Tel: 737-1588
My personal favourite. There are some expensive labels like OshKosh, but there's always a good sale rack at the back; it's an excellent source for good cotton pajamas and stuff for newborns.

Lil'Putian's Fashions for Kids
4406 W. 10th Ave (at Arbutus), Tel: 222-3321
2029 W. 4th Ave (at Arbutus), Tel: 738-2483
Top designers; for infant to preteen.

Maybo Children's Wear
229 Keefer St (at Main)
Tel: 683-8898
Newborn to preteen; casual wear, pants, shirts are reasonably priced.

Miki House
375 Water St (at Richards)
Tel: 681-6454
Japanese designers; clothing and accessories for ages six months to eight years.

Mountain Equipment Co-Op
130 W. Broadway (at Columbia)
Tel: 872-7858
Specializes in outdoor wear. You must buy a lifetime membership ($5) to purchase items here, but it has a large kids' section and is a great place for high-quality rain gear, fleece items, coats and other outdoor stuff.

Oh Baby!
3475 Cambie St (at 18th Ave)
Tel: 873-5808
Both classic and funky clothes for newborn to age six; gifts.

Pagasa Children's Wear
185 E. 16th Ave (at Main)
Tel: 708-4166
Very reasonably priced clothes of all types for ages six months to three years.

Peppermintree Children's Wear
4243 Dunbar St (at 26th Ave)
Tel: 228-9815
High-end, designer clothes for newborns and up.

Please Mum
2951 W. Broadway (at Bayswater), Tel: 732-4574
2041 W. 41st Ave (at West Blvd), Tel: 264-0366
Expensive but great-quality, Please Mum clothes are made in Canada and you can get great deals during their frequent sales.

Popi Childrenswear
701 W. Georgia St (at Howe), in Pacific Centre
Tel: 688-9194
Cute, fun clothing.

The Ralph Lauren Polo Store
375 Water St (at Richards)
Tel: 682-7656
Classic Polo attire for ages four to adult.

Roots
1001 Robson St (at Burrard), Tel: 683-4305
650 W. 41st Ave (at Cambie), in Oakridge Centre, Tel: 266-6229
701 W. Georgia St (at Howe) in Pacific Centre, Tel: 683-5465
3695 Grandview Hwy (at Boundary), Tel: 433-4337
Canadian-designed clothes for newborns to adult; sturdy cottons, great sweatshirts. The Grandview Highway location is Roots' factory outlet.

Scallywags
1496 Cartwright St, in the Kids Only Market on Granville Island
Tel: 682-3364
Lots of reversible clothing with flowery prints, as well as dresses with petticoats; newborn to age eight.

Spoilt Children's Wear
650 W. 41st Ave (at Cambie), in Oakridge Centre
Tel: 261-2311 or 261-2377
Made in Vancouver, their functional kids' clothes last a long time.

Suzy Shier (Suzy Girl)
701 W. Georgia St (at Howe), in Pacific Centre
Tel: 685-1237
Traditional middle-ground children's clothes.

Timeké
3080 W. Broadway (at Balaclava)
Tel: 738-5393
Fun, Canadian-made wear for newborns and up; bright coloured cottons and quirky designs.

Under the Monkey Tree
1496 Cartwright St, in the Kids Only Market on Granville Island
Tel: 685-7226
Casual, locally made clothes for ages two to 14.

Vicky's Childrens Wear
2618 W. Broadway (at Trafalgar)
Tel: 731-8919
Both casual items and dress-up stuff for newborns and up.

The AT Factor
4406 W. 10th Ave (at Trimble)
Tel: 222-3321
Trendy clothing for boys eight to adult; connected with Lil'Putian's next door.

North Shore

Angels on Bellevue
1463 Bellevue Ave (at 15th St), **West Vancouver**
Tel: 926-8737
Mainly European brands for newborn to age 12.

Boomers & Echoes
1709 Lonsdale Ave (at 17th Ave), **North Vancouver**
Tel: 984-6163
Huge stock of both new and consignment clothes plus maternity and furnishings.

Colors of Europe Clothing
1425 Marine Dr (at 15th St), **West Vancouver**
Tel: 926-8828
Largely European brands; newborn to age 12.

The GAP Kids
640 Park Royal North (at Taylor Way), in Park Royal Shopping Centre, **West Vancouver**
Tel: 925-3929
(See Vancouver entry for description.)

Kidz Biz
1199 Lynn Valley (at Mountain Hwy), in Lynn Valley Centre, **North Vancouver**
Tel: 988-7466
Brand names "for less"; newborn to size 14.

kuddel muddel kids
4342 Gallant Ave (at Panorama), in Deep Cove, **North Vancouver**
Tel: 929-2524
Both new and consignment clothes for newborn to size 12; a small selection of toys, too.

Please Mum
807 Park Royal North (at Taylor Way), in Park Royal Shopping Centre, **West Vancouver**
Tel: 925-0338
(See Vancouver entry for description.)

Popi Childrenswear
935 Marine Dr (at Hamilton), in Capilano Mall, **North Vancouver**
Tel: 986-2087
(See Vancouver entry for description.)

Roots
790 Park Royal North (at Taylor Way), in Park Royal Shopping Centre, **West Vancouver**
Tel: 925-2166
(See Vancouver entry for description and factory outlet location.)

Suzy Shier (Suzy Girl)
935 Marine Dr (at Hamilton), in Capilano Mall, North Vancouver Tel: 980-5540
986 Park Royal South (at Taylor Way), in Park Royal Shopping Centre, West Vancouver, Tel: 926-3610
(See Vancouver entry for description.)

Burnaby

Buddies
4800 Kingsway (at McKay), in Metrotown Centre
Tel: 436-0607
Babies' and children's clothing; mainly dress-up items such as First Communion outfits and party dresses.

The GAP Kids
4700 Kingsway (at McKay), in Eaton Centre Metrotown
Tel: 431-6577
(See Vancouver entry for description.)

Helen's Children's Wear
4142 Hastings St (at Gilmore)
Tel: 298-5141 or 298-0715
A fixture since 1948 (its original girl-on-a-swing sign is worth a look). Lots of girls' dresses and boys' dress suits are here, as well as brand-name casual wear for infant to age 16.

Hoppla Hopp Kids Wear
4820 Kingsway (at McKay), in Metrotown Centre
Tel: 433-1771
Clothing for six months and up; a wide variety of both casual and dress wear.

Jacob Jr.
4700 Kingsway (at McKay), in Eaton Centre Metrotown
Tel: 435-5233
(See Vancouver entry for description.)

Just Kid'n Children's Wear
4820 Kingsway (at McKay), in Metrotown Centre
Tel: 436-2575
Lots of casual clothing with fun prints, cute dresses, and pants you can roll up. This company makes their own clothing for newborns to age eight.

Kangaroo Children's Fashions
4008 Hastings St (at Gilmore)
Tel: 298-1166
Clothing for newborns to size 14; some casual wear, but this store's strong point is its dress-up clothing, from flower girl dresses to boys' tuxedos.

Mother Love
4800 Kingsway (at McKay), in Metrotown Centre, Tel: 451-0398
9855 Austin Rd (at North Rd), in Lougheed Mall, Tel: 420-6533
A wide choice of both casual and dress wear, with lots of name brands like OshKosh, Polo and Calvin Klein; from newborn to size 12.

Please Mum
4700 Kingsway (at McKay), in Eaton Centre Metrotown, Tel: 430-1702
9855 Austin Rd (at North Rd), in Lougheed Mall, Tel: 420-0199
(See Vancouver entry for description.)

Popi Childrenswear
1219A Kingsway (at McKay), in Eaton Centre Metrotown
Tel: 436-9262
(See Vancouver entry for description.)

Roots
4700 Kingsway (at McKay), in Eaton Centre Metrotown
Tel: 435-5554
(See Vancouver entry for description and factory outlet location.)

Suzy Shier (Suzy Girl)
4567 Lougheed Hwy (at Willingdon) in Brentwood Mall, Tel: 291-6553
4700 Kingsway (at McKay), in Eaton Centre Metrotown, Tel: 439-1968
9855 Austin Rd (at North Rd) in Lougheed Mall, Tel: 420-4505
4800 Kingsway (at McKay) in Metrotown Centre, Tel: 439-1693
(See Vancouver entry for description.)

New Westminster

Captain Mickey Fashions
610 6th St (at 6th Ave)
Tel: 526-8228
Their own Captain Mickey fashions are sold here – locally-made casual clothing and fleece jackets – as well as a few other brands, for infants to age eight.

Tri-Cities

Hoppla Hopp Kids Wear
2929 Barnet Hwy (at Pinetree Way) in Coquitlam Centre, **Coquitlam**
Tel: 464-1766
(See Burnaby entry for description.)

Please Mum
2929 Barnet Hwy (at Pinetree Way) in Coquitlam Centre, **Coquitlam**
Tel: 945-8592
(See Vancouver entry for description.)

Roots
2929 Barnet Hwy (at Pinetree Way) in Coquitlam Centre, **Coquitlam**
Tel: 945-6771
(See Vancouver entry for description.)

Suzy Shier (Suzy Girl)
2929 Barnet Hwy (at Pinetree Way) in Coquitlam Centre, Coquitlam
Tel: 942-6773
(See Vancouver entry for description.)

Richmond

Bambini Kids Wear
6060 Minoru Blvd (at Westminster Hwy), in the North Mall of Richmond Centre
Tel: 278-3106
European designers; newborn to size 16.

The GAP Kids
6551 No. 3 Rd (at Westminster Hwy), in the South Mall of Richmond Centre
Tel: 270-6412
(See Vancouver entry for description.)

Hoppla Hopp Kids Wear
5300 No. 3 Rd (at Alderbridge Way) in Lansdowne Park Shopping Centre
Tel: 278-7830
(See Burnaby entry for description.)

Jacob Jr.
6551 No. 3 Rd (at Westminster Hwy), in the South Mall of Richmond Centre
Tel: 244-9192
(See Vancouver entry for description.)

Kidz Biz
6551 No. 3 Rd (at Westminster Hwy), in the South Mall of Richmond Centre
Tel: 276-8289
(See North Vancouver entry for description.)

Please Mum
5300 No. 3 Rd (at Alderbridge Way), in Lansdowne Park Shopping Centre
Tel: 270-0837
(See Vancouver entry for description.)

Popi Childrenswear
5300 No. 3 Rd (at Alderbridge Way), in Lansdowne Park Shopping Centre
Tel: 270-2224
(See Vancouver entry for description.)

Roots
6551 No. 3 Rd (at Westminster Hwy), in the South Mall of Richmond Centre
Tel: 244-9113
(See Vancouver entry for description.)

Suzy Shier (Suzy Girl)
6551 No. 3 Rd (at Westminster Hwy), in the South Mall of Richmond Centre
Tel: 270-1356
(See Vancouver entry for description.)

Surrey

The GAP Kids
2232 Guildford Town Centre (at 104th Ave)
Tel: 582-2522
(See Vancouver entry for description.)

Kidz Biz
2112 Surrey Place Mall (at King George Hwy)
Tel: 583-8358
(See North Vancouver entry for description.)

Please Mum
1382 Guildford Town Centre (at 104th Ave)
Tel: 585-7742
(See Vancouver entry for description.)

Popi Childrenswear
2153 Surrey Place Mall (at King George Hwy)
Tel: 930-9669
(See Vancouver entry for description.)

Roots
2203 Guildford Town Centre (at 104th Ave)
Tel: 583-0689
(See Vancouver entry for description and factory outlet location.)

Suzy Shier (Suzy Girl)
2224 Guildford Town Centre (at 104th Ave), Tel: 582-2042
2188 Surrey Place Mall (at King George Hwy), Tel: 581-4041
(See Vancouver entry for description.)

Clothing – Secondhand

Most kids' secondhand clothing shops carry a little of everything: children's, infants' and maternity clothes, as well as toys and accessories. Stores tend to be very strict about what they will and will not take, so you will find excellent-quality merchandise (i.e., **OshKosh**, **The Gap**, **Please Mum** stuff) at good prices. I find that smaller kids like secondhand stuff better; it's a bit worn in and not as scratchy as new clothing. If you're interested in selling your kids' used items (but in clean, good condition, please!), phone your local consignment shop to find out if and when they accept items.

As these shops are somewhat similar to one another, I haven't provided individual descriptions. **Value Village** (branches of which are listed below) is a huge thrift store chain with great deals on kids' clothing and supplies (although you'll have to hunt a bit to find the best quality); part of the proceeds are donated to charity. Also keep in mind the **Salvation Army Thrift Stores**. There are 14 stores in the Lower Mainland; one of the most central is at 261 East 12th Avenue (874-4721) in Vancouver; proceeds go to its family and social services centres. **kuddel muddel kids** (see page 144) also sells secondhand clothes.

Vancouver

For A While
1838 W. 4th Ave (at Burrard)
Tel: 730-0232

Happy Kids Consignment Clothes
3633 W. 4th Ave (at Alma)
Tel: 730-5507

Liberty Thrift
1035 Commercial Dr (at 15th Ave)
Tel: 255-3080

MacGillycuddy's for Little People
4881 Mackenzie St (at 33rd Ave)
Tel: 263-5313

Nippers Tog 'n Toy
3712 W. 10th Ave (at Alma)
Tel: 222-4035

Puddleduck Lane
3554 W. 41st Ave (at Alma)
Tel: 267-0926

Pumpkins' Consignment
5026 Joyce St (at VanNess Ave), near Joyce SkyTrain station
Tel: 433-0664

Raggs & Rerunzzs
903 Commercial Dr (at Venables)
Tel: 251-9447

Tiggy-Winkle's
3776 Oak St (at 22nd Ave)
Tel: 731-8647

Toy Traders
1650 E. 12th Ave (at Commercial)
Tel: 708-0322

Value Village
1820 E. Hastings St (at Commercial), Tel: 254-4282
6415 Victoria Dr (at 49th Ave), Tel: 327-4434

Wee Ones Reruns
612 Kingsway (at Fraser)
Tel: 708-0956

North Shore

Boomers & Echoes
1709 Lonsdale Ave (at 17th St), **North Vancouver**
Tel: 984-6163

Secret Closet
1844 Marine Dr (at 18th St), **West Vancouver**
Tel: 926-1630

Burnaby

Value Village
7350 Edmonds St (at Kingsway)
Tel: 540-4066

New Westminster

Fit 4 A Queen & Moms-To-Be
476 E. Columbia St (at 6th St)
Tel: 524-1707

For Kids Only Consignment Store
27 8th Ave (at McBride)
Tel: 526-4113

Tri-Cities

Hiccups
1111 Austin Ave (at Marmont), **Coquitlam**
Tel: 931-5595

Jelly Beans
520 Clarke Rd (at Como Lake), **Coquitlam**
Tel: 939-4846

Kids Korner
2579 Lougheed Hwy (at Lansdowne), **Port Coquitlam**
Tel: 464-7111

Merry-Go-Round
2279 Elgin Ave (at Shaughnessy), **Port Coquitlam**
Tel: 944-0304V

Value Village
540A Clarke Rd (at Como Lake), in Burquitlam Plaza, **Coquitlam**
Tel: 937-7087

Richmond

The Clothes Encounter
3891 Chatham St (at 1st Ave), **Steveston**
Tel: 271-0310

Thrift City
11080 Williams Rd (at Shell), in Shellmont Plaza
Tel: 241-1975

Surrey
Little Tykes Consignment Boutique
6199 136th St (at 60th Ave)
Tel: 591-2606

Value Village
10642 King George Hwy (at 106th Ave), in Dell Shopping Centre
Tel: 588-5225

Shoes

Many of the children's clothing shops listed previously in this chapter also sell shoes; stores listed in this section sell only shoes, boots and sandals.

Kerrisdale Bootery
2182 W. 41st Ave (at Arbutus), **Vancouver**
Tel: 261-6371
Expensive selection of fabulous kids' shoes; good quality.

Kiddie Kobbler Shoes
2024 Park Royal South (at Taylor Way), in Park Royal Shopping Centre, **West Vancouver**
Tel: 926-1616
2748 Lougheed Hwy (at Westwood), Coquitlam, Tel: 464-2115
A fixture since 1946 with a good variety of stock; they specialize in orthopedic footwear.

Lady Sport
3545 W. 4th Ave (at Collingwood), **Vancouver**
Tel: 733-1173
Running shoes and other athletic footwear for kids.

Panda Shoes
650 W. 41st Ave (at Cambie), in Oakridge Centre, **Vancouver**,
Tel: 266-0025
935 Marine Dr (at Hamilton), in Capilano Mall, **North Vancouver**,
Tel: 986-4450
4700 Kingsway (at McKay), in Eaton Centre Metrotown, **Burnaby**,
Tel: 439-9777
5300 No. 3 Rd (at Alderbridge Way), in Lansdowne Park Shopping Centre, **Richmond**, Tel: 278-4800
A wide variety of styles; great quality.

Shoe Warehouse
3010 W. Broadway (at Carnarvon), **Vancouver**
Tel: 738-1843
Excellent, inexpensive choices, helpful staff; numerous other locations.

Toys

There are many, many toy shops in the Greater Vancouver area, so this section has two components: general and specialty. General toy stores are grouped by municipality. These stores sell everything from teddy bears to science kits; those that do focus on a particular type of toy are noted. The bigger stores, such as **Toys "R" Us**, are listed here. A selection of good specialty stores follow, grouped by type of toy.

If you have a complaint about a toy you've bought, you might want to call Product Safety in the **KidsCare National Program** (666-5003). They investigate consumer complaints related to toys and inspect toys that are manufactured in (or imported into) Canada and sold here.

General

You'll find a wide variety of toys in almost every store listed here. Be sure to check out the children's clothing consignment shops listed in this chapter as well (such as **kuddel muddel kids**); they often carry good-quality used toys.

Vancouver

All Aboard
1496 Cartwright St, in the Kids Only Market on Granville Island
Tel: 684-1633
Thomas the Tank merchandise.

China West
41 E. Pender St (at Gore), in Chinatown
Tel: 681-9665
Kites, wooden snakes, inexpensive toys.

Dunbar Toy Store
4292 Dunbar St (at 27th Ave)
Tel: 739-6899
Well-chosen toys with a lot of variety.

The Everything Wet Store
1496 Cartwright St, in the Kids Only Market on Granville Island
Tel: 685-5445
Water-related toys.

The Games People
157 Water St (at Cambie), in Gastown
Tel: 685-5825
Board games, card games; all varieties of games

The Granville Island Toy Co.
1496 Cartwright St, in the Kids Only Market on Granville Island
Tel: 684-0076
Small but well-chosen assortment of Playmobil, games, and other kids' toys; no junk here.

Hyperlight Enterprises
3845 Rupert St (at 22nd Ave)
Tel: 454-0695
Star Trek, Star Wars, X-Files and other science fiction merchandise.

It's All Fun & Games
1417 Commercial Dr (at Grant)
Tel: 253-6727
A small shop with a nice selection of games, educational toys and more.

Just For Kids
650 W. 41st Ave (at Cambie), in Oakridge Centre
Tel: 263-2717
Toys, stuffed animals and more.

Just Imagine
4253 Dunbar St (at 26th Ave)
Tel: 222-3523
Dress-up and dance stuff, plus Barbie doll clothes.

Kaboodles
4449 W. 10th Ave (at Sasamat), Tel: 224-5311
1496 Cartwright St, in the Kids Only Market on Granville Island
Tel: 684-0066
Something for everyone, from construction toys to party supplies to travel games.

Kites & Puppets Only
1496 Cartwright St, in the Kids Only Market on Granville Island
Tel: 685-9877
Just as the name says!

Kites On Clouds
131 Water St (at Abbott), in Gastown
Tel: 669-5677
Kites and wind socks.

Knotty Toys
1496 Cartwright St, in the Kids Only Market on Granville Island
Tel: 683-7854
Wooden toys.

Stay Tooned
1496 Cartwright St, in the Kids Only Market on Granville Island
Tel: 689-8695
Cartoon-related toys.

Toy Traders
1650 E. 12th Ave (at Commercial)
Tel: 708-0322
New and used toys, clothes and baby equipment.

The Toybox
3002 W. Broadway (at Carnarvon)
Tel: 738-4322
Excellent assortment of toys and games; an emphasis on the creative and educational.

Toys "R" Us
1154 W. Broadway (at Oak)
Tel: 733-8697
Huge stock of toys, toys, toys, plus bikes, electronic games and more; low prices.

Van-Hobbies
5675 S.E. Marine Dr (at Fraser)
Tel: 327-3210
Crafts and hobbies.

North Shore

B.C. Playthings
3070 Edgemont Blvd (at Highland), in Edgemont Village, **North Vancouver**
Tel: 986-4111
Toys, art supplies, trains, magic, puzzles.

Bears Toy Store
1459 Bellevue Ave (at 15th St), **West Vancouver**
Tel: 926-2327
Good, well-thought-out selection of creative, imaginative toys.

Creative Kidstuff Toys
1199 Lynn Valley (at Mountain Hwy), in Lynn Valley Centre, **North Vancouver**
Tel: 987-3210
High-quality, educational toys such as Brio, Playmobil and Lego.

The Games People
123 Carrie Cates Court (at Lonsdale), in Lonsdale Quay, **North Vancouver**
Tel: 986-5110
(See Vancouver entry for description.)

Girder & Beam's Construction Toys
123 Carrie Cates Court (at Lonsdale), in Lonsdale Quay, **North Vancouver**
Tel: 984-9200
Construction toys of all types.

The Toy Soldier
3197 Edgemont Blvd (at Connaught Court), in Edgemont Village,
North Vancouver
Tel: 980-8697
High-quality toys, arts supplies and creative items.

Burnaby

Games Workshop
4800 Kingsway (at McKay), in Metrotown Centre
Tel: 435-0111
Tabletop strategy games good for kids 12 and up.

Kid's Wonderland Toys Ltd.
9855 Austin Rd (at North Rd), in Lougheed Mall
Tel: 421-9836
Large selection of games, puzzles, collectibles, Brio and Playmobil.

Mishra's Game Factory
7474 Edmonds St (at Kingsway)
Tel: 521-4471
Collectible trading card games, science fiction model kits, role-playing games.

Sanrio Surprises
4700 Kingsway (at McKay), in Eaton Centre Metrotown
Tel: 436-3887
Hello Kitty and related merchandise.

Star World Toys
4820 Kingsway (at McKay), in Metrotown Centre
Tel: 432-7375
Good variety of toys and art supplies.

Tazmanian Comic Connection
4702 Hastings St (at Beta)
Tel: 298-6208
Non-sports cards, toys, action figures, supplies and memorabilia.

Toys "R" Us
4750 Kingsway (at McKay), in Metrotown Centre
Tel: 668-8330
(See Vancouver entry for description.)

Tri-Cities

Toys "R" Us
1110 Lougheed Hwy, near Brunett Ave and the Cape Horn Interchange,
Coquitlam
Tel: 654-4775
(See Vancouver entry for description.)

Richmond

Imperial Hobbies
5451 No. 3 Rd (at Alderbridge Way)
Tel: 273-4427
Historical, fantasy and science fiction board games.

Kid's Wonderland Toys Ltd.
6060 Minoru Blvd (at Westminster Hwy), in Richmond Square Shopping
Centre
Tel: 273-8398
(See Burnaby entry for description.)

Splash Toy Shop
3580 Moncton St (at 2nd Ave), **Steveston**
Tel: 241-0234
Small but charming shop with a good variety of toys.

Toys "R" Us
5300 No. 3 Rd (at Alderbridge Way)
Tel: 654-4790
(See Vancouver entry for description.)

Treasure Isle Toys
8120 No. 2 Rd (at Blundell)
Tel: 271-5656
Good selection of toys of all varieties.

Surrey

Toys "R" Us
10232 E. Whalley Ring Rd (at 104th Ave)
Tel: 586-1000
(See Vancouver entry for description.)

Arts and Crafts

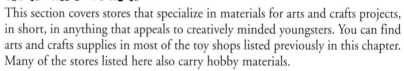

This section covers stores that specialize in materials for arts and crafts projects,
in short, in anything that appeals to creatively minded youngsters. You can find
arts and crafts supplies in most of the toy shops listed previously in this chapter.
Many of the stores listed here also carry hobby materials.

Abbey Arts & Crafts
4118 Hastings St (at Gilmore), **Burnaby**
Tel: 299-5201
A multitude of beads and other crafts materials oriented to older kids and adults.

Creative Children Furniture & Art Supplies
3005 Murray (at Moody), **Port Moody**
Tel: 469-6403

Creative Hobbycraft Stores
43 6th St (at Columbia), **New Westminster**
Tel: 525-6644
Three floors of crafts and a great selection of model kits.

Dundee Hobby Craft Ltd.
6551 No. 3 Rd (at Westminster Hwy), in the South Mall of Richmond Centre,
Richmond
Tel: 278-5713
A variety of crafts, hobbies and models.

Eastside Datagraphics Ltd.
1458 Commercial Dr (at Grant), **East Vancouver**
Tel: 255-9559
Artists' materials and watercolours. This is a good shop for young serious artists,
but doesn't have much for smaller kids.

Grand Prix Hobbies & Crafts
3038 W. Broadway (at Carnarvon), **Vancouver**
Tel: 733-7114
A comprehensive selection of crafts supplies, plus lots of model kits and miniature trains.

I'm Impressed
1496 Cartwright St, in the Kids Only Market on Granville Island,
Vancouver
Tel: 684-4657
Stamps and stamp pads of every variety.

Maxwell's Artists Materials
206 Cambie St (at Water), in Gastown, **Vancouver**
Tel: 683-8607
One of Vancouver's premier art and graphic supply stores; it has a selection of
crayons and the like for smaller kids.

Opus Framing & Art Supplies
1360 Johnston St, on Granville Island, **Vancouver**
Tel: 736-7028
A do-it-yourself frame shop with an excellent and extensive selection of artists'
materials.

Pioneer Arts & Crafts
2601 Westview Dr (at the Upper Levels Hwy), in Westview Mall, **North
Vancouver**
Tel: 988-9968
Art supplies and crafts projects for kids and adults.

Urban Source
3126 Main St (at 15th St), **East Vancouver**
Tel: 875-1611
An unusual shop that sells unique materials collected from industries. It's great
for arts and crafts, particularly for small kids; worth a special visit.

Computer and Video Games

All computer stores carry computers and games but these stores have particularly good selections of stuff for kids. Some sell only kids' software; others have computers as well, but aside from that, there's not too much difference between these stores.

If you or your child is web-literate, check out *www.discoverlearning.com*, BC Tel's on-line educational community for kids, parents, and teachers; they have games, software, and on-line learning.

Discovery Multi-Media
7966 Granville St (at 64th St), **Vancouver**
Tel: 263-2377
Software titles.

InterAction
120 E. 3rd St (at Lonsdale), **North Vancouver**
Tel: 987-3472
Computers and kids' software titles.

Microplay Video Game Store
2379 W. 41st Ave (at Balsam), **Vancouver**, Tel: 264-7529
6200 McKay Ave (at Kingsway), in Station Square Metrotown, **Burnaby**, Tel: 451-7529
3025 Lougheed Hwy (at Barnet Hwy), **Coquitlam**, Tel: 464-4263
8040 Garden City Rd (at McKay), **Richmond**, Tel: 244-1969
10033 136A St (at 104th Ave), **Surrey**, Tel: 589-7529
Video games and software.

Wiz Computers for Kids
20148 Park Royal South (at Taylor Way), in Park Royal Shopping Centre, **West Vancouver**
Tel: 925-1440
Hundreds of kids' software titles.

Educational Supplies

These stores sell educational supplies, not only for teachers, but for parents who are home schooling or who simply want to enhance their child's learning.

ADS Academic Distribution Services Ltd.
528 Carnarvon St (at 6th St), **New Westminster**
Tel: 524-9758
Reading, writing and mathematics materials for parents and teachers; kindergarten to grade 12.

Artel Educational Resources
5528 Kingsway (at Royal Oak), **Burnaby**
Tel: 435-4949
Educational materials for parents and teachers.

Collins Educational
8358 St George St (at S.E. Marine Dr), **Vancouver**
Tel: 325-5005
Workbooks and educational materials for parents and teachers.

Hobbies

Although these shops stock art supplies and simpler crafts, they tend to specialize in model construction, an activity best suited to kids aged eight to 10 and
up. (See also under Arts and Crafts, page 156.)

Burnaby Hobbies
5209 Rumble St (at Royal Oak), **Burnaby**
Tel: 437-8217
Model kits, radio-controlled boats and more; huge selection.

Granville Hobbies & Crafts
2642 Granville St (at 10th Ave), **Vancouver**
Tel: 738-8331
Models, miniatures, crafts, artists' supplies.

Imperial Hobbies
5451 No. 3 Rd (at Alderbridge Way), **Richmond**
Tel: 273-4427
Specialists in science fiction and historical fantasy board games; also models and
miniatures.

RC Pit Stop
8386 120th St (at 84th Ave), **Surrey**
Tel: 597-4670
Specialists in radio-controlled cars and planes, plus models of all varieties.

Stealth Hobbies
1049 Ridgeway Ave (at Blue Mountain), **Coquitlam**
Tel: 931-7177
Wooden model kits, books, model trains.

Science and Nature

Most of the general toy stores listed in this chapter stock a good supply of projects related to science and nature, but shops listed here are truly devoted to the
earth and its environment, with imaginative, innovative toys and books for both
kids and adults.

Science-oriented kids can check out ***YES MAG: Canada's Science Magazine
for Kids*** at *http://www.islandnet.com/~yesmag/homepage.html.* It has news, at-home
projects and other science information for kids.

Exsciting Worlds
2022 Park Royal South (at Taylor Way), in Park Royal Shopping Centre, **West
Vancouver**
Tel: 925-3563

A great selection of educational materials that educate kids about science, technology and nature.

Science & Nature Co.
2929 Barnet Hwy (at Pinetree Way), in Coquitlam Centre, **Coquitlam**
Tel: 945-8740
Books, crafts and games related to the Earth.

Science World
1455 Quebec St (at Terminal), Main Street/Science World SkyTrain station,
Vancouver
Tel: 268-6363
Science World's gift shop has a great selection of educational toys, projects and books.

Techno-Kids
4424 Dunbar St (at 28th Ave), **Vancouver**
Tel: 730-9449
Science, nature and art projects.

Vancouver Aquarium
Off Georgia St, east of Denman, in Stanley Park, **Vancouver**
Tel: 659-3474
The aquarium's gift shop has lots and lots of toys and books related to aquatic life.

Books

These stores either specialize in children's books or have a good selection of them. Both **Vancouver Kidsbooks** and the UBC **Bookstore** offer children's readings. For other readings, call your local library (see page 222).

Blackberry Books
1663 Duranleau St, in Granville Island Public Market, **Vancouver,**
Tel: 685-4113
While you're at the Market, why not buy a book to read while you sit in the sun and watch the boats go by?

Book Warehouse
Three **Vancouver** locations:
632 Broadway (west of Cambie), Tel: 872-5711
1181 Davie St (west of Burrard), Tel: 685-5711
2388 W. 4th Ave (west of Arbutus), Tel: 734-5711

Metrotown Centre, 4820 Kingsway, **Burnaby**, Tel: 434-5711

1524 Lonsdale Ave, **North Vancouver**, Tel: 904-5711

Remaindered books, including recent bestsellers. A bit of a hit or miss, but you can't beat the prices!

Cody Books
810 Quayside Dr (at 8th St), in New Westminster Quay Public Market, **New Westminster**, Tel: 525-9850
3000 Lougheed Hwy (at Barnet), in Westwood Mall, **Coquitlam**, Tel: 464-5515
Large bookstore with excellent kids' section.

The Comicshop
2089 W. 4th Ave (at Arbutus), **Vancouver**
Tel: 738-8122
Fantastic selection of comic books for both kids and adults.

Duthie Books
2239 W. 4th Ave (at Vine), **Vancouver**, Tel: 732-5344
Website: *www.litrascape.com*
Duthie's is a Vancouver fixture, but unfortunately, this former mini-chain of bookstores now has only one location. It's probably a good idea to call ahead to their toll-free number (1-800-663-1174) if you're looking for one of the French and Spanish children's books that they used to carry at Manhattan Books & Magazines on Robson Street. Duthie's selection is good, with a wide range of children's books.

East End Book Co.
1470 Commercial Dr (at Grant), **Vancouver**
Tel: 251-5255
A small neighbourhood shop with a nice selection of children's literature.

Golden Age Collectables
830 Granville St (at Robson), **Vancouver**
Tel: 683-2819
New and rare comic books plus toys, model kits and role playing games.

Hager Books
2176 W. 41st (west of W. Boulevard), **Vancouver**, Tel: 263-9412
A quality selection of children's books.

Humpty Dumpty Books & Music
1496 Cartwright St, in the Kids Only Market on Granville Island, **Vancouver**
Tel: 683-7009
A small shop with lots of fiction, workbooks and music CDs and cassettes.

Iwase Books Canada
3700 No. 3 Rd, in Yaohan Centre, **Richmond**
Tel: 231-0717
Japanese-language books.

Kidsbooks
3083 W. Broadway (at Balaclava), **Vancouver**, Tel: 738-5335
3040 Edgemont Blvd (at Queens), in Edgemont Village, **North Vancouver**, Tel: 986-6190

Kidsbooks is *the* place to buy kids' books in Vancouver. They also have reference materials for parents, readings, music, videos, games, puppets, a lot of books in French, and a few in Spanish, and a very helpful, knowledgeable staff.

Sino
78 E. Pender St (at Main), **Vancouver**
Tel: 688-3785
Chinese language children's books.

UBC **Bookstore**
6200 University Blvd (at East Mall), **Vancouver**
Tel: 822-2665
A huge bookstore with a surprisingly good selection of kids' books. Readings and activities are often scheduled.

Musical Instruments — Sales and Rentals
These are a few of the top music shops in Vancouver, all of which have a big selection of instruments available for sale or rent. For information on music and vocal lessons, see page 201.

Long & McQuade
2301 Granville St (at 7th Ave), **Vancouver**, Tel: 734-4886
2215 Coquitlam Ave (at Shaughnessy), **Port Coquitlam**, Tel: 464-1011
10560 King George Hwy (at 106th Ave), in Dell Shopping Centre, **Surrey**, Tel: 588-9421,
Sales and rentals, including band instruments.

Prussin Music
3607 Broadway (at Dunbar), **Vancouver**
Tel: 736-3036
Woodwinds, string and brass instruments.

Tom Lee Music
929 Granville St (at Nelson), **Vancouver**, Tel: 685-8471
3631 No. 3 Rd (at Cambie), **Richmond**, Tel: 273-6661
2635 Barnet Hwy (at Lansdowne), **Coquitlam**, Tel: 941-8447
8356 120th St (at 84th Ave), **Surrey**, Tel: 599-0844
Guitars, pianos, band instruments; rentals, sales and instruction.

Ward Music
412 W. Hastings St (at Richards), **Vancouver**, Tel: 682-5288
1615 Lonsdale Ave (at 16th St), **North Vancouver**, Tel: 986-0911
Huge selection, especially of sheet music; rentals and sales.

Furnishings
Places to put all those clothes, shoes and toys! Don't forget to check out children's clothing consignment shops (see page 148) for good-quality, used baby furniture.

Friendly Bears
4411 No. 3 Rd (at Alderbridge Way), **Richmond**
Tel: 276-8278
Bunk beds, twin beds and other kids' furniture.

Ikea
3200 Sweden Way (at Bridgeport), **Richmond**
Tel: 273-2051
Enormous Swedish store selling everything from infant bedding to bunk beds to toys. Their kids' activities room, with a ball pit, video room and activities, is available for kids to play in while you shop.

Kid's Furniture World
12680 Bridgeport Rd (at Sweden Way), **Richmond**
Tel: 278-7654
Good prices on wooden bunk beds, captain beds and more.

MB Furniture Ltd.
8678 120th St (at 88th Ave), **Surrey**
Tel: 594-9313
Kids' bedroom furniture including wall units, desks and closets; they'll custom paint and stain.

Majestic Futon & Frame
1828 W. 4th Ave (at Burrard), **Vancouver**, Tel: 731-8226
388 W. Broadway (at Yukon), **Vancouver**, Tel: 879-7398
5072 Kingsway (at Royal Oak), **Burnaby**, Tel: 430-2258
13566 77th Ave (at King George Hwy), **Surrey**, Tel: 590-2228
Mainly adult-size furniture, but good prices on solid pine bunk beds and single beds.

Soothers Kids Boutique
935 Marine Dr (at Hamilton), in Capilano Mall, **North Vancouver**,
Tel: 980-7229
4567 Lougheed Hwy (at Willingdon), in Brentwood Mall, **Burnaby**,
Tel: 205-0030
Mainly furniture, strollers and bedding, but lots of other miscellaneous kids' stuff.

T.J.'s The Kiddies Store
3331 Jacombs Rd (at Sweden Way), **Richmond**, Tel: 270-8830
16050 Fraser Hwy (at 160th St), **Surrey**, Tel: 599-6999
Huge selection of everything for babies and kids, from soothers and cribs to bedding and rocking chairs.

Sporting Goods — New

These are good places for finding a range of sporting goods – anything from soccer cleats to baseball bats to running shoes. For stores that specialize in bicycles, camping equipment, dance supplies, martial arts supplies, skateboards, snowboarding and skating equipment, see individual listings.

Abbie's Sporting Goods
4895 Main St (at 33rd Ave), **Vancouver**
Tel: 874-6910
A great spot for team uniforms as well as hockey, softball and soccer gear plus more; they also do skate sharpening.

Skyline Sports
5395 West Blvd (at 38th St), **Vancouver**
Tel: 266-1061
From cleated footwear to in-line skates to ski clothing, they also have a junior equipment trade-in program and service skis and snowboards.

Sport Chek
792 Beatty St (at Robson), Tel: 684-7669, **Vancouver**
2105 Park Royal South (at Taylor Way), in Park Royal Shopping Centre, Tel: 922-3336, **West Vancouver**
6200 McKay Ave (at Kingsway), in Metrotown, Tel: 433-1115, **Burnaby**
2929 Barnet Hwy (at Pinetree Way), in Coquitlam Centre, Tel: 464-5122, **Coquitlam**
3000 Lougheed Hwy (at Barnet Hwy), in Westwood Mall, Tel: 944-1100, **Coquitlam**
5300 No. 3 Rd (at Alderbridge Way), in Lansdowne Park Shopping Centre, Tel: 231-9610, **Richmond**
1901 Guildford Town Centre (at 104th Ave), in Guildford Town Centre, Tel: 585-7293, **Surrey**
A bit of everything is sold at this chain.

Sport Mart Discount Superstores
495 W. 8th St (at Cambie), **Vancouver**, Tel: 873-6737
735 Thurlow St (at Alberni), **Vancouver**, Tel: 683-2433
1331 Marine Dr (at Bridgman), **North Vancouver**, Tel: 984-8494
2755 Lougheed Hwy (at Westwood), **Coquitlam**, Tel: 942-3163
5381 No. 3 Rd (at Alderbridge Way), **Richmond**, Tel: 244-0317
15280 101st Ave (at 152nd St), **Surrey**, Tel: 582-1133
Excellent prices, helpful staff; good selection.

The Sports Exchange
2151 Burrard St (at 5th Ave), **Vancouver**
Tel: 739-8990
Excellent prices on new sporting goods, trades accepted.

Sporting Goods — Secondhand
Kids love sports of all kinds, but unfortunately equipment is pricey. Luckily Vancouver has a great number of shops that sell (and buy) good, used equipment – perfect for families. You might not find the newest models here (and sometimes you might not find what you want), but the equipment at these stores will all be in good condition.

Cheapskates
3644 W. 16th Ave (at Dunbar), **Vancouver**
Tel: 222-1125
A cluster of three shops selling everything from bikes to ski equipment; prices drop the longer the merchandise stays in the store.

Play It Again Sports
106 2748 Lougheed Hwy (at Westwood), **Coquitlam**
Tel: 464-7529
A wide variety of clean equipment in good condition.

Ride On Sports Consignment
2255 W. Broadway (at Arbutus), **Vancouver**
Tel: 738-7734
A small shop with a helpful staff; a good place for used bikes and more.

Sports Junkies
600 W. 6th Ave (at Ash), **Vancouver**, Tel: 879-0666
3056 St John's St (at Williams), **Port Moody**, Tel: 469-3700
Large selection of both new and used items.

Bicycles — Sales

Besides having a good selection of bikes for adults, all these stores have a good selection of bikes for kids, as well as training wheels, carriers and helmets. The staff at these shops take pride in what they do and they tend to be really helpful, from choosing just the right bike to adjusting the seat and performing repairs. Most importantly, when you buy a bike, it's already put together! For tricycles and other toddler-size wagons and cars, see under Toys (page 152).

Ace Cycle Shop
3155 W. Broadway (at Trutch), **Vancouver**
Tel: 738-9818
My favourite bike shop; a small but good selection; helpful staff.

Bicycle Sports Pacific
999 Pacific St (at Burrard), **Vancouver**, Tel: 682-4537
3026 Mountain Hwy (at Lynn Valley), **North Vancouver**, Tel: 988-1800
Kids' bikes plus mountain and road bikes; kids' clothing and accessories.

Cambie Cycles
3317 Cambie St (at 17th Ave), **Vancouver**
Tel: 874-3616
A shop with a good reputation, they have new and used bikes, accessories, clothing and trade-ins.

Cap's Bicycle Stores
333 W. 2nd Ave (at Yukon), **Vancouver**, Tel: 873-1449
1077 Marine Dr (at Lloyd), **North Vancouver**, Tel: 985-44398
460 Alexandra Rd (at No. 3 Rd), **Richmond**, Tel: 270-2020
Another shop with an excellent reputation, these are only three of their eight stores; good selection of bikes at competitive prices.

Cyclepath
1421 W. Broadway (at Granville), **Vancouver**
Tel: 737-2344
A shop with a sense of humour, they have a good selection of mountain bikes plus more.

Dunbar Cycles
4219 Dunbar St (at 26th Ave), **Vancouver**
Tel: 224-2116
Around for over 50 years, they have a complete line of children's bikes plus clothing and accessories.

Newton Rocky Cycle
7143 King George Hwy (at 72nd Ave), **Surrey**
Tel: 591-5333
Kids' bikes plus a great selection of mountain bikes.

Reckless The Bike Store
1810 Fir St (at 3rd Ave), **Vancouver**
Tel: 731-2420
Right at the entrance to Granville Island, this shop does quick repairs, has rentals and loaners, plus they sell both adult and kids' bikes. Really helpful staff.

West Point Cycles
3771 W. 10th Ave (at Alma), **Vancouver**, Tel: 224-3536
6069 W. Blvd (at 45th Ave), **Vancouver**, Tel: 263-7587
Since 1930; they have kids' bikes, trailers and parts, as well as rentals.

Camping Equipment
The following places have good stocks of camping and outdoor equipment. Some of them offer rentals, so if you're new to camping, you don't have to invest a lot of money in tents, sleeping bags and the like. **Mountain Equipment Co-Op** (see page 142) has excellent-quality outdoor cycling, boating, climbing skiing and camping equipment; they also rent sleeping bags, tents and backpacks.

Altus Mountain Gear
137 W. Broadway (at Columbia), **Vancouver**
Tel: 876-5255
Huge selection of camping and climbing equipment, children's outerwear, plus full rental program including tents and sleeping bags.

Europe Bound Travel Outfitters
555 Seymour (at Dunsmuir), **Vancouver**, Tel: 683-2282
555 W. 8th Ave (at Ash St), **Vancouver**, Tel: 874-7456
Camping and hiking equipment; inexpensive, good-quality tent and equipment rentals.

Great Outdoors Equipment Ltd.
222 W. Broadway (at Columbia), **Vancouver**
Tel: 872-8872
Camping, backpacking, travel gear.

Three Vets Ltd.
2200 Yukon St (at 6th Ave), **Vancouver**
Tel: 872-5475
Camping gear as well as a big fishing department plus more.

Dance Supplies

Whether your daughter (or son) is serious about ballet or tap lessons or just wants to pretend they are, these stores carry everything you might want.

Avalon Dance Shop
4532 Main St (at 29th Ave), **Vancouver**
Tel: 874-2461
Huge variety of dance costumes and shoes, including children's ballet, tap and jazz clothing and shoes.

Beetles Dance Wear
12501 2nd Ave (at Chatham), **Richmond**
Tel: 277-4528
Dance wear selection includes tights, shoes, ballet and jazz wear, as well as skate wear.

The Dance Shop
1089 W. Broadway (at Oak), **Vancouver**
Tel: 733-6116
In addition to dance wear and shoes, they have a selection of face paints and theatrical makeup.

Just Imagine
4253 Dunbar St (at 26th Ave), **Vancouver**
Tel: 222-3523
Lots of dance clothes as well as dress-up items and other fun stuff.

Limbers' Dancewear
5635 West Blvd (at 41st Ave), **Vancouver**
Tel: 264-0009
Ballet, tap, and jazz dance supplies.

Tiptoe Gym Wear
4132 Hastings St (at Gilmore), **Burnaby**
Tel: 294-5577
Ballet, gymnastics and Highland dance wear and shoes, as well as skating supplies and more.

Martial Arts Supplies

The following places have a good stock of martial arts supplies, whether your child is taking karate or jujitsu.

Golden Arrow Martial Arts Supplies
2234 E. Hastings St (at Garden), **Vancouver**
Tel: 254-6910
Martial arts supplies and boxing equipment.

Mikado Enterprises
701 E. Hastings St (at Heatley), **Vancouver**
Tel: 253-7168
Martial arts supplies, dancing lion equipment, books and videos.

Skateboards and Snowboards

Snowboarding is now the hot sport, and soon your kids may be begging you for their own snowboard, if they haven't already. The following places are among the most respected for the quality of their snowboarding and skateboarding merchandise, as well as their knowledgeable staff. See also "Sporting Goods," page 163, for other sources of new or used boards. I'd recommend renting equipment the first few times you go, just to make sure your kids are really into it. For lessons, see page 85; snowboard rentals are usually available through the ski school as well as at the places indicated below.

The Boarding House
4800 No. 3 Rd (at Alderbridge Way), **Richmond**
Tel: 273-7700
Skateboards and snowboards; sales only.

The Boardroom Snowboard Shop
1717 W. 4th Ave (at Burrard), **Vancouver**
Tel: 734-7669
Snowboard sales and rentals; also ski supplies.

Cypress Mountain Sports
2002 Park Royal South (at Taylor Way) in Park Royal Shopping Centre, **West Vancouver**
Tel: 878-9229
Snowboard sales and rentals.

Northshore Ski & Board
1625 Lonsdale Ave (at 16th St), **North Vancouver**
Tel: 987-7245
New and used snowboards and shred gear; sales only.

Pacific Boarder Sail Snow & Surf
1793 W. 4th Ave (at Burrard), **Vancouver**
Tel: 734-7245
Sailboard, snowboard and surfboard sales and rentals.

RDS Skate & Snow Supply
137 W. 3rd St (at Lonsdale), **North Vancouver**
Tel: 990-4737
Skateboard and snowboards; sales only.

Vert
1020 Granville St (at Nelson), **Vancouver**
Tel: 688-5464
Skateboards and snowboards; sales only.

Westbeach
1766 W. 4th Ave (at Burrard), **Vancouver**
Tel: 731-6449
Snowboards, skateboards and surfboards; sales only.

Skating Equipment

All ice skating rinks rent skates; many of them sell clothing and skating accessories. The following places have the largest stock of skating supplies. Also check out **Beetles Dancewear** and **Tiptoe Gym Wear** under Dance Supplies.

Cyclone Taylor Sporting Goods
6575 Oak St (at 49th Ave), **Vancouver**, Tel: 266-3316
14140 Triangle Rd (at No. 6 Rd), in the Richmond Ice Centre, **Richmond**, Tel: 448-1748
Both stores, the latter of which is located in the **Richmond Ice Centre** (see page 82), have a huge selection of new and used hockey and figure skates, clothing and equipment, and provide skate sharpening, technical repairs and fitting advice.

The Hockey Shop
10369 135th St (at 104th Ave), **Surrey**
Tel: 899-8699
A huge selection of hockey equipment and nothing else.

It Figures
13479 76th Ave (at King George Hwy), **Surrey**
Tel: 594-4454
Excellent selection of all types of skating supplies.

7th Figure Skating Boutique
930 Brunette Ave (at Lougheed Hwy), **Coquitlam**
Tel: 521-5770
Skates and clothing.

Alternative Medicines and Treatments

More and more families are turning to alternative medicines and treatments for their children's ailments. The following places offer natural therapies for childhood ailments; no appointment is necessary. For a list of naturopaths, see page 240. For traditional pharmacies, see page 238.

Bloom Aromatherapy
1854 W. 1st Ave (at Burrard), **Vancouver**
Tel: 736-8960
Besides their regular products, they have a kids' line with essential oils and bath products.

Escents Aromatherapy Bath & Body Products
1172 Robson St (at Bute), **Vancouver**, Tel: 682-0041
2579 W. Broadway (at Trafalgar), **Vancouver**, Tel: 736-7761
650 W. 41st Ave (at Cambie), in Oakridge Centre, **Vancouver**, Tel: 267-7310

2002 Park Royal South (at Taylor Way), in Park Royal Shopping Centre, **West Vancouver**, Tel: 926-7720
Essential oils for adults and children, plus bath products.

Finlandia Natural Healing Centre
1962 W. Broadway (at Maple), **Vancouver**
Tel: 733-0266
Homeopathic and herbal remedies, vitamin and mineral supplements; helpful, knowledgeable staff; Natural Healing Centre upstairs.

Gaia Garden Herbal Apothecary
2672 W. Broadway (at Trafalgar), **Vancouver**
Tel: 734-4372
Herbal apothecary with tinctures, dried herbs, essential oils and nutritional supplements; many products for children. Experienced herbalists on staff.

Candy and Chocolate

Here are both kid-oriented candy stores, with their usual assortment of lollipops and sweets, as well as higher-quality chocolate shops for those who want their children to experience the real thing.

Avril's – The Sugarless Candy Co.
2225 Surrey Place Mall (at King George Hwy), **Surrey**
Tel: 582-1101
Sugar-free hard candies and more.

Bernard Callebaut Chocolaterie
2698 Granville St (at 11th Ave), **Vancouver**, Tel: 736-5890
8120 No. 2 Rd (at Blundell), **Richmond**, Tel: 275-1244
Exquisite, expensive chocolate.

Candy Kitchen
1689 Johnston St, in Granville Island Public Market, **Vancouver**
Tel: 681-7001
Bins full of both modern and old-fashioned candies, from Pez to Smarties to jelly beans and more.

Charlie's Chocolate Factory Ltd.
3746 Canada Way (at Boundary), **Burnaby**
Tel: 437-8221
Slabs of Belgian chocolate plus candies and candy-making supplies

Chocolate Arts
2037 W. 4th Ave (at Arbutus), **Vancouver**
Tel: 739-0475
Much of their chocolate is done in Pacific Northwest designs; good for gifts to bring back home.

Daniel Le Chocolat Belge
1105 Robson St (at Thurlow), **Vancouver**, Tel: 688-9624
2820 Granville St (at 12th Ave), **Vancouver**, Tel: 733-1994
4447 W. 10th Ave (at Sasamat), **Vancouver**, Tel: 224-3361
805 Park Royal North (at Taylor Way) in Park Royal Shopping Centre, **West Vancouver**, Tel: 925-2213
5300 No. 3 Rd (at Alderbridge Way), in Lansdowne Park Shopping Centre, **Richmond**, Tel: 273-8186
The most delicious chocolate in town; one succulent piece just might appease your child in the midst of shopping.

Dutch Girl Chocolates
1002 Commercial Dr (at Parker), **Vancouver**
Tel: 251-3221
A small shop with exquisite, artful chocolate.

Lee's Candies
4361 W. 10th Ave (at Trimble), **Vancouver**
Tel: 224-5450
Candies made by hand in the store; less-expensive seconds are often available.

Olde World Fudge Co. Ltd.
1689 Johnston St, in Granville Island Public Market, **Vancouver**,
Tel: 687-7355
123 Carrie Cates Court (at Lonsdale), in Lonsdale Quay, **North Vancouver**, Tel: 980-8336
810 Quayside Dr (at 8th St), in New Westminster Quay Public Market, **New Westminster**, Tel: 520-3227
Fudge of all varieties plus those coveted chocolate-covered apples; their caramels are exquisite.

Over the Moon Chocolate Company
2868 W. Broadway (at Macdonald), **Vancouver**, Tel: 737-0880
3457 Cambie Stree (at 18th Ave), **Vancouver**, Tel: 872-6673
Delicious, original chocolates; my kids love the hedgehogs or tiny milk chocolate bears and monkeys.

Purdy's Chocolates
2196 W. 4th Ave (at Yew), **Vancouver**, Tel: 730-8669
2189 W. 41st Ave (at Yew), **Vancouver**, Tel: 266-9311
2777 Kingsway St (at Earles), **East Vancouver**, Tel: 454-2700
Ever-popular; you can choose your own chocolates or buy prepackaged boxes. Their kids' ice cream cones are only one dollar. There are numerous Purdy's locations not listed here.

Rocky Mountain Chocolate Factory
1017 Robson St (at Burrard), **Vancouver**
Tel: 688-4100
Kids love the trays of candy apples in the window of this busy Robson Street store and you can often see the staff at work making chocolates; the smell of sugar when you enter this place is overwhelming.

Suckers Candy Shop
1496 Cartwright St, in the Kids Only Market on Granville Island, **Vancouver**
Tel: 682-4240
Candies of every variety plus lollipops and more.

The Sweet Factory
4700 Kingsway (at McKay), in Eaton Centre Metrotown, **Burnaby**, Tel: 430-9730
6551 No. 3 Rd (at Westminster Hwy) in the South Mall of Richmond Centre, **Richmond**, Tel: 273-8689
2249 Guildford Town Centre (at 104th Ave) in Guildford Town Centre, **Surrey**, Tel: 582-0525
Sweets and suckers of every variety; a good mall treat.

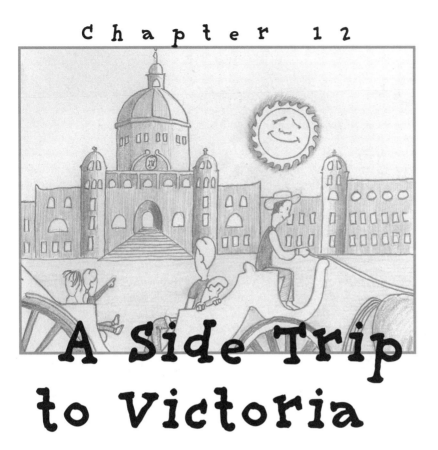

c h a p t e r 1 2

A Side Trip to Victoria

At first glance, Victoria might be considered too stuffy for children. B.C.'s capital is a lovely place with manicured flower gardens and a postcard-perfect atmosphere. Victoria's centrepiece is the **Inner Harbour**, ringed by the **Parliament Buildings**, the **Royal British Columbia Museum** and the **Empress Hotel**. North of the Empress is **Government Street**, where the shops are laden with British merchandise such as tweeds and fine china. None of this sounds very kid-friendly, but this city is actually a fun place to go with children, whether you're a B.C. resident looking for a weekend getaway or a tourist wanting to explore places outside of Vancouver. **Beacon Hill Park**, just south of the Empress, and the museum are two particularly good spots for kids, and there are lots of family-oriented restaurants and interesting attractions.

Having said that, Victoria makes a great two- or three-day trip, but beyond that your kids will probably get bored. Consider taking some time to explore the rest of Vancouver Island, of which Victoria is only a small part. In the summertime, stay at one of the numerous motels or campsites farther up the island, particularly north and south of Nanaimo on the east coast. It's nice to combine a couple of days in Victoria with several more days relaxing by the beach. Keep in mind that Victoria gets very crowded in the summer, and if you plan a trip in the off-season, you can take advantage of lower hotel rates and a less frenetic scene.

Listed below are ideas of what to do and where to stay and eat when in Victoria. For further information, contact the Tourist Information Centre in Victoria at 812 Wharf Street, (250) 953-2033.

Getting There

Victoria is accessible by ferry from both Vancouver and Seattle. Ferry rides, unlike monotonous car trips, can be a lot of fun in themselves. The kids have space to run around, and if you bring your own lunch (the food is usually expensive and mediocre) and a few puzzles and games, everyone will have a pretty good time. If you're travelling from Vancouver, B.C. Ferries has play equipment for smaller kids, plus video games for the older set (don't forget a pocketful of change).

If you're driving a car onto the ferry in the summertime, do make a reservation, for the boats can get quite full. All of the ferries listed below (except Black Ball) accept reservations.

The **Victoria Regional Transit System** is a good bus system that runs throughout the city. For 24-hour recorded transit information, call (250) 382-6161. (Day passes are available for $4 to $5.) If you are travelling with a car, you'll probably end up parking it while you explore much of the city, but it can be handy to explore the perimeter of Victoria or other parts of the island. There are beautiful parks located less than an hour's drive from Victoria that are definitely worth checking out.

From Vancouver, **BC Ferries** offers service between Tsawwassen (about a half-hour drive south of Vancouver) and Swartz Bay (about a half-hour drive from downtown Victoria) and between Horseshoe Bay (a half-hour drive northwest of Vancouver) or Tsawwassen and Nanaimo (about an hour-and-a-half drive from Victoria). For 24-hour schedule information, call BC Ferries at 1-888-223-3779. To make automated reservations (there is a $15 fee per reservation), call BC Ferries' automated line at 1-888-724-5223. In the middle of summer, do spend the $15. If you don't, you and your kids could spend hours in a lineup of cars, which is no way to start or finish a holiday. Prices for ferry rides vary depending on time of year and day of week (it's more expensive in the summer). In the summer months it's $32 to take a car on the ferry to Victoria; passengers in cars as well as walk-ons are $9; kids 5 to 11 are $4.50; kids under five are free. Bicycles attached to a car are free, as long as the car is under seven feet in height; walk-on passengers with a bicycle are charged an additional $2.50. Do check directly with BC Ferries to check on height and length requirements if you're driving to the island with a camper van or other large vehicle. For more information on taking a ferry, see "Getting Around," page 6.

Obviously it can get pretty pricey just for a weekend away with the kids. It's relatively easy to access the ferry by bus. **Translink** (see page 2) goes as far as

Tsawwassen; West Vancouver's **Blue Bus** (see page 3) goes to Horseshoe Bay. There is always a local bus waiting at Swartz Bay to take passengers into Victoria. **Pacific Coach Lines** (see page 7) goes from downtown Vancouver to downtown Victoria, but don't look to save any money over a car ride. (The one-way cost for adults is $26, kids five and up are $13, and kids under five are free.)

Seaplanes are another way to get to Victoria from either Seattle or Vancouver. See page 106 in "Get Up and Go!" for a list of Vancouver-based airplane, seaplane and helicopter companies.

From Seattle, the *Victoria Clipper* provides year-round passenger-only service on a high-speed catamaran. The one-way trip takes two hours. The *Princess Marguerite* provides car and passenger service from mid-May to mid-September, and because it's a slower ferry, the one-way trip takes four-and-a-half hours. The long trip is beautiful, though, with the *Marguerite* like a sort of cruise ship. The food is good and it's got a great play area for the kids. Oftentimes people like to take the *Marguerite* coming over, then the faster *Clipper* going back. For information on both ferries, call (206) 448-5000 from Seattle, (250) 382-8100 from Victoria or Vancouver, or 1-800-888-2535 (within North America). Prices and schedules for the *Clipper* and the *Marguerite* vary widely depending on the time of year, but the last time I checked, a one way-trip on the *Marguerite* with a car and driver was $54, additional adults were $29 each, and kids one to 11 were $14.50. Kids over 11 paid the adult fare. For walk-on service on the *Clipper*, one-way prices started at $58 for adults. Kids one to 11 were $29.

Washington State Ferries provides year-round service for both cars and walk-on passengers. That ferry departs from Anacortes (145 km/90 mi. north of Seattle) and docks in Sydney (27 km/17 mi. out of Victoria). The trip meanders through the San Juan Islands and takes three hours. From Seattle, call (206) 464-6400; from Victoria or Vancouver, call (250) 381-1551.

Black Ball runs a year-round car and passenger ferry from Seattle to Victoria, a trip that takes only 90 minutes. Again, they don't take reservations. For more information, call (206) 622-2222 from Seattle, (250) 386-2202 from Victoria or Vancouver. Fares on Black Ball and Washington State Ferries are comparable with those of the *Clipper* or *Marguerite*. For information on seaplane trips out of Seattle, call **Kenmore Air** at 1-800-826-1890. If you arrive via boat or plane from Seattle, you'll dock in the Inner Harbour, right downtown. From here it's easy to walk to most places.

What to Do

Victoria's most famous landmarks are the **Empress Hotel**, the **Parliament Buildings** and the **Royal British Columbia Museum**. One good approach to Victoria is to take the kids someplace like the museum, go out for lunch at one of the restaurants below, then work off some energy at **Beacon Hill Park** just across the street. If you're in Victoria for more than a day or two and need some non-touristy downtime, try the **Oak Bay Recreation Centre** or **Saanich Commonwealth Place** (both listed below) and go swimming or ice skating. It might seem odd to take your kids to a pool, something they can probably do at home, but in the midst of new and different activities, this can be a real stress-reducer and give the family some fun time together without costing a lot of money.

Also keep in mind that you can walk all around the **Inner Harbour** to **West Bay**. It's about a two- to three-hour walk, so go as far as you're able; there are little parks along the way and opportunities to see shore life. At West Bay, just across the street from the marina, there is a retired sea captain's house whose outside has been heavily decorated with "life at sea" memorabilia, including an anchor, ropes, a mermaid figure and more; it's very cool. West Bay has a little ferry that takes you back downtown if you don't want to walk back.

Beacon Hill Park
Douglas St (at Southgate)
This is a great 74-hectare (184-acre) park with playgrounds, a petting farm, totem poles nearby, and numerous ponds and flower gardens, plus lots of green space for picnicking or running around. Take a break and let your kids loose in one of the playgrounds. They'll like the **Beacon Hill Children's Farm**, a privately operated farm where kids can get close to animals. This is a great place in the spring, when there are baby goats and piglets. A great walk for kids is along the beach at the south side of Beacon Hill Park. You can walk out along a long breakwater to the lighthouse at the end. There are no railings, so keep hold of young ones' hands, but it's a thrill for kids, and you can occasionally see seals poking their snouts out of the water.

Crystal Garden
713 Douglas St, behind the Empress Hotel
Tel: (250) 381-1213
Hours: Daily 10:00 a.m. to 4:30 p.m.
Prices: Adults $7.50; seniors $6.50; kids 5 to 16 $4; kids under 4 free; family (2 adults with 2 kids) $20
A good spot for a rainy day, the Crystal Garden is an indoor paradise with thousands of tropical plants beside koi ponds, a stream and a cascading waterfall. Kids love the world's smallest monkeys (they're only four inches high when fully grown) as well as the brilliant flamingos and macaws.

Empress Hotel
721 Government St, on the Inner Harbour
Tel: (250) 384-8111
This is a gorgeous hotel in the heart of the Inner Harbour. Afternoon tea is popular with tourists, but you have to make reservations and you can't wear jeans, so you can imagine that kids are not *really* welcome, except for exceptionally well behaved ones who like tea (hmmm . . . do you know any?). They do serve tea in a smaller café in a downstairs level of the hotel; it's not as grandiose, but the cakes are just as yummy and you'll feel more comfortable with your kids here. Do walk through the Empress just for a kick; it's very elegant and houses **Miniature World** (see below).

Government Street

North of the Empress Hotel

Here you'll find a load of shops, most of which are, for better or worse, designed with tourists in mind. If you can manage it with children, it's definitely worth taking an hour or two to check out the selection of china, Cowichan sweaters, Scottish tartans, teas and other items to take home. Smaller kids will like the Native dolls and glass figurines and will go nuts over the **British Candy Shoppe** (635 Yates, east of Government Street) or the **Original Christmas Village**, an all-Christmas store located in the 1300 block of Government Street, between Yates and Johnson.

Miniature World

721 Government St, inside the Empress Hotel

Tel: (250) 385-9731

Hours: Daily 8:30 a.m. to 9:00 p.m. in summer, 9:00 a.m. to 5:00 p.m. in non-summer months

Prices: Adults $6.75; kids 5 to 11 $4.75; kids under 5 free

Most kids adore this place, though I haven't found any adults who actually like it. Frankly, it's a tourist trap. But if your kids like dollhouses or anything miniature, take a deep breath and bring them here. There's an extensive collection of dollhouses, including a miniature railway, scenes from Santa's Workshop and more than 80 displays depicting historic scenes of all kinds.

Oak Bay Recreation Centre

1975 Bee St (at Fort)

Tel: (250) 595-SWIM (7946)

Prices: Vary depending on activity

If the kids are tired of being toted around, head to the rec centre for the afternoon. Swimming, ice skating and tennis are all offered year-round, and you don't have to be a member to use the facilities. Call before coming, though; there are designated family swim and skate times.

Pacific Undersea Gardens

490 Belleville St (at Menzies)

Tel: (250) 382-5717

Hours: Daily 9:00 a.m. to 9:00 p.m. in summer; 10:00 a.m. to 5:00 p.m. in winter

Prices: Adults $7; seniors $6.25; students 12 to 17 $5; kids 5 to 11 $3.50; kids under 5 free

This underwater glass structure allows you to view hundreds of unusual creatures underwater. There are also live narrated scuba diving shows. This can be an interesting attraction, but like many things in the area, it is on the touristy side and overpriced for what it is.

Parliament Buildings

501 Belleville Ave, on the Inner Harbour

Tel: (250) 387-3046

Hours: Mon. to Fri. 8:30 a.m. to 5:00 p.m., Sat. and Sun. 9:00 a.m. to 5:00 p.m.

This is the main seat of B.C.'s government. During the summer there are daily guided tours, a good way to introduce your kids to the legislative process. This is a better tour for kids 10 and over; younger ones will get bored too easily. When in session, you can see the Legislative Assembly; the Speaker sits on a gilded throne, and the costumed sergeant-at-arms holds a gold mace.

Royal British Columbia Museum
675 Belleville St (at Government)
Tel: (250) 387-3014, (250) 387-3701 or 1-800-661-5411
Hours: Daily 9:00 a.m. to 5:00 p.m.
Prices: Adults $7; seniors, students (19 and older with valid id) and kids 6 to 18 $4; kids 5 and under free; family (2 adults plus related dependent youth) $18
This museum, the "must-see" attraction in Victoria for kids, manages to teach about B.C.'s history in a way that is fun and interesting for both adults and children. The life-size dioramas are particularly good, complete with appropriate sounds and smells (sometimes too realistic; the underwater exhibit is a bit dark and scary). Walk through a rainforest, sit in a Kwakiutl Native longhouse or stand in the captain's quarters of the HMS *Discovery*. Kids adore the Pioneer Village, complete with silent movies playing in the mini-theatre. There are great kids' books in the museum shop; spend your money here and forego buying cheap kids' trinkets from Government Street.

Royal London Wax Museum
470 Belleville St, on the Inner Harbour
Tel: (250) 388-4461
Hours: Daily 9:00 a.m. to 9:00 p.m.
Prices: Adults $8; students and seniors $6; kids 6 to 12 $3; kids 5 and under free; family (2 adults and their dependent children) $20
Go here if you like wax museums. Some children find them fascinating, and it can give you a chance to teach them a bit of history, if only because kids are constantly asking who all the "people" are. The Chamber of Horrors is too scary for small children (barbaric is more like it), but it's clearly marked so you can avoid it.

Saanich Commonwealth Place
Off Elk Lake Dr (at Royal Oak Dr)
Tel: (250) 727-7108
This facility has a water slide, a wave pool, diving boards, a sauna, a steam room, a whirlpool, family change rooms, a gymnasium, a weight room, a dance studio and a library. If the weather's rotten while you're in Victoria (and it often is), go for a swim to burn off some energy. Call ahead for family swim times.

Where to Eat
Like the restaurants in Vancouver, these restaurants were chosen based on their kid-friendly menus and welcoming attitudes to children. Price ratings are based on dinner for one adult with one nonalcoholic drink, taxes and tip. Lunch usually costs 25 percent less. Prices for children's food tend to be in the $5 range. A rating of Inexpensive/Moderate means that the menu has a range of prices. You'll

note that expensive restaurants are not listed here. I simply didn't find any in the area that fit the criteria for a family-friendly restaurant. Besides, most restaurants in the downtown Victoria area are more casual and geared to visiting families. Many hotels also have restaurants; see the hotel listings below.

Inexpensive – Less than $15

Moderate – $15 to $25

Alzu's Family Restaurant

811 Bay St (at Blanshard)

Tel: (250) 388-5658

Hours: Open 24 hours

Prices: Inexpensive

Regrettably, they've had to remove the toddlers' play area that used to be a highlight here. But they still have a kids' menu. Go on Tiny Tykes Toonie Tuesday, when all kids' meals are, you guessed it, $2. The adult menu is standard coffee shop fare. Breakfast, lunch and dinner are served 24 hours a day.

Blethering Place

2250 Oak Bay Ave (at Monterey)

Tel: (250) 598-1413

Hours: Daily 8:00 a.m. to 9:00 p.m.

Prices: Inexpensive/Moderate

This is a good place to treat the kids to an authentic English tea – the café is casual enough for small children. The scones are excellent, and they also serve traditional English meals, with simple choices kids tend to like.

Cecconi's Pizzeria and Trattoria

3201 Shelbourne (at N. Dairy), across from Hillside Mall

Tel: (250) 592-0454

Hours: Mon. to Sat. 11:30 a.m. to 10:00 p.m., Sun. 5:00 p.m. to 10:00 p.m.

Prices: Moderate

Pizza and pasta are served at this noisy, casual restaurant perfect for families. It can get crowded, so arrive early if you don't want to wait.

Milestone's

812 Wharf St (at Government)

Tel: (250) 381-2244

Hours: Mon. to Fri. 11:00 a.m. to 10:30 p.m., Sat. 10:00 a.m. to 11:00 p.m., Sun. 9:00 a.m. to 11:00 p.m.

Prices: Moderate

Part of the **Milestone's** chain in Vancouver (see page 116), this one is right on the harbour, with a great view.

Millos

716 Burdett, next to the Empress Hotel

Tel: (250) 382-4422 or (250) 382-5544

Hours: Mon. to Sat. 11:00 a.m. to 11:00 p.m., Sun. 4:00 p.m. to 10:00 p.m.

Prices: Inexpensive/Moderate

This is a really good Greek restaurant with a nice selection of seafood, steaks, ribs and pasta. Kids like the Greek dancing and belly dancing, and there's even a children's menu for them to choose from. The lunch specials are really reasonably priced, and there is an early bird dinner special (4:00 p.m. to 6:30 p.m. every day of the week) for $9.95 per adult.

Smitty's Family Restaurant
850 Douglas (at Belleville), near the Empress Hotel, (250) 383-5612
2302 Beacon Ave (at Resthaven), in the Emerald Isle Motel, **Sidney**, (250) 656-2423
6719 W. Saanich Rd (at Keating), **Brentwood Bay**, (250) 652-1764
Hours: Mon. to Sat. 6:30 a.m. to 11:00 p.m., Sun. 7:00 a.m. to 11:00 p.m.
Prices: Inexpensive
This is one of the easiest places in Victoria to take kids. It's old and established (in existence since 1960), noisy as anything and definitely not expensive. Kids 10 and under can order from the kids' menu for only $3.59 and get anything from mini-pancakes to "dinosaur buddies" (more chicken strips) to pasta with marinara sauce. A good spot before heading to **Beacon Hill Park**. The Smitty's in Sidney is good for a quick meal before getting on or after getting off the ferry at Swartz Bay; the one in Brentwood Bay is near **Butchart Gardens**, a formal garden better for adults.

Where to Stay

Like the hotels listed for Vancouver, these were chosen because they're kid-friendly, clean, safe and comfortable. Price ratings below are based on standard accommodations for a family of four in July. Most of the rooms come with kitchens, which are handy and can dramatically cut down on the cost of eating out all the time. For more helpful details on accommodation, see "Where to Stay with Kids," page 131.
Inexpensive – $50 to $125
Moderate – $126 to $200
Expensive – $201 to $300

The Bowery Guest House
310 Huntington Pl (at Avalon St)
Tel: (250) 383-8079
Prices: Inexpensive
A bed-and-breakfast that caters to kids! Unbelievable but true, and this one is particularly charming. The owner, Beverly Dresen, has a heritage house with a self-contained apartment big enough to accommodate the parents, two kids and even a babysitter or grandmother. Aside from the living room (with television and VCR), master bedroom, guest bedroom and loft with two single beds, there's a fully stocked kitchen with a microwave and coffee machine. There's also a portable crib and fold-up bed if you need it. A complimentary breakfast (usually muffins, bagels, cereal, juice, coffee and tea) is included in the price, and Beverly brings it up to your room, which is a lot easier than having to dress to

come down to breakfast. No taxes are charged, so you save the 17 percent that's usually tacked on. The B & B is half a block from **Beacon Hill Park**, and two-and-a-half blocks from the **Royal British Columbia Museum**. There's even a stuffed Paddington bear, complete with sou'wester and boots, on loan to visiting kids. And if you come in on one of the ferries docking downtown, Beverly will come and pick you up if you need a ride. The Bowery is normally open from April 1 through October, but book as early as you can, as it's quite full during summer months.

Canterbury Inn
310 Gorge Rd. East (at Jutland), off Douglas
Tel: (250) 382-2151, (800) 952-2151
Prices: Inexpensive
This is a no-frills hotel with 80 clean and comfortable rooms, half of which are self-contained suites with kitchen facilities. This is a good alternative to some of the pricier downtown hotels, and it's still only two miles from the main action. There's an indoor pool, a restaurant and free cribs. They have excellent off-season specials.

Royal Scot Motor Inn
425 Quebec St (at Menzies)
Tel: (250) 388-5463
Prices: Moderate
This hotel is not luxurious, but it's clean and comfortable. Better yet, most of its 150 units have kitchens. (They're only $10 more a night than suites without, so it's well worth the added cost. If you don't feel like cooking, there's a full-service restaurant downstairs.) Larger suites have one or two bedrooms; smaller ones have a queen-size bed and a sofa bed. Cribs are available. There is an indoor pool, a few arcade games and a coin-operated laundry. Kids really like the fact that all the employees at the Royal Scot wear kilts. Best of all, it's centrally located, only half a block from the **Parliament Buildings**.

Swans Hotel
506 Pandora Ave, near Market Square
Tel: (250) 361-3310 or 1-800-668-7926
Prices: Expensive
This conveniently located hotel has some of the most spacious units around. Staying here is like having your own private condominium. Each of the 29 units is on two levels and has two bedrooms, a fully equipped kitchen and a separate dining and living area. It's a bit pricey but worth it, and more of a bargain in nonsummer months. There's a pub and restaurant downstairs.

chapter 13

Kids' Parties

Children's parties can be a parent's biggest nightmare. What to do? Where to have it? How much will it cost? Not only do you need to entertain a group of kids (a huge challenge), but you need to do it in a way that doesn't make you insane. Most importantly, it should be something the birthday boy or girl actually *enjoys* – it is their special day, after all. Personally, I held off having a large birthday party for my kids until they were old enough to want one. Kids under four or five are usually quite content with the attention of family and one or two friends, as long as there's a cake, balloons and the inevitable presents. Once they start making friends, they'll want a different type of party.

If you've got the space (and the temperament) for it, have a party at your home and bring in live entertainment, hire a party planner or rent an air-inflated play structure. Having a party somewhere else can be a blessing, however, basically because you don't have a horde of kids to clean up after. What you end up choosing will depend on what age your child is, what will make them happy and what you can afford. Younger kids love live entertainment; having a magician or face painter come to your house is a real treat. Artistic six-year-olds like ceramics studios (see page 97); older kids will opt for laser tag (see page 99) or indoor rock climbing (see page 83). Less expensive options include beaches and parks (if the weather's nice). For lots of ideas on outside locales, see page 28. There are also some excellent books on the market that have at-home party activities if you're strapped for cash but want to make it a fun day; these range from making your own ringtoss or beanbag toss to decorating flower pots; in particular, check out your local library.

Entertainers and Party Planners

Bringing an entertainer to your house can be really fun. If you're planning a two-hour party, allow half an hour for the children to greet each other and let off their initial energy, an hour for the entertainer and the last half hour for cake and presents. Entertainers aren't cheap. They run at least a hundred bucks for a visit, although that price can vary. Call to check, but most do parties all over the Lower Mainland. **CirKids**, **Fairy Garden** and **Mad Science** are particularly innovative, fun choices.

All Kids Stuff
Tel: 205-5808
They have your choice of clowns, magicians, face painters and jugglers, as well as different games.

Amazing Scruffles the Clown
Tel: 589-7806

A-Z Events
Tel: 878-0542
This outfit offers clowns, magicians, jugglers or blow-up amusements, depending on your fancy.

Bob Wilson Magic Company
Tel: 240-7241

Butterfly the Clown
Tel: 434-3857

Canadian Folk Puppets
Tel: 277-9177
Puppet shows for kids of all ages.

CastleTop Characters
Tel: 736-0876
Fairies, clowns, princesses, mermaids and genies doing magic, balloon animals, face painting and more.

Cinemazoo
Tel: 299-6963
This top-notch animal agency has everything from exotic animal displays and presentations to a petting zoo and trick dog show. They'll even bring a miniature trout fishing pond to your house so kids can try their hand at angling.

CirKids
Tel: 737-7408
Learn to flip, flop and fly on your birthday. For ages six and up.

The Clownerie
Tel: 328-3311
Offers balloon twisting, face painting, a clown or train rides.

Elwoodettes Marionettes
Tel: 521-0829
Puppet musicals for all ages.

Fairy Garden
Tel: 432-1050
A fairy or wizard handles everything from games, songs and stories to costumes and face painting.

Mad Science
Tel: 924-1061
Fun, science-based parties.

The Magic of Martin DominO
Tel: 836-8749
Magician.

Parties by Us
Tel: 467-8510
Theme-based parties individually tailored to each child. They will design packages for do-it-yourself parties or they'll handle every detail, from invitations to running the party itself.

Par-T-Perfect
Tel: 987-3365
Clowns, face painting, rentals.

Peartree Puppet Theatre
Tel: 734-0537
Scottish puppeteer who entertains kids age four to adult.

Perfect Party Place
Tel: 985-4443
Clowns, magicians, loot bags.

Tickles the Clown and Friends
Tel: 683-3384
Clown.

Play Equipment Rentals

These places rent air-inflated play structures that are delivered to your house and set up. Some of them are small enough to be set up in a large living room, but others require an outside garden. Prices vary widely depending on the structure. If you've got the space for one, they're lots of fun, and kids of all ages love endless amounts of jumping.

Astro Jump Entertainment Services
Tel: 205-5867

Bouncey Castles
Tel: 857-5662

International Creative Entertainment
Tel: 431-0477

It's My Party Shop
Tel: 931-6040

Party Supplies

Balloonery and **The Balloon Shop** sell only balloons (of every style and colour), but all the other places stock a variety of party supplies, from invitations to paper tablecloths. **Bazaar and Novelty** is a particularly good place. It's a huge store full of not only party supplies, but also a great selection of costumes, face paints, masks and other fun things. For party favours, keep in mind the various dollar stores located around town. They have plastic toys, tiny notebooks, pencils, stickers and other fun loot bag items.

The Balloon Shop
2407 Burrard St (at Broadway), **Vancouver**
Tel: 684-0959

Balloonery
991 Marine Dr (at MacKay), **North Vancouver**
Tel: 986-8787

Bazaar and Novelty
215 W. 2nd Ave (at Columbia), **Vancouver**
Tel: 873-5241

The Flying Rhino
3696 W. 8th Ave (at Alma), **Vancouver**
Tel: 738-7447

It's All Fun and Games
1417 Commercial Dr (at Grant), **Vancouver**
Tel: 253-6727

It's My Party Shop
509 Clarke Rd (at Como Lake Ave), **Coquitlam**
Tel: 931-6040

Kaboodles
4449 W. 10th Ave. (at Sasamat), **Vancouver**, 224-5311
1496 Cartwright St, in the Kids Only Market on Granville Island, **Vancouver**, 684-0066

Paper Parade
333 Brooksbank Ave (at Main), in Park and Tilford Centre,
North Vancouver
Tel: 980-5377

The Toybox
3002 W. Broadway (at Carnarvon), **Vancouver**
Tel: 738-4322

WOW Gifts 'N Parties 'N Florals
105 – 14727 108th Ave (at 148th St), **Surrey**
Tel: 589-7849

Places to Have a Birthday Party

The following places, all described elsewhere in this book, offer birthday packages of some sort or are very open to having you host your child's birthday party there. A birthday package refers to a set price that is charged for a set number of kids and includes the use of the facilities, as well as extras like lunch, extra entertainment or a party room. Usually you just bring your own cake. For those who don't want a load of kids in their house (and the cleanup this entails), these places are super.

Indoors

Unless it's the height of summer, indoor places are always a better bet for parties, since it's impossible to know whether it's going to rain or not. Age appropriateness is given for each place, but it's very subjective and depends on your child. When my son turned four, he loved tumbling and romping around at the **Phoenix Gymnastics Club**; on a rainy February day, it was the perfect place for his energy level. Swimming pools are also great places for parties. Even if your child or his friends can't really swim, a place like the **Vancouver Aquatic Centre** has an excellent shallow toddler pool with a lifeguard and a separate party room. **Aquaventures Swim Centre** also has great parties; the pool is deeper but there is plenty of supervision, standing structures in the water, life jackets and other support.

Besides the places listed below, there are a number of other great indoor spots for parties, including bowling lanes, ceramics studios, community centres, family places, indoor rock climbing centres, indoor swimming pools and indoor skating rinks. For these, see the listings "Inside Play," "Sports" and "Organizations and Services."

Adventure Zone and Circuit Circus: indoor playground and arcade (ages 4 to 12)
Aquaventures Swim Centre: indoor pool and party room (ages 3 to 12)
Bonkers: indoor playground (ages 3 to 10)
B.C. Sports Hall of Fame and Museum: interactive museum (ages 7 to 12)
Burnaby Village Museum: carousel (ages 3 to 8)
Crash Crawly's Adventure Fun Centre: indoor playground (ages 3 to 10)
The Gator Pit: indoor playground (ages 3 to 10)
Gymboree: indoor playground (ages 1 to 5)
Hogarth's Sport Chek – The Activity Centre: interactive sports area (ages 7 to 12)

Jolly Genie's Pizza and Play Park: indoor playground (ages 4 to 12)
Kid City: indoor playground (ages 4 to 12)
Lester's Family Amusement Centre: indoor playground (ages 5 to 12)
North Vancouver Museum and Archives: museum (ages 4 to 10)
Omega Gymnastics: gymnastics (ages 1 to 13)
Pacific Space Centre: attraction (ages 5 to 13)
Phoenix Gymnastics Club: gymnastics (ages 3 to 13)
Planet Lazer: laser tag (ages 7 to 13)
Playdium: indoor playground (ages 7 to adult)
Richmond Art Gallery: art activities (ages 3 to 8)
Science World: attraction (ages 5 to 13)
Score-Virtual Sportsworld: interactive sports centre (ages 7 to 13)
Vancouver Aquarium Marine Science Centre: aquarium (ages 5 to 13)
Vancouver Aquatic Centre: toddler pool and party room (3 to 12)

Outdoors

Outdoor areas to have a party include beaches, parks, outdoor swimming pools, riding stables and water parks (see "The Out-of-Doors" and "Sports"). Here are some suggestions, all described elsewhere in this book, that welcome children's parties.

Bear Creek Park Train: miniature train (ages 3 to 9)
Deer Lake Boat Rentals: pedal boats and rowboats (ages 5 to 13)
Greater Vancouver Zoological Centre: zoo (ages 2 to 13)
Maplewood Farm: petting farm (ages 2 to 8)
Playland: amusement park (ages 4 to 10)
Queen's Park Children's Petting Farm: petting farm (ages 2 to 8)
Richmond Go-Kart Track: go-carts (ages 10 and up)
Stanley Park Children's Farmyard and Miniature Railway: train ride and petting farm (ages 3 to 8)
Tsawwassen Paintball Games: paintball (ages 12 and up)

Restaurants

Restaurant parties tend to be better for older kids (it's cruel to make toddlers sit still for long periods), and older kids tend to get a kick out of trendier places such as the **Hard Rock Café** and **Planet Hollywood**. While they don't offer birthday packages, a lot of restaurants are open to family celebrations.

Hard Rock Café (ages 10 and up)
The Old Spaghetti Factory (ages 5 and up)
Planet Hollywood (ages 10 and up)
Romano's Macaroni Grill (ages 7 and up)

Chapter 14

At Your Service

A babysitter for the night? A place that delivers groceries? Someone to clean the bathroom? (I'll take all of the above, please.) Here are places that provide services really important to harried parents – not only babysitters, grocery delivery and maids, but daycares and schools, educational tutors, hair stylists, restaurants that deliver and more. For those who can afford it, any one of these services can be a blessing. For diaper services, see page 208.

Babysitters and Nannies

Finding a good babysitter is one of the hardest things there is; it's difficult to leave your child with a stranger. These licensed services provide childminders and nannies, both temporary and permanent. All are experienced and have been thoroughly screened, which explains why they're so expensive. Babysitters usually cost about $10 per hour, with a four-hour minimum, plus a $10 transportation fee. You can find cheaper babysitters through notices at community centres, neighbourhood houses and family places (see "Organizations and Services," page 213). If they're good, they'll have references you can check out.

For daycares, see below. And if you're a new parent looking for help, see "For Parents of Babies," page 205.

If you're concerned about the price or quality of daycare and want to do something about it, there is an excellent advocacy organization, the **Coalition of Child Care Advocates of B.C.** (709-5661). This organization of volunteers is working together for a non-profit childcare system that is high-quality, affordable, accessible, publicly-funded and accountable.

Canzac Nannies
926-3654
This service provides both babysitting and permanent placements.

Just Like Mum!
325-4225
A friendly outfit that works with some of the major hotels, they provide on-call babysitters or long-term help. I got one of my best babysitters through this agency, who worked for me for four years until she moved away.

Moppet Minders Child and Home Care Services
942-8167
A Coquitlam-based agency that provides both permanent placements and babysitting by the hour.

Nannies and Grannies Placement Agency
688-7767
This is a top-notch agency that provides permanent placements of nannies only.

Optimum Childcare and Nannies
879-2485
This agency provides permanent placements of nannies only.

Daycares

Daycares are places where you can take your child for a full or half day so they can play and interact with other children in a supervised environment. **Information Daycare** (709-5699) is a service of **Westcoast Child Care Resource Centre** (see page 191) and provides referrals to licensed and registered child care programs in Vancouver. They will also give you information on typical costs of daycare, as well as advice on what to look for in a childcare program. For information on childcare in North Vancouver and West Vancouver, call the **North Shore Child Care Resource and Referral Program** (985-2988). For Burnaby and New Westminster, call **Burnaby/New Westminster Child Care Resource and Referral** (294-1109). For childcare in the Richmond area, call **Richmond Connections Child Care Resources and Referral Service** (279-7025). For Surrey, call the **Childcare Support Program** (572-8032).

If you have an infant or preschooler, there are family places and drop-in centres open to caregivers and their children (see page 219). Unfortunately, there is a real lack of drop-in facilities for parents who need emergency daycare. Some family places offer childcare one or two days a week, but it often gets booked up early. Short-term emergency childcare for children from six weeks to six years old is available at YWCA **Crabtree Corner** (101 E. Cordova Street, 689-2808). Seventy-two hours of care per month are allowed. Parents on social assistance get the service free; working parents pay $4.50 per hour per child.

Education

Regarding public school, inquire at the school in your neighbourhood for enrollment procedures. The school boards listed below will tell you which school you should inquire into. Children can enroll in kindergarten if they will turn five by December 31 of the year they want to start kindergarten. Some schools specialize in French or Mandarin immersion, ESL students and students with special needs; for more information, consult your local school board. For more information on B.C. schools, French programs and home schooling, access the website of the B.C. Ministry of Education, Skills & Training at *www.est.gov.bc.ca*.

If you're from outside the country or if English is not your child's first language, visit the **Oakridge Reception and Orientation Centre** at 5445 Baillie Street (at 41st Avenue, 266-8376); they have services in 13 languages.

For information on private schools, consult the *BC Tel Yellow Pages*. If you're looking for specialized classes in art, music and more, see page 197.

If you are home schooling or need parenting resources, check out the **Westcoast Child Care Resource Centre** (709-5661). This is a nonprofit organization that serves as a resource centre to parents and child care providers. Funded largely by the City of Vancouver and the B.C. Ministry for Children and Families, the centre runs a service called **Information Daycare** (see page 190); they also have a comprehensive library that focuses specifically on children and family resources, including parenting books and children's books, in English and other languages. The centre also provides support to family child care providers and to parents who home school, including training and loans of toys and equipment.

An alternative for people who want their children tutored is the **Progressive Learning Centre** at 2050 West 10th Avenue (at Arbutus, 733-4400). This privately-run centre teaches kids from three to nine years old, provides supplementary educational tutoring, and also assists parents who are home schooling their kids. For a listing of other educational tutors, see page 192. For a listing of stores that sell home schooling supplies, see "Shopping," page 158.

In addition to the public school immersion programs, there are dozens of private language schools in Greater Vancouver that teach a variety of languages, including English, French and Mandarin. Unfortunately, they are too numerous to mention and they vary widely by price, style and area; consult the *BC Tel Yellow Pages* for more information. Some of the cultural centres (see page 213), such as the **Goethe Institut**, the **Chinese Cultural Centre** and the **Centre Culturel Francophone de la Colombie-Britannique** (CCFV) either provide or are good links to language classes for children.

There are dozens of private language schools in Greater Vancouver.

So many activities mentioned in this book provide great educational opportunities, from a visit to the **Vancouver Aquarium** (see page 13) to a trip to the UBC **Observatory** to see the stars at night (see page 16). APASE **(Association for the Promotion and Advancement of Science Education** (687-8712) offers free Saturday afternoon science workshops for families with hands-on, discovery-based learning. Both kids and their parent(s) attend; the intention is to bring science into the community and to families. There is also a mentorship component whereby professional scientists and technologists come and work with families. Workshops take place at various elementary schools; call ahead to find out about ones near you.

Finally, another place to keep in mind is **Odin Books**, 1110 West Broadway (at Spruce, 739-8874); they specialize in books relating to psychology, therapy and special needs, with an emphasis on materials relating to attention deficit disorder. This is a great source for resource materials relating to children and families.

Vancouver School Board, 1580 W. Broadway (at Granville), 713-5000
North Vancouver School Board, 721 Chesterfield Ave (at Keith), 903-3444
West Vancouver School Board, 1075 21st St (at Jefferson), 981-1000
Burnaby School Board, 5325 Kincaid St (at Royal Oak), 664-8441
New Westminster School Board, 821 8th St (at 8th Ave), 517-6240
Coquitlam School Board, 550 Poirier St (at King Albert), 939-9201
(for Coquitlam, Port Coquitlam and Port Moody)
Richmond School Board, 7811 Granville Ave (at Minoru Blvd), 668-6000
Surrey School Board, 14225 56th Ave (at 42nd St), 596-7733

Educational Tutors

Everybody needs a little extra help sometimes, and kids are no exception. These places have tutoring in various subjects. Some of it is done at their premises, and in other cases tutors come to your home.

Attention Disorders Neurofeedback Centre
2245 W. Broadway (at Vine), **Vancouver**
Tel: 730-9600
This company specializes in tutoring kids with attention disorders.

British Columbia Tutoring Academy
4549 Hastings St (at Willingdon), **Burnaby**
Tel: 299-2984
They tutor in math, English, ESL, science and reading.

Canadian Tutoring Service
Tel: 983-9009
This service provides in-home tutoring in all levels and subjects throughout Greater Vancouver.

FutureGrads
Tel: 240-6284
Extra tutoring is provided in English, math and science.

The Homework Centre for Academic Achievement
Tel: 467-5519
The focus here is on small-group tutoring in reading, math and ESL. They have locations in Burnaby, Coquitlam and Port Coquitlam.

Kumon Canada
4720 Kingsway (at McKay), in Eaton Centre Metrotown, **Burnaby**
Tel: 454-1001
This top-notch company provides math and reading instruction.

Peak Learning
1107 Homer St. (at Helmcken), **Vancouver**
Tel: 609-7722
This company focuses on accelerated language learning.

Progressive Learning Centre
2050 W. 10th Ave (at Arbutus), **Vancouver**
Tel: 733-4400
Tutoring in all subjects is provided, including ESL, math and writing.

The Reading Foundation
3730 W. Broadway (at Alma), **Vancouver**
Tel: 222-2254
Remedial programs for reading, spelling, comprehension and math.

Sylvan Learning Centre
4255 Arbutus St (at King Edward), in Arbutus Shopping Centre, **Vancouver**,
Tel: 738-7325
3200 E. 54th Ave (at Kerr), in Champlain Mall, **Vancouver**,
Tel: 434-7323
This well-known outfit offers reading, writing and math programs.

Grocery Delivery

The following businesses provide home delivery of groceries, which can be a life-saver when you've got your hands full with kids, you're on foot with a stroller or you have a very full schedule. At some places, you have to shop in person; other businesses allow you to place an order via phone, fax, e-mail or via their website.

If you've run out of ideas for what to cook for dinner, call Recipes to the Rescue's **Dial-A-Menu** at 990-4593 to get menus for Monday-to-Friday meals.

Your three-year-old hasn't eaten green vegetables for five months? You're a nursing mom and don't know if you're getting enough nutrients for you and your baby? Call **Dial-A-Dietitian**. Funded primarily by the B.C. Ministry of Health, as well as the Vancouver Richmond Health Board, this phone line is serviced by volunteer dietitians who are experienced health care providers. Call 732-9191 (in Vancouver) or toll-free 1-800-667-3438 (outside the Vancouver area).

BlueMoon Organics
Tel: 469-3003 or 519-4995

website: *www.bluemoonorganics.com*

Fresh organic food is delivered to Coquitlam, Port Coquitlam, Port Moody and North Burnaby. Boxes of produce are $33.00 with a $20.00 deposit for the container. Customers can make up to two changes to the selection, plus additions can be made.

Canada Safeway

Tel: 1-800-723-3929

Nearly all the Safeways in the Lower Mainland provide a delivery service on certain days. The fee varies depending on the store but is usually no more than a few dollars. Call the number above for the delivery hours and prices of the Safeway closest to you.

Capers

1675 Robson St (at Cardero), **Vancouver**, tel: 687-5288

2285 W. 4th Ave (at Vine), **Vancouver**, tel: 739-6676

2496 Marine Dr (at 25th), **West Vancouver**, tel: 925-3316

A natural foods store with huge selection of grains, breads, fruits and vegetables and more; there is a $3.00 charge for same-day delivery.

Dairyland Home Service

Tel: 421-4663

Home delivery service of dairy products, *plus* everything from bread and bacon to soaps and cleaners. Prices are comparable to corner grocers and the delivery is free. Call for a brochure.

Dial-A-Bottle Services

Tel: 688-0348

Will deliver wine, beer or liquor for the price of the booze plus a $7 delivery charge. Available in the Vancouver area.

EverGreen Organics

Tel: 871-1132

They deliver fresh organic produce; weekly boxes depend on availability. Substitutions can be made.

IGA

2949 Main St (at 10th Ave), **Vancouver**

Tel: 873-8377

This IGA offers free delivery with a minimum $30 order Monday to Saturday. If you shop in the morning, you'll get delivery the same day, though they can't guarantee at what time. There is a $3 charge for orders of less than $30. Numerous IGAs in the Lower Mainland provide this service as well. Times and prices vary; call the head office at 421-4242 to find out the store closest to you.

Organics To You
Tel: 473-5001
They deliver fresh organic fruits and vegetables. There is a refundable deposit on the bin and weekly delivery dates; call for a brochure. It's pricey, but they offer a good selection of produce, suitable for a small family. They often have bread and eggs available as well.

Stong's Market
4560 Dunbar (at 30th Ave), **Vancouver**
Tel: 266-5191
Fax: 266-5199
Website: *www.stongs.com*
For a $10 charge, you can shop for groceries Monday to Friday by phone, fax, website or e-mail (cori_bonina@bc.sympatico.ca) . The website gives a listing of the store's products; you can simply click off what you want. In many areas, if orders are received before 11:00 a.m., delivery is made the same day. Service extends from Steveston and Surrey to Lions Bay. Customers who shop in the store can get their groceries delivered for $1.50.

Super Valu
1255 Davie St (at Bute), **Vancouver**
Tel: 688-0911
This is a 24-hour supermarket with delivery service Monday to Saturday from 9:00 a.m. to 6:00 p.m. There is a $5 delivery fee; orders must be over $25.

Hair Stylists

There are lots of hair stylists in the Lower Mainland, but the ones below not only concentrate specifically on kids, they also make getting a haircut a fun experience, with colourful decorations and toys, kids' videos, lollipops or cute chairs to sit in. This might sound excessive unless you've got a kid who absolutely hates having their hair cut, when these places are a godsend. The stylists at these places are really used to kids and nothing seems to surprise them; they give good, quick haircuts. Prices vary widely depending on the place, but expect to spend at least $15 to $20. Also popular are barber shops, no-nonsense places that give decent boys' haircuts, usually for less than $10. A word of warning: when you go to a barber, don't say you want your son's hair short unless you want it *short*. My son ended up with a buzz cut that way.

The Hairloft
1496 Cartwright St, in the Kids Only Market on Granville Island, **Vancouver**
Tel: 684-6177

Kid's Kut Land
2624B St. John's St (at Grant), **Port Moody**
Tel: 937-7455

2 Cute 4 U Children's Hair Care
1433 Bellevue Ave (at 15th St), **West Vancouver**
Tel: 926-4345

Maid Services

I love maid services (and wish I could afford one; these places tend to be about 50 bucks a pop). Although you can find maid services advertised at community centres, these ones offer employees who are bonded and insured – good if you're concerned about your valuables. For childcare providers who also do light housekeeping, see "Parents of Babies," page 206.

Miss Molly House Cleaning Services

Vancouver	730-2700
North Shore	985-5643
Tri-Cities	945-1033
Richmond	273-5420
Surrey	582-7888

Molly Maid

Vancouver	734-7260
North Shore	987-4112
Burnaby and New Westminster	433-6634
Tri-Cities	469-2015
Richmond	241-8466
Surrey	534-9697

Summit Maid Services
Tel: 291-1001

The Three Houseketeers
Tel: 899-8625

Restaurants That Deliver

Takeout Taxi delivers food from a wide number of restaurants for a nominal charge. Call 451-4491 to get a brochure with full menu listings of the restaurants closest to you. See "Where to Eat with Kids," page 109, for a list of restaurants that cater to kids. Of these, **Tio Pepe's**, **Thai House** and the **Robson Street Hon's Wun-Tun House** all deliver. Aside from that, if you live somewhere long enough, delivery menus will start appearing on your doorstep, or collect them from local restaurants when you go out.

Chapter 15

Classes
in the Arts

One of the best ways to encourage creativity in children is through art classes – drawing, ballet, learning a musical instrument or acting out a part in a play. Creating art is also an excellent method of self-expression and helps build confidence and self-esteem. The arts are great for younger kids in this respect, but high school kids also really benefit from classes in which they're *interested*. Not only do art classes inspire creativity and confidence in teens, but parents know their kids are actively involved with a healthy, motivated peer group. My only piece of advice here is never to push a child into a lesson they don't want to take; it's a recipe for disaster. While it's good to encourage kids, they should be the ones who express an interest. Luckily, the arts classes offered these days are quite different from those given when I was a kid; a lot more care seems to be put into the selection of teachers and the appropriateness of the material, and classes nowadays seem to be *fun*. (Isn't that what this activity is supposed to be all about?)

Vancouver has so many wonderful schools that cater specifically to kids; this is a city where art is respected and encouraged in its youth. Many classes are geared toward to kids as young as five, and there are even classes for two- and three-year-olds. Prices vary widely depending on the age of the child and the length of the class; it's best to call each establishment for a schedule. In addition to the list given here, bear in mind that community centres offer lessons in a wide variety of areas and their prices are usually quite reasonable. For a list of community centres, see page 214. For sports-related lessons, including gymnastics, ice skating, martial arts, horseback riding, sailing, skiing, tennis and yoga, see "Sports," page 73. For academic classes and tutors, see "At Your Service," page 192.

Visual Arts

These companies offer everything from drawing to web page design. Call for their brochures to get specific information as to class times and age levels. A non-class activity to keep in mind is ceramic painting; see page 97.

Art Therapy
1645 W. 5th Ave (at Pine), **Vancouver**
Tel: 733-9221
Both caregivers and their kids aged four to eight are welcome to their art and storytelling sessions.

Arts Umbrella
1286 Cartwright St, on Granville Island, **Vancouver**
Tel: 681-5268
This company's reputation for its visual and performing arts classes for kids aged two to 19 is excellent; they offer theatre, film, painting, sculpture, architecture, animation, dance and more.

Bodwell Multimedia School
640 W. Pender St (at Seymour), **Vancouver**
Tel: 602-7600
Classes in 3-D modelling, animation and graphics and CD-ROM and web page design are given for kids aged eight and up.

Place des Arts
1120 Brunette Ave (at Marmont), **Coquitlam**
Tel: 664-1636
A well-respected school offering painting, drawing, cartooning, graphic design and more, for ages four and up.

Richmond Arts Centre
7700 Minoru Gate (at Granville), **Richmond**
Tel: 231-6429 or 231-6457
Their classes range from clay exploration for three-year-olds to cartooning, painting and pottery for the older set.

Shadbolt Centre for the Arts
6450 Deer Lake Ave (at Canada Way), in Deer Lake Park, **Burnaby**
Tel: 291-6864
Well-respected centre with classes in painting, drawing, sculpture and lots more; ages vary depending on class.

Surrey Arts Centre
13750 88th Ave (at King George Hwy), **Surrey**
Tel: 501-5566
Classes in drawing, painting, clay, stencils, mixed media and more; ages four and up.

Vanarts
837 Beatty St (at Robson), **Vancouver**
Tel: 682-2787
This high-tech facility offers drawing instruction and computer animation training for ages 13 and up.

Dance

Like the other arts, dance is a great way to encourage creativity, and to develop body confidence and poise. Ballet, jazz and tap are popular with all ages; teens particularly favour hip-hop and modern dance. Several of the facilities listed under Visual Arts also offer dance classes. These include **Arts Umbrella** (see page 198), **Place des Arts** (see page 198), the **Richmond Arts Centre** (jazz and ballet from age three to teen; see page 198), and the **Shadbolt Centre for the Arts** (creative dance, jazz, tap, ballet and modern dance for ages three and up; see above). Bear in mind that if your child gets interested in dance, the lessons can get expensive as time goes by and, as well, you'll need to buy dance costumes (see page 167 for a list of shops). But if you can afford it, you'll never regret it.

Boswell Dance Academy
303 3rd Ave (at 2nd St), **New Westminster**
Tel: 522-4424
Classes in classical ballet, jazz and modern dance are offered for ages four and up.

Caulfield School of Dance
2813 Spring St (at Moody), **Port Moody**
Tel: 469-9366
Ballet, jazz, tap and more is offered for ages four and up.

Centro Flamenco
3398 Dunbar St (at 18th Ave), **Vancouver**
Tel: 737-1273
An innovative school offering flamenco classes for ages six and up.

Dance Co.
4255 Arbutus St (at King Edward Ave), in Arbutus Shopping Centre, **Vancouver**
Tel: 736-3394
A top-notch company offering jazz, tap, ballet, modern, hip-hop, musical theatre, flamenco and more for ages three and up; there are competitions and year-end performances.

Goh Ballet Academy
2345 Main St (at 8th Ave), **Vancouver**
Tel: 872-4014
Ballet, jazz, character and Chinese dance are offered for preschool ages and up.

Anne Gordon Ballet School
286 Pemberton Ave (at Marine Dr), **North Vancouver**
Tel: 988-5811
Ballet only is offered for preschool ages and up.

JCC Performing Arts School
950 W. 41st Ave (at Oak), **Vancouver**
Tel: 257-5111, extension 203
The Jewish Community Centre offers excellent classes in ballet, jazz, hip-hop and tap and theatre (plus lots of other types of classes) for preschoolers to adults.

Lorita Leung Dance Association
2268 No. 5 Rd (at Bridgeport), **Richmond**
Tel: 279-2306
Ages four and up can take lesson in classical, minority, fold, ballet and Chinese ballet.

North Shore Academy of Dancing
1819 Capilano Rd (at Upper Levels Hwy), **North Vancouver**
Tel: 987-3814
Ballet, tap and more are offered for ages three and up.

Pacific Ballet Theatre School
456 W. Broadway (at Cambie), **Vancouver**
Tel: 873-5024
Ballet and jazz are offered for ages three and up.

Paul Latta Dance Studios
Tel: 533- 2315, **Surrey**
Tap, jazz and modern dance classes, as well as Polynesian dance, are offered for kids ages three and up.

Spotlight Dance Centre
6637 Hastings St (at Sperling), **Burnaby**
Tel: 299-6111
Ballet, jazz, tap and modern dance classes are offered, as well as classes in musical theatre for ages three and up.

Vanleena Dance Academy
1152 Welch St (at Pemberton), **North Vancouver**
Tel: 983-2623
Ballet, jazz, tap, hip-hop and musical theatre are offered to kids as young as two.

Anna Wyman School of Dance Arts
1457 Marine Dr (at 15th St), **West Vancouver**
Tel: 926-6535
Lessons in ballet, jazz, contemporary, musical theatre, flamenco and more for
preschool ages and up.

Music

Even if they missed out on Mozart in utero, it's never too late to introduce children to the pleasure of making music. Studies have shown that learning music
helps kids concentrate better and makes them feel better about themselves, while
it also helps them develop an appreciation of music as a whole. Some studies also
show that music helps children with the skills necessary for learning math and
science. Music lessons are offered for kids as young as three, with a few exceptions. **JCC Performing Arts School** (see page 200) and **Place des Arts** (see page
199) also offer music lessons. For further referrals, contact the **B.C. Registered
Music Teachers Association** (733-5531).

Allegro Music School
5481 Mackie St (at 37th Ave), **Vancouver**
Tel: 327-7765
Both in-home or studio lessons are offered in singing as well as in numerous
instruments, ranging from piano to violin to drums.

British Columbia Boys Choir
Tel: 322-5240
This is a well-respected choral music education program with various perfor-
mances throughout the year.

British Columbia Conservatory of Music
4549 Hastings St (at Willingdon), **Burnaby**
Tel: 299-2984
A well-respected music school registered with the B.C. Ministry of Education
offering lessons in voice and most instruments.

City Academy of Musical Arts
555 W. 12th Ave (at Cambie), at Dorset College in City Square Mall,
Vancouver, Tel: 872-8820
1393 Austin Ave (at Gatensbury), **Coquitlam**, Tel: 872-8820
Voice and instrumental lessons are offered, including lessons at the preschool
level. The academy also has a string orchestra and flute choir.

Coquitlam Music
2819 Shaughnessy St (at Lougheed Hwy), **Port Coquitlam**
Tel: 942-9312
Voice and instrumental lessons are offered.

Grace Notes Drum School
1632 W. 4th Ave (at Fir), **Vancouver**
Tel: 730-9493
Both drum set and hand drumming classes are given to kids of all ages.

Main Music School
4331 Quebec St, near 27th Ave and Main, **Vancouver**
Tel: 872-2485
European-trained teachers give lessons in piano, guitar, organ, theory and voice to students aged five to adult.

Mount Royal Music
5280 Minoru Blvd (at Alderbridge Way), **Richmond**
Tel: 273-0436
Voice and instrumental lessons are given; this is a government-registered private postsecondary educational institution.

Music for Young Children
Tel: 1-800-828-4334
Lessons are specifically geared to younger kids, with piano and singing for kids age three to nine.

Richmond Community Music School
11371 No. 3 Rd (at Steveston Hwy), **Richmond**
Tel: 272-5227
A nonprofit music school offering voice and instrumental lessons.

Vancouver Academy of Music
1270 Chestnut St (at Whyte), **Vancouver**
Tel: 734-2301
All instruments are taught, including band and orchestra; classes in voice and ballet are also given.

Vancouver Adapted Music Society
770 Pacific Blvd, at the foot of Cambie Bridge in the Plaza of Nations, **Vancouver**
Tel: 688-6464
This society offers children's programs for the physically challenged.

Vancouver Youth Band
206 – 6715 Burlington Ave (at Imperial), **Burnaby**
Tel: 430-3120
This children's band performs at various venues throughout the year.

Vancouver Youth Symphony Orchestra Society
3214 W. 10th Ave (at Trutch), **Vancouver**
Tel: 737-0714
This society provides orchestral experience to ages seven to 23, with intensive coaching. There are also concert performances.

Performing Arts

If your child wants to be an actor or performer, there are some very cool opportunities for them in Vancouver. Of particular note are the **Young Shakespeareans Summer Workshops**, **Be Scene**, **Carousel Theatre Company & School**, **CirKids** and **Vancouver Youth Theatre**, all of which offer innovative, inspiring theatrical opportunities for children. **Arts Umbrella** (see page 198) and the **JCC Performing Arts School** (see page 200) also offer classes in the performing arts. Kids who learn to be comfortable performing in front of an audience are bound to carry that with them through life. If you want to get your child into television or movie acting, contact **Global Model & Talent Agency** (685-8842) in Vancouver; they represent children.

Most of us put photos of our babies and children into drawers or shoe boxes, but here's a better option. **Scrapbook Warehouse** (266-4433), at 8932 Oak Street, has workshops that help you make scrapbooks of your kids' photos and other memorabilia; construction materials are provided.

Bard on the Beach, Young Shakespeareans Summer Workshops

Ogden Ave (at Chestnut St), in Vanier Park, **Vancouver**
Tel: 737-0625

In conjunction with the long-running summer theatre company, this two-week program enables kids to create an abridged version of a Shakespearean play. Book early, as it's popular.

Be Scene

280 E. Cordova St (at Gore), in the Firehall Arts Centre, **Vancouver**
Tel: 689-0926

An annual competition for actors around 12 and up, Be Scene also provides a showcase for talent, giving young actors the opportunity to have their audition videotaped and critiqued by professional directors.

Carousel Theatre Company & School

1411 Cartwright St, on Granville Island, **Vancouver**
Tel: 669-3410

Vancouver's oldest theatre school; professional actors and directors teach classes here.

Cirkids

1820 Trafalgar St (at 2nd Ave), **Vancouver**
Tel: 737-7408

This noncompetitive program is based on circus arts and teaches skills such as acrobatics, juggling, clowning and tightrope walking.

The Gateway Theatre

6500 Gilbert Rd (at Westminster Hwy), **Richmond**
Tel: 270-6500

Musical theatre, dance and acting are taught here.

Tarlington Training
525 Seymour St (at Pender), **Vancouver**
Tel: 664-0315
Acting for film and television are taught here.

Theatrix Youtheatre Society
Tel: 939-6992, **Tri-Cities**
Theatrix focuses on theatre for kids aged three to 16.

Vancouver Film School Acting Studio
510 Seymour St, downtown, **Vancouver**
Tel: 685-5808
Acting workshops are given for ages six and up.

Vancouver Youth Theatre
Tel: 877-0678
Kids and teens turn their *own* ideas into theatre here; programs take place in Vancouver, the North Shore, Burnaby and Surrey.

c h a p t e r   1 6

For Parents
of Babies

Every parent needs a little help from time to time, but new parents are particularly overwhelmed by the care of a little one. The first half of this chapter is devoted to services for new parents, including all types of pregnancy support, from prenatal classes to breastfeeding support to postpartum depression counselling, as well as diaper services and exercise classes. For babysitting and nanny services, see "At Your Service," page 189. For places to meet other parents of young children in a relaxed atmosphere, see under Family Places, Drop-Ins and Resources, in "Organizations and Services," page 219. The second half of this chapter is a guide to where to shop for your little one. This is the place to turn to for shops that sell clothing, accessories, equipment, furniture, rentals, breastfeeding supplies, diapers and maternity clothing.

Pregnancy Support and Prenatal and Postnatal Care

Many support services for parents (other than those listed here), such as counselling services, crisis centres and family services, as well as health units (which offer child health clinics, parent groups, breastfeeding drop-in centres and more) are located in "Emergency, Medical and Other Resources," page 229.

B.C. Women's Hospital and Health Centre
4500 Oak St (at 33rd Ave), **Vancouver**
Tel: 875-2383
This health centre provides prenatal and postnatal care, prenatal classes, breastfeeding support, counselling and help for women with financial or social difficulties.

Burnaby General Hospital
3935 Kincaid St, east of Boundary Rd, south of Canada Way, **Burnaby**
Tel: 434-4211
This hospital offers prenatal classes.

Crisis Pregnancy Centres
Tel: 731-1122, **Vancouver**
Tel: 525-0999, **Burnaby** and **New Westminster**
Tel: 939-2633, **Coquitlam**
Tel: 596-3611, **Surrey**
These centres provide options in counselling, testing, education, prenatal help and more.

Douglas College Prenatal Program
Tel: 527-5476
Prenatal classes are given in New Westminster, Coquitlam and Port Coquitlam.

Doula Services Association
Tel: 527-5335, then press 2
They provide referrals to doulas, women who are labour support persons.

Drake Medox Health Services
Tel: 682-2801
They provide postpartum depression counselling, plus doulas for baby care, breastfeeding support, meal preparation and light housekeeping.

Facts of Life Line
Tel: 731-4252, then press 8
This confidential, toll-free telephone service gives information and referrals on sexuality and reproductive health concerns.

The Greater Vancouver Childbirth Education Association
Tel: 437-9968
This association offers prenatal classes.

The Healthiest Babies Possible
10256 154th St (at 104th Ave), **Surrey**
Tel: 583-1017
This pregnancy outreach program offers pregnancy support and nutrition coun-selling, as well as a lunch program.

Kwantlen College
Tel: 599-2570
Prenatal classes are offered by this college in Richmond and Surrey.

La Leche League
Tel: 736-3244
Support and breastfeeding information are given; this is an excellent organiza-tion run by volunteers and a great resource for nursing moms.

Lower Mainland Childbearing Society
Tel: 882-9192
Prenatal classes are offered at various locations.

Heather Martin
Tel: 733-2121
Experienced midwife, childbirth educator and yoga teacher; classes held in Vancouver.

Midwives Association of B.C. (MABC)
1675 W. 8th Ave (at Fir)
Tel: 736-5976
This association provides a list of midwives who practice in your area.

Mother Nurture
Tel: 462-8169 or 462-0984
They provide in-home postpartum care, support with breastfeeding, baby care, sibling care and light housework.

Newborn Hotline
Tel: 737-3737
This is a telephone service for new parents in Vancouver, Richmond and Burnaby.

North Shore Maternity Care Hot Line
Tel: 984-3813
This is a 24-hour line for parents of babies under four weeks old, for residents of North Vancouver, West Vancouver, Lions Bay and Bowen Island.

Pacific Post-Partum Support Society (PPSS)
1416 Commercial Dr (at Grant), **Vancouver**
Tel: 255-7999
They offer confidential help with postpartum depression, including support groups, counselling and information packs.

Planned Parenthood Association of B.C.
Tel: 731-4252
They offer a variety of family planning services; offices all over the Lower Mainland.

Pregnancy Yoga with Janice Clarfield
Tel: 739-6664
Couples yoga workshops for birth preparation.

Richmond General Hospital
7000 Westminster Hwy (at Gilbert), **Richmond**
Tel: 278-9711
This hospital holds prenatal classes.

Sheway Project
449 E. Hastings St (at Dunlevy), **Vancouver**
Tel: 254-9951
This is a pregnancy outreach program for Vancouver women trying to get off alcohol and drugs; the facility offers prenatal care and counselling, a drop-in centre, daily hot lunch, clothing and food donations.

St. Paul's Hospital
1081 Burrard St (at Helmcken), **Vancouver**
Tel: 682-2344
This hospital holds prenatal classes.

Surrey Memorial Hospital
13750 96th Ave (at King George Hwy), **Surrey**
Tel: 581-2211
Prenatal classes are held here.

The Vancouver Breastfeeding Centre
690 W. 11th Ave (at Ash), **Vancouver**
Tel: 875-4678
They provide assistance with breastfeeding difficulties.

Vancouver Health Services
Tel: 877-4673 or 267-2690 (English) or 215-3900 (Cantonese)
They provide prenatal care, support and classes.

Diaper Services and Stores

Having a cloth diaper service is the best choice for the environment and the service is actually cheaper than buying disposable diapers. The first place listed provides diapers, dirty diaper pick-up and clean diaper delivery; the other three establishments sell cloth diapers (that you wash yourself), diaper covers, wipes and other baby items.

Diapers Naturally Cotton Diaper Service
Tel: 682-8860 (Vancouver) or 980-7167 (North Vancouver)

Absolutely Diapers
2110 W. 4th Ave (at Arbutus), Tel: 737-0603, **Vancouver**
1099 Marine Dr (at Lloyd), Tel: 990-5880, **North Vancouver**

Discount Diapers
3031 Beckman Pl (at Bridgeport), **Richmond**
Tel: 278-5223

TC Kidco
6851 Elmbridge Way (at Gilbert), **Richmond**
Tel: 276-2004

Exercise Classes

The organizations listed here have exercise classes, but be sure to check at your community centre as well (see page 214); they often schedule exercise programs for moms and moms-to-be.

The Fitness Group
3507 W. 4th Ave (at Collingwood), **Vancouver**
Tel: 738-4169
They provide some of the area's best prenatal and postnatal exercise classes, with good childcare available. Like all fitness centres, they require that you buy a membership.

Mom & Me Network
Tel: 922-0415
Classes in aerobics, weights, stretch and relaxation; babysitting available.

Baby Supplies

The shops listed here stock nearly everything you'll need for a baby; stores that specialize in particular areas are indicated. Many other stores also supply baby needs, however, so be sure to check out "Shopping for Kids." Page 148 has children's clothing consignment shops, most of which carry baby clothing and accessories. Page 140 has new clothing shops, most of which also sell baby items. Page 162 has places to get furnishings; good spots for baby supplies are **Friendly Bears**, **Soothers Kids Boutique** and **Kid's Furniture World**; **T.J.'s The Kiddies Store** has a great supply of baby products and furnishings. See also under Toys in the same chapter (page 152); many carry baby rattles and other infant development toys. Both **T.J.'s The Kiddies Store** and **Toy Traders** (page 153) rent baby equipment, such as car seats, playpens, strollers and more. **Absolutely Diapers**, listed under Diaper Services and Stores (page 208), also sells feeding systems, infant clothing and other environmentally-friendly products in addition to cloth diapers.

For information or advice regarding the correct use of infant or child car seats, call the **Infant/Child Car Seat Information Line** (298-2122.)

Bobbit's for Kids
2951A W. 4th Ave (at Bayswater), **Vancouver**
Tel: 738-0333
Kids up to age three are catered to here; clothing, baby toys, bibs, etc.

Camelot Kids
1496 Cartwright St, in the Kids Only Market on Granville Island, **Vancouver**
Tel: 688-9766
They specialize in toys and products for infant and early childhood development; their high-quality selection comes from all around the world.

Cribs & Carriages
1849 Lonsdale Ave (at 18th St), **North Vancouver**
Tel: 988-2742
They buy, sell and rent good-quality used furniture and equipment.

Kiddie Proofers
Tel: 536-5437 (Vancouver, Burnaby, Richmond, Surrey)
or 922-2273 (North Vancouver and West Vancouver)
They sell and install baby-proofing supplies.

Breastfeeding Supplies
In addition to these stores, **Absolutely Diapers** (page 209), **Bobbit's for Kids** (page 209) and **Room for Two Maternity Apparel** (page 211) sell breastfeeding supplies.

Mom's Pumps and Videos Rental
3333 Regent St (at 29th St), **North Vancouver**
Tel: 980-0562

Mother's Komfort Breast Feeding & Pump Supplies
Tel: 572-5545

Maternity Clothing and Accessories — New
Luckily over the years maternity clothing has gotten more fashionable, and now is more than an oversized T-shirt or a dress with a big bow. The following stores carry a variety of outfits, from casual to urban, suiting a wide variety of styles. The owners of **Hazel & Co. Maternity & Kids** (page 141 in "Shopping for Kids") have excellent taste in both their maternity and children's clothing: they have a wide range of maternity wear, from office to casual to evening wear, including some really nice cotton leggings and shirts.

Benetton
650 W. 41st Ave (at Cambie), in Oakridge Centre, **Vancouver**
Tel: 266-1135
They carry a small line of maternity outfits in the Benetton style: simple, clean, fashionable.

Boomers & Echoes
1709 Lonsdale (at 17th Ave), **North Vancouver**
Tel: 984-6163
Besides a good selection of new maternity wear, this enormous store carries children's clothing and furniture, both new and used.

Formes
2985 Granville St (at 14th Ave), **Vancouver**
Tel: 733-2213
This Paris-based shop carries easily the loveliest, most stylish maternity clothing
I've ever seen (but at prices to match).

Maternal Instinct
3673 W. 4th Ave (at Alma), **Vancouver**
Tel: 738-8300
Their specialty is urban maternity clothing: suits, blouses, slacks.

Room For Two Maternity Apparel
1409 Commercial Dr (at Kitchener), **Vancouver**
Tel: 255-0508
They have really reasonable prices for their maternity clothing and also carry
some used items.

Shirley K. Thyme Maternity
700 W. Georgia St (at Howe), in Pacific Centre, **Vancouver**,
Tel: 689-9481
4700 Kingsway (at McKay), in Eaton Centre Metrotown, **Burnaby**,
Tel: 430-6821
9855 Austin Rd (at North Rd), in Lougheed Mall, **Burnaby**,
Tel: 420-7661
2929 Barnet Hwy (at Pinetree Way) in Coquitlam Centre), **Coquitlam**,
Tel: 464-6238
6060 Minoru Blvd (at Westminster Hwy), in the North Mall of Richmond
Centre, **Richmond**, Tel: 278-6544
1388 Guildford Town Centre (at 104th Ave) in Guildford Town Centre, **Surrey**,
Tel: 584-1122
This chain sells both casual and office wear at reasonable prices.

Maternity Clothing and Accessories — Secondhand

Be sure to consider buying secondhand maternity clothing if money is a con-
cern. Consignment shops in Vancouver are usually quite good and only sell merchandise in clean, good condition. Most children's clothing consignment shops
(see "Shopping for Kids," page 148) carry maternity items as well. **Puddleduck
Lane** (page 149), on the Westside, has a good selection and **Fit 4 A Queen &
Moms-To-Be**, in New Westminster, is worth checking out (page 150).

   Boomers & Echoes (page 150) and **Room For Two Maternity Apparel**
(see above) sell both new and used maternity clothing. The consignment shop
Encore Fashion Boutique (922-2020), at 2445 Marine Drive (at 24th Street)
in West Vancouver, also has a selection of maternity wear.

c h a p t e r   1 7

Organizations and Services

Vancouver has a rich supply of community services for families, from classes and workshops to libraries to places to get support or just to hang out with other parents. This chapter includes a comprehensive list of community and recreation centres, family places and drop-ins, libraries, neighbourhood houses and organizations for kids such as **Girl Guides** and the **Boys' and Girls' Club**. Community centres and libraries are arranged alphabetically within municipality. For services such as babysitting, maid services and delivery services, see "At Your Service." Youth Centres are drop-in centres where teenage kids can hang out, visit with one another and participate in the various programs offered by the centre, such as sports and dances, job clubs, girls' groups and more. For more information, contact your local community centre (see page 214); they can guide you to the youth centre closest to you.

There are numerous cultural centres located in Greater Vancouver, which are good sources for various cultural communities, providing resources, classes and information of all sorts. Some of the bigger ones include the **Centre Culturel Francophone de la Colombie-Britannique** (CCFV), 1551 W. 7th Avenue at Fir

(736-9806), which has a children's book and videotape library, art classes, Saturday-morning storytimes and other French-language programs for kids. The **Chinese Cultural Centre of Vancouver**, 555 Columbia Street at Pender (687-0282) has classes and art exhibitions relating to Chinese culture; the **Jewish Community Centre**, 950 W. 41st Avenue at Oak (257-5111), has social, recreational, educational and cultural programs for all age groups. Also keep in mind the **Goethe Institut**, the **Italian Cultural Centre**, the **Russian Cultural Centre** and the **Richmond Chinese Cultural Centre Society**. For more information, check out the website *www.culturalexpress.com* for listings of multicultural centres, societies and events.

Community and Recreation Centres

Community centres are the first place to go if you're looking for a class or service in your community. Highly reflective of the needs of their local community, centres vary in the services they offer, which, depending on the centre, include classes and workshops for both adults and kids, ice skating rinks, swimming pools, fitness centres, preschools and day cares, as well as many family- and kid-oriented events. Recreation guides are usually published four times a year and are available at each community centre and local libraries. As well, many communities centres publish a schedule each season of the programs and events they offer; these are usually available at the front desk of the centre.

Vancouver

Details of community centres, including facilities and classes, can be found in the *Vancouver East Recreation Guide* or *Vancouver West Area Recreation Guide*, available at any of the centres below and at libraries.

Britannia Community Centre
1661 Napier St (at Commercial)
Tel: 253-4391

Carnegie Centre
401 Main St (at Hastings)
Tel: 665-2220

Champlain Heights Community Centre
3350 Maquinna Dr (at Champlain)
Tel: 437-9115

Douglas Park Community Centre
810 West 22nd Ave (at Heather)
Tel: 257-8130

Dunbar Community Centre
4747 Dunbar St (at 33rd Ave)
Tel: 222-6060

False Creek Community Centre
1318 Cartwright St, on Granville Island
Tel: 257-8195

Hastings Community Centre
3096 E. Hastings St (at Renfrew)
Tel: 718-6222

Kensington Community Centre
5175 Dumfries St (at 18th Ave)
Tel: 718-6200

Kerrisdale Community Centre
5851 West Blvd (at 41st Ave)
Tel: 257-8100

Killarney Community Centre
6260 Killarney St (at 49th Ave)
Tel: 434-9167

Kitsilano War Memorial Community Centre
2690 Larch St (at 10th Ave)
Tel: 257-6976

Marpole–Oakridge Community Centre
990 W. 59th Ave (at Oak)
Tel: 257-8180

Mount Pleasant Community Centre
3161 Ontario St (at 16th Ave)
Tel: 713-1888

Ray-Cam Co-Operative Centre
920 E. Hastings St (at Clark)
Tel: 257-6949

Renfrew Park Community Centre
2929 E. 22nd Ave (at Rupert)
Tel: 257-8388

Riley Park Community Centre
50 E. 30th Ave (at Main)
Tel: 257-8545

Roundhouse Community Arts and Recreation Centre
181 Roundhouse Mews (at Pacific)
Tel: 713-1800

Strathcona Community Centre
601 Keefer St (at Princess)
Tel: 713-1838

Sunset Community Centre
404 E. 51st Ave (at Main)
Tel: 718-6505

Thunderbird Neighbourhood Community Centre
2311 Cassiar St (at Broadway)
Tel: 713-1818

Trout Lake Community Centre
3350 Victoria Dr (at 19th Ave)
Tel: 257-6955

West End Community Centre
870 Denman St (at Barclay)
Tel: 257-8333

West Point Grey Community Centre at Aberthau
4397 W. 2nd Ave (at Trimble)
Tel: 257-8140

North Shore

Get schedule information from the *Leisure Activities Guide*, available at all North Vancouver recreation centres, or the *Leisure Guide*, available at all West Vancouver recreation centres.

Delbrook recCentre
660 W. Queens Rd (at Westview), **North Vancouver**
Tel: 987-7529

Eagle Harbour Community Centre
5575 Marine Dr (at Gallagher), **West Vancouver**
Tel: 921-2100

Karen Magnussen recCentre
2300 Kirkstone Pl (at Lynn Valley), **North Vancouver**
Tel: 987-7529

Lonsdale Recreation Centre
123 E. 23rd St (at Lonsdale), **North Vancouver**
Tel: 987-7529

Lynn Valley recCentre
3590 Mountain Hwy (at Lynn Valley), **North Vancouver**
Tel: 987-7529

Park Gate Community Centre
3625 Banff Court (at Mount Seymour Rd), **North Vancouver**
Tel: 929-7981

Ron Andrews recCentre
931 Lytton St (at Mount Seymour Pkwy), **North Vancouver**
Tel: 987-7529

Seycove Community Centre
1204 Caledonia Ave (at Strathcona), **North Vancouver**
Tel: 929-7981

Seylynn recCentre
605 Mountain Hwy (at Keith), **North Vancouver**
Tel: 987-7529

West Vancouver Community Centre
780 22nd St (at Marine Dr), **West Vancouver**
Tel: 925-7270

William Griffin recCentre
851 W. Queens Rd (at Westview), **North Vancouver**
Tel: 987-7529

Burnaby

Details for these centres are in the *Burnaby Parks and Recreation Leisure Guide*, available at Burnaby community centres and libraries.

Bonsor Recreation Complex
6550 Bonsor Ave (at Central)
Tel: 439-1860

Burnaby South Fitness and Leisure Center
5455 Rumble (at MacPherson)
Tel: 439-1860

Cameron Recreation Centre
9523 Cameron St (at Bartlett)
Tel: 421-5225

Eastburn Community Centre
7435 Edmonds St (at Kingsway)
Tel: 525-5361

Eilleen Dailly Leisure Pool and Fitness Centre
240 Willingdon Ave (at Triumph)
Tel: 298-7946

Kensington Recreation Office
6159 Curtis St (at Fell)
Tel: 299-8354

Willingdon Heights Community Centre
1491 Carleton Ave (at Grant)
Tel: 299-1446

New Westminster

Get schedules and information from the *Active Living Guide* or *Family Matters* brochures, available at New Westminster community centres.

Centennial Community Centre and Fitness New West
65 E. 6th Ave (at McBride)
Tel: 526-2751

Queen's Park Arenex
1st St (at 3rd Ave)
Tel: 525-0485

Queensborough Community Centre
920 Ewen Ave (at Lawrence)
Tel: 525-7388

Tri-Cities
Coquitlam, Port Coquitlam and Port Moody all put out their own Recreation Guides, available at the community centres as well as local libraries.

Hyde Creek Centre
1379 Laurier Ave (at Regina), **Port Coquitlam**
Tel: 927-7946

Kyle Centre
125 Kyle St (at St Johns), **Port Moody**
Tel: 469-4561

Old Orchard Hall
6444 Bentley Rd (at Ioco), **Port Moody**
Tel: 469-4555

Pinetree Community Centre
1260 Pinetree Way (at Guildford Way), **Coquitlam**
Tel: 927-6960

Port Coquitlam Recreation Centre
2150 Wilson Ave (at Kingsway), **Port Coquitlam**
Tel: 927-7933

Social Recreation Centre
630 Poirier St (at Foster), **Coquitlam**
Tel: 933-6010

Town Centre Recreation Centre
1290 Pinetree Way (at Guildford Way), **Coquitlam**
Tel: 927-6960

Richmond
The *Richmond Leisure Guide* is available at all community centres and libraries.

Cambie Community Centre
4111 Jacombs Rd (at Cambie)
Tel: 273-3394

City Centre-Lang Community Centre
8279 Saba Rd (at Frontage)
Tel: 214-7716

Hamilton Community Centre
5140 Smith Dr (at Gilley)
Tel: 524-0631

Sea Island Community Centre
7140 Miller Rd (at Aylmer)
Tel: 278-5820

218

South Arm Community Centre
8880 Williams Rd (at No. 3 Rd)
Tel: 277-1157

Steveston Community Centre
4111 Moncton St (at No. 1 Rd)
Tel: 277-6812

Thompson Community Centre
5151 Granville Ave (at Railway)
Tel: 272-5338

West Richmond Community Centre
9180 No. 1 Rd (at Francis)
Tel: 277-9812

Surrey

The *Surrey Leisure Guide* is available at all community centres and libraries.

Cloverdale Recreation Services
6220 184th St (at 64th Ave)
Tel: 502-6400

Fleetwood Recreation Services
15996 84th Ave (at Fraser Hwy)
Tel: 501-5030

Guildford Recreation Services
15105 105th Ave (at 152nd St)
Tel: 502-6360

Newton Recreation Services
7120 136B St (at King George Hwy)
Tel: 501-5040

North Surrey Recreation Services
10275 135th St (at Old Yale)
Tel: 502-6300

South Surrey Recreation Services
2199 148th St (at 24th Ave)
Tel: 502-6200

Whalley Recreation Services
10665 135th St (at 108th Ave)
Tel: 502-6340

Family Places, Drop-Ins and Resources

There are numerous family resource programs in and around Vancouver available for families wanting general support as well as those experiencing difficulties. Most of the programs focus on parents and their young children (ages newborn to six), but some programs are open to all caregivers. Services include counselling, parent education, drop-in programs, community kitchens, prenatal

219

programs, crisis intervention, childcare options, children's workshops, parent support groups and toy and resource libraries. Each centre listed here reflects the needs of the community, so services vary, but the focus is on the promotion of family well-being. The most up-to-date information on family places, drop-in programs and neighbourhood houses can be found by contacting either **Family Services of Greater Vancouver** at 731-4951 (Vancouver), 874-2938 (East Vancouver), 279-7100 (Richmond), 525-9144 (New Westminster) or **Family Services of the North Shore** (988-5281). Many community centres have parent and toddler/infant groups that run off and on throughout the year; see the list of community centres in this chapter. Other good sources of community support are neighbourhood houses (see page 221). For more support services for families, see "Emergency, Medical and Other Resources."

Burnaby Family Place
410 Clare Ave (at Hastings), **Burnaby**
Tel: 299-5112

Collingwood Neighbourhood House Family Place
5288 Joyce St (at VanNess), **Vancouver**
Tel: 435-0323

East Burnaby Family Place
9528 Erickson Dr (at Bartlett), **Burnaby**
Tel: 444-1090

Eastside Family Place
1661 Napier St (at Commercial), **Vancouver**
Tel: 255-9841
Website: *www.vcn.bc.ca/eastside*

Hastings Family Centre
3096 E. Hastings St (at Lillooet), **Vancouver**
Tel: 718-6222

Kinder House
819 Chesterfield Ave (at Keith), **North Vancouver**
Tel: 990-9401

Marpole-Oakridge Family Place
1305 W. 70th Ave (at Oak), **Vancouver**
Tel: 263-1405

Mount Pleasant Family Centre
2910 St George St (at Kingsway), **Vancouver**
Tel: 872-6757

New Westminster Family Place
611 Agnes St (at 6th St), **New Westminster**
Tel: 520-3666

Park Gate Community Centre
3625 Banff Court (at Mount Seymour Rd.), **North Vancouver**
Tel: 929-7981

Richmond Family Place
6560 Gilbert Rd (at Granville), **Richmond**
Tel: 278-4336

South Vancouver Family Place
2295 East 61st Ave (at Nanaimo), **Vancouver**
Tel: 325-5213

Sunrise Family Drop-In
1931 Windermere St (at 4th Ave), **Vancouver**
Tel: 251-2913

Surrey Family Place
10310 154th St (at 152nd St), **Surrey**
Tel: 583-3844

Touchstone Family Association
6411 Buswell St (at Cook), **Richmond**
Tel: 279-5599

Tri-City Family Place
3435 Victoria Dr (at Cedar), **Coquitlam**
Tel: 945-0048

West Coast Energy Children's Centre
2151 Lonsdale Ave (at 22nd St), **North Vancouver**
Tel: 986-9311

West Side Family Place
2819 W. 11th Ave (at MacDonald), **Vancouver**
Tel: 738-2819

Neighbourhood Houses

Neighbourhood houses focus on providing programs and services to enhance family and neighbourhood life throughout Greater Vancouver. Services vary by community, but range from drop-ins and day camps to support groups, immigrant services and immunization clinics. Programs reflect a variety of races, religions, cultures, abilities, economic levels and sexual orientations. For more information, contact the **Association of Neighbourhood Houses of Greater Vancouver** (875-9111).

Cedar Cottage Neighbourhood House
4065 Victoria Dr (at Kingsway), **Vancouver**
Tel: 874-4231

Collingwood Neighbourhood House
5288 Joyce St (at VanNess), **Vancouver**
Tel: 435-0323

221

Frog Hollow Neighbourhood House
2131 Renfrew St (at 6th Ave), **Vancouver**
Tel: 251-1225

Gordon Neighbourhood House
1019 Broughton St (at Pendrell), **Vancouver**
Tel: 683-2554

Kitsilano Neighbourhood House
2325 W. 7th Ave (at Vine), **Vancouver**
Tel: 736-3588

Kiwassa Neighbourhood House
2425 Oxford St (at Nanaimo), **Vancouver**
Tel: 254-5401

Little Mountain Neighbourhood House
3981 Main St (at King Edward), **Vancouver**
Tel: 879-7104

Mount Pleasant Neighbourhood House
800 E. Broadway (at Fraser), **Vancouver**
Tel: 879-8208

North Shore Neighbourhood House
225 E. 2nd St (at Lonsdale), **North Vancouver**
Tel: 987-8138

South Vancouver Neighbourhood House
6470 Victoria Dr (at 49th Ave), **Vancouver**
Tel: 324-6212

Step-By-Step Child Development Society
101F-508 Clarke Rd (at Como Lake), **Coquitlam**
Tel: 939-7436

Libraries

If you're looking for storytelling events, keep in mind that they take place all over the city, including the libraries listed below. Many bookstores, including the UBC **Bookstore** and **Kidsbooks,** have children's readings; see "Shopping for Kids," page 160. The **Dr. Sun Yat-Sen Classical Chinese Garden** has afternoon storytelling in the garden on summer afternoons; see page 47 for more information. Also be sure to check out the daily *Vancouver Sun* or the *Georgia Straight,* which comes out on Thursdays, storytelling events are often listed.

Libraries in the Lower Mainland vary in their size and selection of children's materials, but many have not only books but magazines, compact discs, audio-cassettes, materials in languages other than English and more. Kids can even obtain their own library card and there are no late fees for children's books taken out on these cards. For information on events and other library-related information, access *http://www.vpl.vancouver.bc.ca* or call **The Events Line** (331-3602). Library hours vary from one branch to another, so be sure to call ahead.

Vancouver

Central Library
350 W. Georgia St (at Homer)
Tel: 331-3600 (main information line) or 331-3660 (children's library)

Britannia Branch
1661 Napier St (at Commercial)
Tel: 665-2222

Carnegie Reading Room
401 Main St (at Hastings)
Tel: 665-3010

Champlain Heights Branch
3200 E. 54th Ave (at Kerr)
Tel: 665-3955

Collingwood Branch
2985 Kingsway (at Rupert)
Tel: 665-3953

Dunbar Branch
4515 Dunbar St (at 30th Ave)
Tel: 665-3968

Firehall Library
1455 W. 10th Ave (at Hemlock)
Tel: 665-3970

Fraserview Branch
1950 Argyle Dr (at Victoria)
Tel: 665-3957

Hastings Branch
2674 E. Hastings St (at Penticton)
Tel: 665-3959

Joe Fortes Branch
870 Denman St (at Robson)
Tel: 665-3972

Kensington Branch
3972 Knight St (at King Edward)
Tel: 665-3961

Kerrisdale Branch
2112 W. 42nd Ave (at West Blvd)
Tel: 665-3974

Kitsilano Branch
2425 MacDonald St (at Broadway)
Tel: 665-3976

Marpole Branch
8386 Granville St (at 67th Ave)
Tel: 665-3978

Mount Pleasant Branch
370 E. Broadway (at Main)
Tel: 665-3962

Oakridge Branch
650 W. 41st Ave (at Cambie), in Oakridge Centre
Tel: 665-3980

Renfrew Branch
2969 E. 22nd Ave (at Renfrew)
Tel: 257-8705

Riley Park Branch
3981 Main St (at King Edward)
Tel: 665-3964

South Hill Branch
6076 Fraser St (at 45th Ave)
Tel: 665-3965

Strathcona Community Library
592 E. Pender St (at Jackson)
Tel: 665-3967

West Point Grey Branch
4480 W. 10th Ave (at Trimble)
Tel: 665-3982

North Shore

Capilano Branch
3045 Highland Blvd (at Edgemont), **North Vancouver**
Tel: 987-4471

Lynn Valley Main Library
1280 E. 27th St (at Lynn Valley), **North Vancouver**
Tel: 984-0286

North Vancouver City Library
121 W. 14th St (at Lonsdale), **North Vancouver**
Tel: 980-0581

Parkgate Branch
3675 Banff Court (at Mount Seymour), **North Vancouver**
Tel: 929-3727

West Vancouver Memorial Library
1950 Marine Dr (at 19th St), **West Vancouver**
Tel: 925-7400

Burnaby
Cameron Branch
9523 Cameron St (at North Rd)
Tel: 421-5454

Kingsway Branch
7252 Kingsway (at Edmonds)
Tel: 522-3971

McGill Branch
4595 Albert St (at Willingdon)
Tel: 299-8955

Bob Prittie Metrotown Branch
6100 Willingdon Ave (at Kingsway)
Tel: 436-5400

New Westminster
New Westminster Public Library
716 6th Ave (at 6th St)
Tel: 527-4660

Tri-Cities
City Centre Branch
3001 Burlington Dr (at Glen), **Coquitlam**
Tel: 927-3561

Poirier Branch
575 Poirier St (at Foster), **Coquitlam**
Tel: 931-2416

Port Moody Public Library
100 Newport Dr (at Ioco), **Port Moody**
Tel: 469-4575

Terry Fox Library
2470 Mary Hill Rd (at Wilson), **Port Coquitlam**
Tel: 927-7999

Richmond
Brighouse–Main Branch
7700 Minoru Gate (at Granville Ave)
Tel: 231-6401

Steveston Branch
4111 Moncton St (at No. 1 Rd)
Tel: 274-2012

Surrey
Cloverdale Library
5642 176A St (at 60th Ave)

Tel: 576-1384

Fleetwood Library
15996 84th Ave (at 156th St)
Tel: 572-5922

Guildford Library
15105 105th Ave (at 152nd St)
Tel: 585-5015

Newton Library
13795 70th Ave (at King George Hwy)
Tel: 596-7401

Ocean Park Library
12854 17th Ave (at 128th St)
Tel: 531-5044

Port Kells Library
18885 88th Ave (at 192nd St)
Tel: 882-0733

Whalley Library
10347 135th St (at 108th Ave)
Tel: 588-5951

Organizations for kids

If your child has a great interest in nature or animals or you simply want them to become involved in a healthy peer group, you may be interested in one of the organizations listed here. For musical groups such as the **B.C. Boys' Choir** and other arts-oriented associations, see "Classes in the Arts," page 197. For support groups like **Big Brothers of Greater Vancouver** or the **Gifted Children's Association of B.C.**, see "Emergency, Medical and Other Resources," page 229.

Boys' and Girls' Club of Greater Vancouver
Tel: 879-6554
There are numerous branches of this club all over Vancouver and its environs; they focus on programs and summer camps for underprivileged kids.

Girl Guides of Canada
Tel: 734-4877
This association for five- to 18-year-old girls focuses on leadership and community skills.

Junior Achievement of British Columbia
Tel: 688-3887
This is a nonprofit business educational organization for young people.

Junior Forest Wardens Association of B.C.
Tel: 685-7788
Outdoor-oriented programs are developed for kids six to 18 to help them understand and appreciate the natural environment.

LIFE – Leadership Initiative for Earth
Tel: 687-5558
This association hosts nature expeditions and learning adventures for kids to help them become active in the development of an ecologically sustainable society.

Outward Bound Western Canada
Tel: 737-3093
This non-profit organization has mountaineering adventures for kids age 15 and up, with a focus on personal growth.

Scouts Canada
Tel: 879-5721 (Vancouver office)
Similar to Girl Guides in its focus, this association is for five- to 26-year-old boys.

Sierra Club Lower Mainland Group
Tel: 915-9600
The Sierra Club puts on a variety of hikes and nature-oriented programs throughout the year, many of which are open to families.

SPCA Youth Program
Tel: 599-PAWS (7297)
The SPCA puts on a variety of programs and summer camps for kids who love animals; open to a variety of age groups.

YMCA of Greater Vancouver
Tel: 681-9622

YWCA of Greater Vancouver
Tel: 895-5800

c h a p t e r   1 8

Emergency, Medical and Other Resources

Here you'll find everything from basic emergency numbers for an ambulance or poison control to crisis centres and a variety of support services. When an emergency happens, it's a relief to know that there are professionals trained to handle such things. You'll feel even more confident if you yourself (as a parent) or your kids have had some first aid training. One group that offers courses in emergency first aid and CPR is **St. John Ambulance** (321-2651). Vancouver firefighters also offer instruction in CPR (call 822-8283). Contact your community centre (see page 214) for other classes.

In case of an emergency, the main number to know (and to teach your kids) is **911** (for fire, police or ambulance). The number for the **Poison Control Centre** is 682-5050. Visitors, see the "Introduction," page xii.

For a comprehensive list of services, consult *The Red Book: Directory of Services for the Lower Mainland,* published by Information Services Vancouver, and *The Red Book Online,* accessible via Information Services' web site at *www.vcn.bc.ca/isv/*

Crisis Centres and Helplines

If someone you know is being abused, has a drug problem, needs food or is experiencing a serious crisis, call one of the following numbers. This is by no means a comprehensive list of emergency and support services available to parents. There are many more crisis centres and support groups available to people who are referred through the Ministry for Children and Families. For more information on these and other programs, consult the list of support services that appears later in this chapter. For support for pregnant women and new parents, see "For Parents of Babies," page 205.

Alcohol and Drug Information and Referral Service
Tel: 660-9382
A 24-hour help line. Information and referral specialists respond to enquiries on all aspects of alcohol and drug abuse.

Battered Women's Support Services
Tel: 687-1867
A free service providing phone counselling and referrals.

B.C. Parents in Crisis Society
Tel: 669-1616 or 1-800-665-6880
This is a free, confidential service to help parents cope more effectively with children.

Child and Youth Advocate
Tel: 871-6032
They provide referrals for help and information to youths in any type of crisis.

Children Who Witness Abuse
Tel: 951-0688 or 572-7411
A Surrey-based group for children who need help and counselling concerning abuse that they have either experienced or witnessed.

Chimo Crisis Services
Tel: 278-8283 (Cantonese), 279-8882 (Mandarin), 279-7070 (English)
This is a crisis line for Chinese families.

Covenant House Vancouver
Tel: 1-800-999-9999
This is a crisis intervention centre for homeless and runaway kids ages 16 to 24 that offers food, shelter, clothing and counselling.

Crisis Centre
Tel: 872-3311
This 24-hour line provides help with emotional distress and suicide prevention.

Crisis Pregnancy Centre
Tel: 731-1122
A confidential service for women who require pregnancy-related help.

Dusk to Dawn
Tel: 688-0399
This teen shelter at St. Paul's Hospital, 1056 Comox Street at Thurlow, provides food and a place to stay.

Family Services of Greater Vancouver
Vancouver, 731-4951
East Vancouver, 874-2938
Richmond, 279-7100
New Westminster, 525-9144
Various branches of Family Services provide support services, counselling, street youth services, youth detox, incest and sexual abuse counselling, parent-teen mediation and more. Services are available in multiple languages.

Family Services of the North Shore
Tel: 988-5281
Support services similar to those listed above.

Greater Vancouver Food Bank Society
Vancouver, **Burnaby**, the **North Shore** and **New Westminster**, 876-3601
Richmond, 271-5609
Surrey, 581-5443
They also have a line for single parents (463-6767).

Helpline for Children
Tel: Dial "0," ask for Zenith 1234
To report child abuse or neglect.

Kids Help Phone
Tel: 1-800-668-6868
Free, anonymous counselling and referral available 24 hours.

Lawyer Referral Service
Tel: 687-3221
Referrals to lawyers familiar with child protection. There is a consultation fee of $10 per half hour.

Native Courtworkers and Counselling Association of B.C.
Tel: 687-0281
Legal information and advice for abused women of aboriginal ancestry.

Option Services to Community Society
Tel: 596-4321
This Surrey-based society operates two transition houses for abused women and their kids. They also offer counselling for abused women.

PACE 2 (Parents and Children for Education and Employment)
Tel: 254-2223
Career education and training for income-assisted Eastside parents is offered here.

Port Coquitlam Area Women's Centre Society
Tel: 941-6311
This society runs a transition house and also offers counselling and a drop-in centre for women in the Tri-Cities area.

Rape Crisis Centre
Tel: 255-6344
This is a 24-hour line run by Women Against Violence Against Women.

Rape Relief and Women's Shelter
Tel: 872-8212
A number to call for immediate help, counselling and a safe place to go.

Stop the Violence, Face the Music (STV) Society
Tel: 1-800-647-STOP (1-800-647-7867)
This society provides free, confidential counselling to kids and parents who are dealing with violence and gives kids healthy alternatives to deal with their problems.

Vancouver-Richmond Incest and Sexual Abuse Centre (VISAC)
Tel: 874-2938
They provide help to people who are experiencing, or have experienced, incest and abuse.

Victims Information Line
Tel: 1-800-563-0808
A province-wide, toll-free service that provides information and assistance to victims of crime.

Violence Prevention Information Line
Tel: 1-888-606-LIVE (1-888-606-5483)
A province-wide, toll-free information and referral service for people who want to contribute to the prevention of violence in society.

Women's Resource Centre Richmond
Tel: 279-7060
Single mothers' support, babysitting exchange and other help.

Youth Action Centre
342 E. Hastings St (at Gore)
Tel: 602-9747
This is a place for street youth to go for three meals a day, clean showers, laundry facilities, food bank services, lockers, mailboxes, recreational activities and advocacy referral services. It's run by the Downtown Eastside Youth Activities Society.

YouthCo
Tel: 688-1441
Support and fun for HIV-positive youth ages 15 to 30.

Youth Crisis Hotline
Tel: 1-800-448-4663
Counselling and referrals for teens in crisis.

Support Services

Here you'll find a variety of support services, including information and referral services and societies for parents and children facing challenges ranging from learning disabilities to alcohol or drug problems. They may also provide help in areas such as job training and immmigrant support. Community centres (page 214) often provide a variety of support services and can be an excellent place to turn to. See also Education under "At Your Service" (page 191) for language classes and home schooling, and "Organizations and Services" (page 213) for the names of some cultural centres and groups that often offer community-based support.

Al-Anon-Alateen Family Groups
Tel: 688-1716
For teenagers and parents with alchohol problems.

Attention Disorders Neurofeedback Centre
Tel: 730-9600
Provides effective training methods to overcome the symptoms of ADD.

Autism Society of BC
Tel: 434-0880
Support services for parents of autistic children.

Big Brothers of Greater Vancouver
Tel: 876-2447
This service organization matches up young fatherless boys with young men who can provide them with guidance and companionship.

Big Sisters of B.C. Lower Mainland
Tel: 873-4525
Like Big Brothers, except for girls and women.

B.C. Council for Families
Tel: 660-0675
Clearinghouse for information about family programs and resources.

B.C./Yukon Society of Transition Houses
Tel: 669-6943
A nonprofit association that offers transition houses (first- and second-stage), safe homes and other home-placement services to battered women and their children.

Burnaby Information and Community Services Society
Tel: 299-5778
This society offers referrals for, and help with, community services and organizations.

Canadian Parents for French
Tel: 254-0134
An advocacy group promoting the learning of French.

Cancer Support Groups
Tel: 877-6000, local 2194
A main reference number for referrals to cancer support groups.

C.H.A.D.D. (Children and Adults with Attention Deficit Disorders)
Tel: 271-9285
They provide support for children and adults with attention deficit disorder.

Facts of Life Line
Tel: 731-4252, then press "8"
This toll-free, confidential telephone service provides information and referrals on sexuality and reproductive-health concerns.

Family Support Institute
Tel: 875-1119
Information, referrals, training and networking for families of people with disabilities.

FAS Support Network
Tel: 589-1854
Support for parents and caregivers of children with FAS (Fetal Alcohol Syndrome).

Fathers' Support Group
Tel: 526-9015
A self-help group for fathers going through child custody issues.

Gab Youth Services Program
Tel: 684-4901
For lesbian, gay, transgendered, bisexual and questioning youth.

Gifted Children's Association of B.C.
Tel: 736-2705
This association helps develop awareness of and support for gifted and talented children. It offers parent support groups and telephone counselling and has multiple offices.

Immigrant Services Society of B.C.
Tel: 684-7498
Help for new immigrants. Multiple languages spoken.

Infant Development Programmes of B.C.
Tel: 822-4014
For families with children from birth to three years who are at risk for developmental problems or have developmental delay. Services include home visits, support, education and assessments.

Information Children
Tel: 291-3548
A parenting resource centre that offers workshops, a telephone helpline and more.

Information Services Vancouver
Tel: 875-6431 or 875-6381 (information and referrals), 875-0885 (information and referrals for deaf and hard-of-hearing callers)
Web sites: *informbc@vcn.bc.ca* or *www.vcn.bc.ca/isv*
This organization provides free and confidential information and referral services to British Columbians. They maintain a resources database and library on community services, and they publish *The Red Book: Directory of Services for the Lower Mainland.* ISV can provide assistance and referrals in many different areas for both parents and their children (other ISV services are listed throughout this section).

Jewish Family Service Agency
Tel: 257-5151
Provides counselling and therapy.

Kidsafe
Tel: 469-4965
Informs and educates families about sexual abuse and ways to talk to children. Workshops offered.

Learning Disabilities Association of B.C.
Tel: 873-8139
Support group for parents of kids with learning disabilities.

Nisha Family and Children Services Society
Tel: 412-7950
Family counselling program in Vancouver for families experiencing conflict.

Pacific Coast Family Therapy Training Association
3021 Arbutus St (at 15th Ave), **Vancouver**
Tel: 736-3664
Services include parenting workshops and a daycare for kids with learning disabilities.

Parents Without Partners
Tel: 945-2407
Support services, community events and dances for single parents.

Queerlings East Side Youth Group
Tel: 718-5800
East Side group for gay, lesbian and transgendered youth from 16 to 26.

Richmond Connections Caregivers Support Program
Tel: 279-7034
A nonprofit program that offers caregivers education, emotional support and referrals to appropriate resources.

Richmond Connections Information and Volunteer Society
Tel: 279-7020
A nonprofit, charitable organization that brings people and services together through volunteerism and the dissemination of community information. They offer a number of programs and services, including community referrals, a caregivers' support program (see listing above), a child care resource and referral service (see page 190) and leadership programs for young adults.

Society for Children and Youth of B.C.
Tel: 433-4180
A nonprofit, voluntary organization that provides information to increase the understanding and knowledge of all types of child abuse.

Society of Special Needs Adoptive Parents (SNAP)
Tel: 687-3114
Services for parents who have adopted children with special needs.

Support to Parents of Young Children
Tel: 583-3852
Surrey-based parent-support program with parenting classes and in-home support.

Surrey-Delta Immigrant Services Society
Tel: 597-0205
This society provides counselling for immigrant families. Multiple languages are spoken.

Surrey Family Centre
Tel: 584-5811
They have a variety of community support programs, such as a family support outreach program that sends a professional into a family's home to work with parents on parenting issues such as discipline and nutrition.

Surrey Parks and Recreation Outreach and Support Services
Tel: 502-6321
Provides information on community clubs and organizations, as well as to immigrants, people new to the area and people with special needs.

Vancouver and Lower Mainland Multicultural Family Support Services Society
Tel: 436-1025
A service organization for immigrant and visible minority women (and their families), who are experiencing domestic violence. Services are provided in numerous languages.

Vancouver Multicultural Society of B.C.
Tel: 731-4648
This is a nonprofit umbrella society comprised of about 130 different cultural groups, associations and immigrant-servicing societies. They provide referrals to various groups and also conduct special events and public education activities on multiculturism, anti-racism and human rights.

Western Society for Children with Birth Disorders
515-0810
This society's goal is to help children with birth disorders realize their full potential. They provide assistance, care and information in areas such as special medical equipment, academic competence, medical resources and emotional support.

Youth Options B.C.
Tel: 1-800-784-0055
Website: *www.youth.gov.bc.ca*
This information centre is a government-sponsored organization providing information to teens on jobs, training and education.

Youthquest! Lesbian and Gay Youth Society of B.C.
Tel: 944-6293
This is a social support and educational advocacy agency serving queer youth. Drop-in centres are located around the Lower Mainland; for a list of centres, along with their drop-in times, call 688-WEST (9378), ext. 2065.

Hospitals

Please note that callers cannot get emergency medical information over the phone. Call your general practitioner (even after hours) to get their emergency number. If you don't have a GP and require medical attention, go to the emergency department of your nearest hospital or call an ambulance (dial 911) if you can't get there yourself.

Vancouver
British Columbia Children's Hospital
4480 Oak St (at 30th Ave)
Tel: 875-2345

British Columbia's Women's Hospital and Health Centre
4500 Oak St (at 30th Ave)
Tel: 875-2424 or 875-3750

St. Paul's Hospital
1081 Burrard St (at Helmcken)
Tel: 682-2344

University Hospital
2211 Wesbrook Mall, south of University Blvd on the UBC campus
Tel: 822-7121

Vancouver General Hospital and Health Science Centre
855 W. 12th Ave (at Oak)
Tel: 875-4111

North Shore
Lions Gate Hospital
231 E. 15th St, east of Lonsdale, **North Vancouver**
Tel: 988-3131

Burnaby
Burnaby General Hospital
3935 Kincaid St, east of Boundary, south of Canada Way
Tel: 434-4211

New Westminster
Royal Columbian Hospital
330 E. Columbia St, south of Braid
Tel: 520-4253

Tri-Cities
Eagle Ridge Hospital
475 Guildford Way (near Ungless), **Port Moody**
Tel: 461-2022

Richmond
Richmond General Hospital
7000 Westminster Hwy (at Gilbert)
Tel: 278-9711

Surrey
Surrey Memorial Hospital
13750 96th Ave (at King George Hwy)
Tel: 581-2211

24-Hour Pharmacies
Shoppers Drug Mart
1125 Davie St (at Thurlow), **Vancouver**, 669-2424
2302 W. 4th Ave (at Vine), **Vancouver**, 738-3138

Super Valu
1255 Davie St (at Jervis), **Vancouver**, 688-0911
7155 Kingsway (at Salisbury), **Burnaby**, 526-7632

Health Units
Health units offer a variety of services, including child health and immunization clinics, breastfeeding drop-ins and parent groups. Services vary, so call ahead to find out what each unit offers.

Vancouver
Burrard/West End Health Unit
1770 W. 7th Ave (at Pine)
Tel: 736-9844

East Unit
2610 Victoria Dr (at 11th Ave)
Tel: 872-251

North Unit
1651 Commercial Dr (at 1st Ave)
Tel: 253-3575

South Unit
6405 Knight St (at 49th Ave)
Tel: 321-6151

West-Main Unit
2110 W. 43rd Ave (at E. Blvd)
Tel: 261-6366

North Shore
North Shore Health Unit
171 W. Esplanade St (at Lonsdale), **North Vancouver**
Tel: 983-6700

Burnaby
Burnaby Health Unit
4946 Canada Way (at Ledger)
Tel: 918-7605

New Westminster
New Westminster Health Unit
537 Carnarvon St (at 6th St)
Tel: 525-3661

Tri-Cities
Coquitlam Health Unit
644 Poirier St (at Foster), **Coquitlam**
Tel: 937-4000

Port Coquitlam Health Unit
2266 Wilson Ave (at Shaughnessy), **Port Coquitlam**
Tel: 941-3451

Port Moody Health Unit
221 Ioco Rd (at Murray), **Port Moody**
Tel: 461-2705

Richmond
Richmond Health Unit
7000 Westminster Hwy (at Gilbert)
Tel: 276-4050

Surrey
Surrey Health Unit
14265 56th Ave (at 144th St)
Tel: 572-2600

Other Medical Resources

There are walk-in clinics all over Vancouver. To find out the one closest to you, call the **City of Vancouver Health Services** (736-2033). To obtain a list of doctors accepting patients, call the **College of Physicians and Surgeons of B.C.**, at 733-7758.

Some alternative health care services, such as homeopathic, naturopathic, chiropractic and massage therapy, are partially or fully covered by the **Medical Services Plan of B.C.** (MSP). To find out what's covered, call the college at 733-7758. For names of naturopaths, call the **B.C. Naturopathic Association** at 736-6646. For a list of Chinese practitioners, call the **Traditional Chinese Medicine Association of B.C.** at 602-9603.

For names of pediatric dentists, call the **College of Dental Surgeons of B.C.** at 736-3621. For kids under 19 who are in a low-income family, contact the **Healthy Kids Program** at 1-800-748-1144.

Chapter 19

Calendar of Events

Here, arranged by month, is a guide to annual events that occur in the Lower Mainland. Small community events, ever-changing and too numerous to mention here, are listed in community centre schedules and programs. (See page 214 for a listing of community centres.)

Artists in our Midst, a series of events where you can walk through artists' studios, is good for older kids. This series takes place periodically in different parts of the Greater Vancouver area; check the newspapers to keep track of them. I've also included a few events that are out of the area covered by this book, simply because they're such big and noteworthy ones.

Summer events and other seasonal performances are also listed in "Live Entertainment" (see page 53). Also be sure to check out *B.C. Parent*, *Westcoast Families* and the *Georgia Straight*, good sources of up-to-date information on local events and happenings, particularly those at museums and other attractions. These are all free publications; the first two come out monthly, the *Straight* every Thursday. The Thursday edition of the *Vancouver Sun* also has a section that lists things to do over the weekend with kids. Both *B.C. Parent* and

Westcoast Families also do an annual rundown of summer camps, usually in their May issues. Many of the events listed here are advertised widely in advance, but do not have permanent contact information or fixed annual dates and times. If this information is not in the description, a note suggests that you check the publications mentioned in this introduction to get current information.

As well as the seasonal events noted in this calendar, events are usually planned for statutory holidays (and the "long" weekends that often result from them). Check the newspapers for information on events planned in the city. As well as spring, summer and Christmas breaks, statutory holidays mean a day off school for kids. In B.C. the statutory holidays are as follows:

New Year's Day ....Fixed, on January 1
Good Friday ....Floats, in March or April
Easter Monday ....Floats, in March or April
Victoria Day...............................Floats, first Monday following April 23
Canada Day ....Fixed, on July 1
B.C. Day...............................Floats, first Monday in August
Labour Day...............................Floats, first Monday in September
Thanksgiving...............................Floats, second Monday in October
Remembrance Day...............................Fixed, on November 11
Christmas Day ....Fixed, on December 25
Boxing Day ....Fixed, on December 26

January
Polar Bear Swim
English Bay, at Denman and Beach, **Vancouver**
Tel: 732-3204
A free yearly New Year's Day event in which bold Vancouverites, some in flashy costumes, dash into the cold waters of English Bay in the West End. It's fun for kids to watch adults being silly.

Penguin Plunge
Panorama Park, end of Gallant off Deep Cove Rd, **North Vancouver**
This is the same kind of event as the Polar Bear Swim, taking place in Deep Cove.

Chinese New Year
Festival Hotline: 687-6021
Celebrations take place all over the city between late January and early February. Most notable is the parade in Chinatown and the celebration in the Plaza of Nations.

February
Women in View Festival
Tel: 685-6684
A showcase of work by women, ranging from dance to storytelling to music and more, held at different venues in Vancouver. Some of the work is suitable for kids.

242

March

Easter Egg Hunts
Hunts are held all over the Lower Mainland, such as the **Historic Stewart Farm**, various community centres and the **Vancouver Aquarium**. Check publications mentioned in introduction.

Hyack Antique Car Easter Parade
Queen's Park, at 1st St and 3rd Ave, **New Westminster**
This parade happens on Easter Sunday.

Festival du Bois
Blue Mountain Park, at King Albert and Blue Mountain, **Coquitlam**
Tel: 936-0039
This festival features traditional French-Canadian entertainment and food.

Spring Break Theatre Festival
Granville Island, **Vancouver**
Tel: 669-0631
This Granville Island event features three to four kid-friendly shows daily, including performances by theatre companies such as **Axis Theatre**, Carousel Theatre, **Green Thumb Theatre**, **Hooked on Books** and the **Vancouver Theatresports League**.

April

Playland
In PNE exhibition grounds, E. Hastings, west of Cassiar, **Vancouver**
This amusement park has rides for all ages and a midway for the older crowd. It's open each summer. Check publications mentioned in introduction.

Baisaki
Sikh Temple, 8000 Ross (at S.E. Marine Dr), **Vancouver**
Tel: 324-2010
The birth of Sikhism is celebrated in this festival, a parade with costumes and floats.

International Earth Day
Events occur all over the Lower Mainland on April 22 in recognition of our planet. Check publications mentioned in introduction.

Vancouver Sun Run
Tel: 689-9441
Vancouver's biggest run, it's a great spectator sport that takes place downtown, with a mini-Sun Run of 1.5 km (1 mile) that's perfect for those under 12.

SuperCities Walk
Tel: 689-3144
This long-standing walk supports multiple sclerosis.

May

Cedar Cottage Community Carnival
Cedar Cottage Neighbourhood House, 4065 Victoria Dr (at Kingsway),
Vancouver
Tel: 874-4231
This annual kids' carnival has a dunk tank, face painting, garage sale, ethnic
lunch and bake sale.

CityFest
Vancouver Community College King Edward Campus, 1155 E. Broadway (at
Clark), **Vancouver**
Tel: 922-5084
This annual performing arts festival is free and features performers from different cultural groups.

The Great Canadian Pet Fair
Plaza of Nations, 750 Pacific Blvd S. (at Stadium Rd E.) **Vancouver**
Tel: 682-0777
An annual pet fair with kids' place, petting farm, crafts, face painting, pony
rides, police dog demonstrations and more.

Hyack Festival
Tel: 522-6894
Website: *www.arc.bc.ca/hyack.index.html*
New Westminster's annual festival with a May Day celebration, parade, fireworks and other events.

Celebrate the Colour of Children
Queensborough Community Centre, 920 Ewen Ave (at Lawrence), **New
Westminster**
Tel: 591-7200
An annual event, with a focus on African and Caribbean culture, featuring products, services, music, face painting, hair braiding and more.

Granville Island Bluegrass Festival
Tel: 931-7194
Two-week festival of performances with free weekend concerts.

Music West
Tel: 684-9338
Several days of music at various venues, ranging from folk to hip-hop. Older
kids like the international skateboarding event held at the Plaza of Nations in
Vancouver.

Partnership Walk
Lumberman's Arch, at Stanley Park, **Vancouver**
Tel: 986-0075
Barbecue lunch, live band, children's centre with face painting, games and activities. A 15-year-old tradition, this walk around the seawall is put on to raise funds
for projects in Asia and Africa and to raise awareness of international development.

244

Sheep Fair
Maplewood Farm, 405 Seymour River Pl (at Mount Seymour Pkwy), **North Vancouver**
Tel: 929-5610
An annual sheep-shearing event, with activities and games.

Cloverdale Rodeo and Exhibition
6050 176th St (at 60th Ave), **Cloverdale**
Tel: 576-946
A huge rodeo that happens on the Victoria Day long weekend. The 150 acres of family-oriented entertainment includes a trade show, safety fair, arts and crafts, live entertainment and agricultural and horticultural exhibits, as well as traditional rodeo events.

Vancouver International Children's Festival
Vanier Park, at the foot of Chestnut St, **Vancouver**
Tel: 687-7697
A huge festival with children's performers and events over a week-long period. International music, dance, theatre, storytelling and arts and crafts.

Vancouver Rape Relief & Women's Shelter Walkathon & Picnic
Stanley Park, **Vancouver**
Tel: 879-9989 or 872-8212
An annual event with proceeds going to the shelter. Participants walk or cycle around the seawall; a picnic lunch is provided and childcare is available.

June

Fraser River Festival
Deas Island, off Hwy 99, south of **Richmond**
Tel: 432-6350
A GVRD-hosted event, this festival celebrates the river with scenic boat rides, live music, interactive entertainment and storytelling.

Oceans Day Family Festival
Whytecliff Park
Off Marine Dr., west of Horseshoe Bay, **West Vancouver**
Tel: 925-7219
Hosted by the West Vancouver Parks and Recreation Department, this festival celebrates the ocean. There are bins of marine life for kids to look at and a Canadian Coastguard hovercraft which comes up to the beach.

Alcan Dragon Boat Festival
Plaza of Nations, False Creek, behind B.C. Place Stadium, **Vancouver**
Tel: 688-2382
Music and dance performances, as well as dragon boat racing, are featured at this festival.

du Maurier International Jazz Festival.
Tel: 682-0706
Performances by over 1,000 musicians at venues in and around Vancouver. This event is mainly an adult-oriented one, but there are lots of free outdoor events, which gives kids a good introduction to various types of jazz in a fun atmosphere.

Festival d'été francophone de Vancouver
Tel: 736-9806
French Cultural Centre, 1551 W. 7th Ave (at Fir), **Vancouver**
Vancouver Public Library, 350 W. Georgia St (at Homer), **Vancouver**
Ten years running, this festival features Francophone music and performances.

Kitsilano Soap Box Derby
4th Ave (at Balsam), **Vancouver**
Tel: 731-4454
A race of hand-built soap box cars.

North Vancouver Folkfest
Centennial Theatre Centre, 2300 Lonsdale Ave (at 23rd Ave), **North Vancouver**
Tel: 987-6085 or 983-6455
Three nights of multicultural shows with a variety of songs, dances and choral programs.

24-Hour Relay for the Kids
Swangard Stadium, Central Park, Boundary Rd (at Kingsway), **Burnaby**
Tel: 873-1865
A 20-year-old fundraiser for the B.C. Lions Society for Children, in which a team of 20 runners run relay-style for 24 hours. Open to the public, the event has on-site activities for families.

Summer Solstice Parade
Kitsilano War Memorial Community Centre, 2690 Larch St (at 10th Ave), **Vancouver**
Tel: 257-6976
In association with Kits Day, an event with games, food, crafts and more, this parade celebrates the onset of summer.

July
Canada Day
Every July 1st, events are held throughout the Lower Mainland; the biggest is at Canada Place, with fireworks and entertainment. Call 666-7200 for information and check the publications mentioned in the introduction to see what events are scheduled.

Family Day at the UBC Museum of Anthropology
Tel: 822-3825
Dance and musical performances, an outdoor picnic, face painting, talks and demonstrations. 1999 marked the 1st Annual Family Day; it's a lot of fun and very educational so hopefully the tradition will continue.

246

Bard on the Beach
Vanier Park, Chestnut St (at Ogden), **Vancouver**
Tel: 737-0625 or 739-0559
Two Shakespearean plays are performed over the summer. It's a great open-air venue in Vanier Park appropriate for older kids.

Wreck Beach Fun Run/Walk
Tel: 432-6350
An annual event with your choice of a 3.5-km or 7-km course, this one is open to kids and proceeds go to the Wreck Beach Preservation Society.

Dancing on the Edge Festival
Firehall Arts Centre, 280 E. Cordova St (at Gore), **Vancouver**
Tel: 689-0926
A 10-day festival of dance shows around the city, with lots of free outdoor performances.

Illuminares
Trout Lake, Victoria Dr (at 19th Ave), **Vancouver**
Tel: 879-8611
A magical evening lantern procession that takes place the last Saturday of July. There are lantern-making workshops during the three weeks preceding the event.

Discovery Days Festival
Deer Lake Park, Buckingham Ave (off Burris), **Burnaby**
Tel: 291-6864
A huge event with musical performances, a children's reading stage, a literary fair, Lego activity, art, food and numerous displays.

Italian Week
Tel: 430-3337
A Commercial Drive event with food, parades and activities.

Caribbean Days Festival
Waterfront Park, **North Vancouver**
Tel: 273-0874
Sponsored by the Trinidad and Tobago Society of B.C., this festival has music, food and dancing; a lot of fun.

Benson & Hedges Symphony of Fire
English Bay
Tel: 738-4304
The world's largest musical fireworks competition takes place at the end of July; the live music is simultaneously broadcast on local radio stations. It's hard to find a bad seat for this event; although the fireworks barge is situated closer to the Denman and Davie street intersection of English Bay (and therefore you get a closer look from this location or from Kits Beach), you can see the fireworks from almost any vantage point around the whole bay.

247

Taiwanese Cultural Festival
The Gateway Theatre, 6500 Gilbert Rd (at Westminster Hwy), **Richmond**
Tel: 276-6506 or 270-1812
An annual event held for two weeks in July with dance, music, videos and art exhibits.

Vancouver Chamber Music Festival
The Crofton House School for Girls, 3200 W. 41st Ave (at Balaclava), **Vancouver**
Tel: 602-0363
Two weeks of chamber music performances in July and August; better for older kids.

Vancouver Folk Music Festival
Jericho Park, at the western end of Point Grey Rd, **Vancouver**
Tel: 602-9798
Folk music from around the world is performed at this weekend festival which has themed workshops and a separate kids' area with crafts, face painting, water play and more.

Vancouver International Comedy Festival
Granville Island, under the Granville Bridge, **Vancouver**
Tel: 683-0883
A Granville Island festival produced by **Axis Theatre Company**, with both ticketed and free performances. The many street performances make it good for kids.

August
Vancouver Gay and Lesbian Pride Day
Tel: 687-0955
This annual event takes place the first Sunday in August and has a parade that goes from Denman and Georgia Streets down to Sunset Beach at the end of Pacific. After the parade there is music, crafts and food at the beach.

Abbotsford International Airshow
Abbotsford Airport, Peardonville Rd (off Hwy 1), east of Surrey, **Abbotsford**
Tel: 857-1142
A fabulous show for families who like planes both on the ground and in the air.

Harmony Arts Festival
Ambleside Park, 13th St (at Marine Dr), **West Vancouver**
Tel: 925-7290
An arts celebration with a craft market and a Creative Kids Day.

Kerrisdale Days
41st Ave, west of West Blvd, **Vancouver**
This yearly celebration of Kerrisdale's birthday has music, sidewalk sales, rides, free balloons, face painting, food and games.

Pacific National Exhibition
Tel: 253-2311
Originally an agricultural fair, the PNE has expanded over the years to include performances, food stands, crafts and home exhibitions and a midway with lots of rides.

Powell Street Festival
Oppenheimer Park, Powell St (at Jackson), **Vancouver**
Tel: 739-9388
A free two-day event celebrating Japanese and Canadian art, culture and history. Dance, crafts, food, theatre and martial arts are offered.

Street Fare
Tel: 685-7811
Buskers provide eclectic entertainment around the Vancouver Art Gallery at the corner of Robson and Hornby Streets.

September

Aboriginal Cultural Festival
Pacific Coliseum, Exhibition Park, Hastings St (at Renfrew), **Vancouver**
Tel: 251-4844
This festival has elders' teachings, a competition powwow, arts and crafts and a children's creative area.

AIDS Walk
Stanley Park, **Vancouver**
Tel: 915-WALK (9255)
This is a fundraiser for men, women and children living with HIV or AIDS. The 10-km walk is in Stanley Park, with a shorter 3-km route suitable for families; there is also a children's tent with crafts and activities.

Circus of Dreams
McLean Park, McLean Dr (at 1st Ave), **Vancouver**
Tel: 879-8611
This vibrant community circus produced by the Public Dreams Society on the Labour Day weekend features stilt walkers, games and fire performances. Prior to the event there are workshops for building circus parade props.

Coho Festival
Ambleside Park, 13th St (at Marine Dr), **West Vancouver**
There is a barbecue with free entertainment and kids' events.

Farm Fair
Maplewood Farm, 405 Seymour River Pl (at Mount Seymour Pkwy), **North Vancouver**
Tel: 929-5610
The farm hosts kid-oriented activities having to do with farm life.

Terry Fox Run

This is an annual run done in honour of Terry Fox, who ran across Canada to raise money for cancer research. This run takes place at more than 5,000 sites in Canada and around the world; it's a huge fundraiser for cancer societies. Check the local paper to find out when the run is taking place. It's usually held the second Sunday following Labour Day.

Festival of Flavours

Vancouver Trade and Convention Centre, 999 Canada Pl (at Howe), **Vancouver**
Tel: 983-2794
This fun event helps kids learn about different foods, decorate cookies and make animals out of donut holes; also storytelling and magic.

Vancouver International Fringe Festival

Tel: 257-0350 or 873-3646
Alternative theatre is celebrated; over 100 groups do over 500 shows in a variety of venues. Some work is suitable for kids; call for show information.

Harvest Fair

Historic Stewart Farm, 13723 Crescent Rd (off Hwy 99), near Crescent Beach, **South Surrey**
Tel: 543-3456
An annual gardening competition with a children's category; also a pie-eating contest.

Mid-Autumn Moon Festival

Dr. Sun Yat-Sen Classical Chinese Garden, 578 Carrall St (at Pender), **Vancouver**
Tel: 662-3207
This is one of the most important festivals in Chinese culture. Admission is free; the garden is decorated by colourful lanterns; there is also theatre and music.

Molson Indy Vancouver

Tel: 280-INDY (4639)
Three days of automobile racing take place through the streets of downtown Vancouver.

Tri-City Children's Festival

Town Centre Park, Pinetree Way (at Guildford), **Coquitlam**
Tel: 931-8821
Music, storytelling, clowns and other activities are offered.

Word on the Street/Vancouver Book & Magazine Fair

Vancouver Public Library, Robson St (at Homer), **Vancouver**
Tel: 684-8266 or 331-3600
A one-day gathering for lovers of literature, this fair also has events for children, such as activities, readings and live entertainment.

October

Apple Festival
UBC Botanical Garden, S.W. Marine Dr (near 16th Ave), **Vancouver**
An annual festival dedicated to the apple: tasting, buying, candy apples and fun stuff for kids.

Cranberry Harvest Festival
Richmond Nature Park, Westminster Hwy (at No. 5 Rd), **Richmond**
Tel: 273-7015
One of Canada's largest cranberry festivals, this has pony rides, games and prizes, as well as bus tours to a commercial cranberry farm. Fresh cranberries for sale, of course.

101 Pumpkins Event
Maplewood Farm, 405 Seymour River Pl (at Mount Seymour Pkwy), **North Vancouver**
Tel: 929-5610
Crafts, fun and activities are featured at this annual event.

Parade of Lost Souls
Grandview Park, Commercial Dr (at Charles), **Vancouver**
Tel: 879-8611
A celebration to honour the dead, wake the living and chase bad luck away. Kids six and up love it; use discretion with smaller ones. Yet another brilliant Public Dreams event, this one takes place the last Saturday of October and has workshops for making lanterns and noisemakers.

Pumpkin Patches
Pick your own pumpkin, go on a hay ride, see farm animals. Patches can be found at **The Pumpkin Patch** (274-0522), 12900 Steveston Highway (at Highway 99), and at **Westham Island Herb Farm** (946-4393), 4690 Kirkland Road, on Westham Island.

Science and Technology Week
Website: *www.ei.gov.bc.ca/stweek* or *www.irta.gov.bc.ca*
Math and science-related activities happen at a variety of venues in the Lower Mainland.

Vancouver International Film Festival
Tel: 685-0260
Films from around the world are shown at a variety of venues in Vancouver. Some are suitable for older children, but check in with the festival before making firm plans to see a film with kids in tow. A membership of $1 (sold to those 18 years of age and older), is required for attendance.

Vancouver International Writers (& Readers) Festival
Granville Island, **Vancouver**
Tel: 681-6330 or 685-0260
A five-day event with international writers reading from and discussing their works. There are numerous children's readings during the day, and poetry and performances in French.

Vancouver Snowshow
B.C. Place Stadium, Pacific Blvd (at Robson), **Vancouver**
Tel: 878-0754
This is a huge trade and consumer show which raises money for junior snow sports in B.C.; a great opportunity to buy new and used equipment or clothing for children. Child minding and a kids' corner with various activities.

Halloween
Various Halloween events take place at community centres and other locations throughout the Lower Mainland. Consult one of the publications mentioned in the introduction. Halloween is, of course, a big night out for kids, as they get to traipse from door to door collecting free candy and treats. It's fun for four-to-14-year olds. Younger kids get nervous and older kids start feeling a bit too old for it. It's usually a neighbourhood activity, but basic precautions still apply. Younger kids should be accompanied by an adult, of course; older kids often go out in groups. If porch lights are on, the house is open to trick-or-treaters; dark houses mean there is no-one "at home." Kids should wear warm, bright-coloured (preferably reflective) clothing, have a curfew and refrain from sampling their treats until an adult has checked over the goodies.

November

Canadian Living Parents and Kids Show
Vancouver Trade and Convention Centre, 999 Canada Pl (at Howe), **Vancouver**
Tel: 878-8388
Over 150 interactive exhibits are featured for parents and kids, an arts festival, a computer zone, cooking demonstrations and a sports zone with wall climbing. Also excellent parenting seminars and free childcare.

Hadassah Bazaar
Tel: 257-5160
A huge event put on by the Jewish community, this flea market has everything from books to shoes, with various auctions held throughout the day. Traditionally held at the PNE, the venue will change in the year 2000; call for current location.

Winter Tales
Tel: 876-2272
A yearly event put on by the Vancouver Society of Storytelling, with storytelling in several languages with a variety of cultures represented. Events take place at various locations. (This event formerly took place over the summer and was called the Vancouver Storytelling Festival.)

December

Here is a list of places that hold Christmas events; dates vary from year to year. Be sure to check the newspapers and at your community centre for more events. If your child wants to write a **Letter to Santa**, don't worry about the letter never reaching its destination. Send the letter to your local post office and Santa will write back. Consult the phone directory for your local post office; the deadline for letters is usually around December 15. Christmas lights are a big feature of many private homes and public and commercial buildings during this season. Check the newspaper; they usually have list (with addresses) of the year's more impressive displays.

Burnaby Village Museum
6501 Deer Lake Ave (at Hwy 1), **Burnaby**
Tel: 293-6500 or 293-6501
Their Heritage Christmas has music, drama, crafts, lights, carousel rides and Santa himself.

Canada Place
Canada Pl (at Howe), **Vancouver**
Tel: 666-8477
A miniature train ride that passes 16 animated displays (a bit dated and bedraggled now), from the old Woodward's department store; proceeds go to local children's charities

Christmas Carol Ships Parade
Tel: 879-9988 or 682-2007
Boat owners from Vancouver decorate their vessels and cruise the waters of Vancouver; carol singers onboard add to the magical effect of the procession.

Festival of Trees
Four Seasons Hotel, Granville Mall (at Georgia St), **Vancouver**
Tel: 689-9333
An annual fundraising event for the B.C. Children's Hospital. Decorated Christmas trees are displayed in the hotel in December; proceeds from ballots cast for the best tree are given to the hospital, with one prize being given to a lucky winner.

Granville Island
Under Granville Bridge, **Vancouver**
Sing-alongs, magic, storytelling, a Kids' Market Wishing Tree and Santa, strolling through the premises, all take place throughout December.

Stanley Park Miniature Railway
Tel: 257-8438 or 878-9274
Transformed into a Christmas train over the holidays; the route is decorated with lights and other displays. Call ahead to find out the hours and go early; the line-ups can be horrific. Be sure to dress warmly.

VanDusen Botanical Garden Festival of Lights
5251 Oak St (at 37th Ave), **Vancouver**
Tel: 878-9274
The garden is transformed by 20,000 lights and various displays. There is a special price available as part of a package that includes a ride on the Stanley Park Miniature Train.

Westwood Plateau Golf and Country Club
3251 Plateau Blvd, in the Westwood Plateau, **Coquitlam**
Tel: 945-4007
Their Christmas Carol cart gives visitors a trip to a winter wonderland complete with Santa and his workshop, elves, reindeer and an enormous Christmas tree.

Winter Wonderland
13766 63A (at Hwy 99), **Surrey**
This private home is lit up by 400,000 lights and 20 animated scenes during the festive season. It's worth a look, with an electric train, a forest of candy canes, a waterfall and a miniature village.

Got any ideas?
Did we miss something?
We welcome your
comments and suggestions,
and will incorporate the
best ideas into future editions.
Address your comments to:
Kids' Vancouver Editor
Raincoast Books
8680 Cambie Street
Vancouver, B.C.
Canada V6P 6M9

Acknowledgements

This book was a massive project and would not have been possible without the assistance of a great number of people who helped me along the way. My sincere thanks go out to: James Applegate, Theresa Best, Nicole Buckman, Mary Bushnell, Katharine Dickinson, Scott Dunlop, Perci Embree, Nikki Groocock, Rachelle Kanefsky, the staff and parents at Kitsilano Area Childcare Society, Lauren MacKenzie, Bob Mercer, Shani Mootoo, Natalie Ochmanek, Oraf Oraffson, Naomi Pauls, Marina Princz, Aubin Raunet, Kerry Tamm, Bree Willson and to Vicki Williams, who inspired me to do this book in the first place. I am also in gratitude to Kevin Williams, Brian Scrivener, Derek Fairbridge and the staff at Raincoast Books for their enthusiasm and help with this project, as well as to the scores of other people who offered advice and suggestions and to my young assistants Susan, Catherine, Francis, Pamela and Joe, who "kid-tested" this book and accompanied me to multitudes of venues around the city. I am eternally grateful to Brent Boates for his unwavering support and kindness. This book is in memory of Audrey Rodgers Boates and is dedicated to my two children, Charlotte and Alexander Bushnell-Boates.

Index

For listings with multiple page references, boldface numbers indicate the principal entries.

263

and now...

the COUPONS!

Kids' Vancouver

Bill Copeland Sports Centre
3676 Kensington Avenue
Burnaby, B.C. V5B 4Z6
Phone 291-1261
Fax 291-0979

City of **Burnaby**
Parks, Recreation
& Cultural Services

Bill Copeland Sports Centre
3676 Kensington Avenue
Burnaby, B.C. V5B 4Z6
Phone 291-1261   Fax 291-0979

Multi-purpose Facility — ice/floor rentals, skating/inline lessons, public skates, reception and meeting room space

Valid for one complimentary ADMISSION when a second ADMISSION of equal or greater value is purchased.

Valid during any public, family, or adult skating session.

Kids' Vancouver

A Children's
Gift Store

2951-A West 4th Avenue
(at Bayswater)
Vancouver V6K 1R3
tel/fax 604 738 0333

Bobbits

2951-A West 4th Avenue, Vancouver V6K 1R3 tel/fax 604 738 0333

This coupon entitles you to **10% off** any item in the store.
(does not include sale merchandise)

- Baby Sling by Kindersling
- Designer Diaper Bags
- Medela Breast Pump
  Sales & Rentals

- Baby Registry
- Nursing Pillows
- Family Baby Picture Frames
- Really Neat & Eclectic Gift Ideas

Kids' Vancouver

Boomers & Echoes
Kids & Maternity Ltd.

1709 Lonsdale Ave.,
North Vancouver
(at 17th Street)

Phone/Fax (604) 984-6163

Boomers & Echoes
Kids & Maternity Ltd.

1709 Lonsdale Ave., North Vancouver
(at 17th Street)
Phone/Fax (604) 984-6163

20% OFF
REGULAR PRICED (NEW) KIDS' OR MATERNITY WEAR
(ACCESSORIES NOT INCLUDED)

Not valid in combination with any other promotional offer.

Kids'
Vancouver

Kids'
Vancouver

Kids'
Vancouver

Kids'
Vancouver

Burnaby Village Museum
6501 Deer Lake Avenue
Burnaby, B.C. V5G 3T6
Phone (604) 293-6500
Fax (604) 293-6525

Kids' Vancouver

Burnaby's
HERITAGE VILLAGE
& Carousel

Burnaby Village Museum
6501 Deer Lake Avenue
Burnaby, B.C. V5G 3T6
Phone (604) 293-6500
Fax (604) 293-6525
www.city.burnaby.bc.ca

Home of Burnaby's Heritage Village and Vintage Carousel

$1⁰⁰ Off

Regular Admission

(up to Max. 4 people)

Canadian Craft Museum
Cathedral Place Courtyard
639 Hornby St.,
Vancouver, B.C. V6C 2G3
Phone (604) 687-8266
Fax (604) -7174

Hours:
Mon – Sat, 10 am – 5 pm
Sun & Holidays, Noon – 5 pm
Closed Tuesdays Sept 31 – May 1

Kids' Vancouver

COME AND LEARN ABOUT THE WORLD OF CRAFT!
OUR CHANGING EXHIBITS PROVIDE FUN FOR
KIDS OF ALL AGES.
CALL TO FIND OUT ABOUT UPCOMING
KIDS' ACTIVITIES AT THE CCM.

Canadian Craft Museum
Cathedral Place Courtyard
639 Hornby St., Vancouver, B.C.

FREE ADMISSION TO CHILDREN 12 AND UNDER
WHEN ACCOMPANIED BY A PARENT OR GUARDIAN.

CN IMAX Theatre
201-999 Canada Place
Vancouver, BC V6C 3C1
Phone (604) 682-4629

April – September:
12 noon – 10 pm
October – March:
12 noon – 3 pm; 7 – 10 pm

Kids' Vancouver

CN IMAX THEATRE AT CANADA PLACE — GET A **SENSE** OF THE **IMMENSE.**

$1.00 Off Regular Admission
(up to max. 4 people)

A Giant Screen 5 Stories High IMAX and IMAX 3D films put YOU in the Picture

---

Delta Museum and Archives

4858 Delta Street
Delta, BC V4K 2T8
Phone (604) 946-9322

Open 10:00 a.m. to 3:30 p.m.
Tuesdays through Saturdays
Sundays 2:00 to 4:00 p.m.

Kids' Vancouver

D I S C O U N T   C O U P O N

25% Off

the Cost of a Children's Workshop, Activity,
or Event of Your Choice.

Step back in time on a fun-filled visit to
the Delta Museum and Archives.

Attend a craft workshop, holiday celebration, or tour.
Call 946-9322

kids'
Vancouver

kids'
Vancouver

kids'
Vancouver

kids'
Vancouver

**Kids'
Vancouver**

**Kids'
Vancouver**

**Kids'
Vancouver**

**Kids'
Vancouver**

Kids'
Vancouver

Kids'
Vancouver

Kids'
Vancouver

Kids'
Vancouver

kids'
Vancouver

kids'
Vancouver

kids'
Vancouver

kids'
Vancouver

kids'
Vancouver

kids'
Vancouver

kids'
Vancouver

kids'
Vancouver

Techno-Kids

Techno-Kids
4424 Dunbar Street,
Vancouver, BC V6S 2G5
Tel/Fax (604) 730-9449

10% OFF

NOT VALID WITH ANY OTHER PROMOTION

FOR CURIOUS MINDS AND CLEVER HANDS; TECHNO-KIDS —

VANCOUVER'S SCIENCE, NATURE, ART AND EDUCTIONAL STORE OFFERS

A LARGE SELECTION OF UNUSUAL ITEMS FOR ALL AGES AND SEASONS

TECHNO-KIDS
The Science and Nature Centre
Art Supplies

Vancouver
Aquatic Centre

1050 Beach Avenue
Vancouver, BC V6E 1T7

Phone 665-3424
Fax 681 8397

vancouver aquatic centre

Valid for one complimentary **ADMISSION**
when a second **ADMISSION**
of equal or greater value is purchased
— or —
one admission at 50% off the regular price

VALID ANYTIME

Vancouver Art Gallery
750 Hornby Street
Vancouver

Phone 662-4700
Fax 682-1086

VANCOUVER ART GALLERY

2 for 1 Admission

The Vancouver Art Gallery is the
largest home of Art in Western Canada,
focusing on Dynamic Contemporary Works

Vancouver East
Cultural Centre

1895 Venables Street
Vancouver V5L 2H6

Tickets: 254-9578

VANCOUVER EAST CULTURAL CENTRE

Kids' Series Special Offer

4 tickets to Kids'
Series for only

$18.00

kids'
Vancouver

kids'
Vancouver

kids'
Vancouver

kids'
Vancouver